# Transnational Mobility and Identity in and out of Korea

# Korean Communities across the World

**Series Editor**
Joong-Hwan Oh, Hunter College, CUNY

*Korean Communities across the World* publishes works that address aspects of (a) the Korean American community, (b) Korean society, (c) the Korean communities in other foreign lands, or (d) transnational Korean communities. In the field of (a) the Korean American community, this series welcomes contributions involving concepts such as Americanization, pluralism, social mobility, migration/immigration, social networks, social institutions, social capital, racism/discrimination, settlement, identity, or politics, as well as a specific topic related to family/marriage, gender roles, generations, work, education, culture, citizenship, health, ethnic community, housing, ethnic identity, racial relations, social justice, social policy, and political views, among others. In the field of (b) Korean society, this series embraces scholarship on current issues such as gender roles, age/aging, low fertility, immigration, urbanization, gentrification, economic inequality, high youth unemployment, sexuality, democracy, political power, social injustice, the nation's educational problems, social welfare, capitalism, consumerism, labor, health, housing, crime, environmental degradation, and the social life in the digital age and its impacts, among others. Contributors in the field of (c) Korean communities in other foreign lands are encouraged to submit works that expand our understanding about the formation, vicissitudes, and major issues of an ethnic Korean community outside of South Korea and the Unites States, such as cultural or linguistic retention, ethnic identity, assimilation, settlement patterns, citizenship, economic activities, family relations, social mobility, and racism/discrimination. Lastly, contributions relating to (d) transnational Korean communities may touch upon transnational connectivity in family, economy/finance, politics, culture, technology, social institutions, and people.

# Transnational Mobility and Identity in and out of Korea

Edited by
Yonson Ahn

LEXINGTON BOOKS
Lanham • Boulder • New York • London

Published by Lexington Books
An imprint of The Rowman & Littlefield Publishing Group, Inc.
4501 Forbes Boulevard, Suite 200, Lanham, Maryland 20706
www.rowman.com

6 Tinworth Street, London SE11 5AL

British Library Cataloguing in Publication Information Available

**Library of Congress Cataloging-in-Publication Data**

Name: Ahn, Yonson, 1963–, editor.
Title: Transnational mobility and identity in and out of Korea / edited by Yonson Ahn.
Description: Lanham: Lexington Books [2020] | Series: Korean communities across the world | Includes bibliographical references and index. | Summary: "Through a series of empirical studies, this edited volume examines socio-cultural aspects of transnational mobility in and out of Korea as well as the process in which overseas Koreans, returnees, and marriage migrants in South Korea gain agency and negotiate multiple identities"—Provided by publisher.
Identifiers: LCCN 2019040476 (print) | LCCN 2019040477 (ebook) | ISBN 9781498593328 (cloth) | ISBN 9781498593335 (epub) | ISBN 9781498593342 (pbk)
Subjects: LCSH: Koreans—Foreign countries—Ethnic identity. | Koreans—Social networks—Foreign countries. | Koreans—Ethnic identity. | Return migration—Korea (South) | Korea—Emigration and immigration—Social aspects. | Korean diaspora. | Transnationalism.
Classification: LCC DS904.7 .T73 2020 (print) | LCC DS904.7 (ebook) | DDC 305.8957—dc23
LC record available at https://lccn.loc.gov/2019040476
LC ebook record available at https://lccn.loc.gov/2019040477

# Contents

**Part III: Return Migration**

**Part IV: Transnational Mobility from a Historical Perspective**

# Acknowledgments

This work was supported by the Seed Program for Korean Studies through the Ministry of Education of Republic of Korea and Korean Studies Promotion Service of the Academy of Korean Studies (AKS 2015-INC-2230004).

# Introduction

In the age of globalization, which has been described as "time-space compression" (Harvey 1990), the way diasporas, returnees to the ancestral homeland, or migrants maintain networks and connections with both homeland and host-land through transnational mobility has become a topic of interest to researchers and the general public. This is a multi-dimensional process involving both the physical mobility of individuals and a more intangible flow of ideas, cross-cultural exchanges, remittances, or counter-remittances and electronic communication. Furthermore, migration arguably has a significant impact on both the identity of the individuals involved and the diversity of the local demographic landscape.

Transnational migration and mobility have been influenced by the social, cultural, and political conditions of the corresponding countries and regions. The specific context relevant to the Korean peninsula arising from issues including the colonial past and the Korean War (1950–1953) has produced distinct migration and remigration phenomena, trajectories, and outcomes, thereby making it necessary for scholars working in the field to conceptualize the associated underlying empirical cases.

Recent research interest in transnational mobility, migration, and the Korean diaspora has increased in parallel with heightened awareness of the conditions and identities of the Korean diaspora and returnees to the ancestral homeland, together with a shift in Korea's stance from being predominantly a migrant-sending to a migrant-receiving country. According to Korean demographic statistics, the diaspora amounted to 7.4 million in December 2017 (Ministry of Foreign Affairs 2017, 14), and the number of the foreign-born population in South Korea (hereafter Korea), including ethnic Korean returnees, reached almost 2.4 million in May 2019, which represents approximately 4.6% of the country's total population (Ministry of Justice 2019, 18).[1]

Considering the previously relatively homogenous population of Korea compared to the West, these demographic statistics show increased transnational mobility in and out of Korea in the age of globalization. The increase in population mobility can be attributed to the increasing numbers of the Korean diaspora residing outside the country, together with rising numbers of diasporic returnees and a new wave of incoming migrants. Both outbound and inbound rates of transnational mobility demonstrate patterns of diversification. This trend is evidenced by the breakdown of demographic statistics into a range of categories; ethnic Korean returnees, return visits of the mobile Korean diaspora drawn by their ties to the "homeland," migrant workers, and marriage migrants in Korea. These trajectories have generated a new landscape characterized by a populace perpetually "in motion" and have generated shifting subjectivities which constitute their relation both to the "homeland" and the country of settlement.

*  *  *

Through a series of empirical studies, this edited volume aims to examine important socio-cultural aspects of transnational mobility in and out of Korea as well as the process by which overseas Koreans, returnees, and foreign-born migrants in Korea gain agency and negotiate multiple identities. Investigated groups include migrant workers, returnees of Korean diasporic descendants, marriage migrants, adoptees, professionals, and entrepreneurs, along with students outside Korea.

This publication project has evolved from the AKS Seed Program for Korean Studies entitled "Identity and Transnational Mobility in and out of Korea" funded by the Ministry of Education in South Korea and the Academy of Korean Studies (AKS) (July 2015 to June 2018). At the project-concluding conference held at Goethe University of Frankfurt (22 to 23 February 2018), preliminary versions of most of the contributions in this volume were presented, revised, and expanded.

The core theme of this volume is the identity and transnational mobility of the Korean diaspora across the globe, spanning many countries and regions such as Japan, the Philippines, Germany, the U.S., the UK, and Korean diaspora returnees to the ancestral homeland like *Chosŏnjok* (ethnic Koreans from China), *Koryŏ saram* (ethnic Koreans from the Commonwealth of Independent States, CIS), and Korean Americans. The time period extends from the colonial occupation of Korea by Japan to the Korean War (1950–1953) and includes coverage of the current situation.

Authors in this collection focus on contemporary mobility associated with employment or education (Y. Kim, Ahn, Lim), marriage (S. Lee and M. Kim), desire to return to the ancestral land (Suh, Song, Wei, J. Lee), and past mobility during the colonial period (Patterson, Neuhaus) by various groups of the Korean diaspora. First of all, ethnic Korean returnees like *Koryŏ saram, Chosŏnjok*, Korean Americans, and their social relations with the ethnic homeland. Second, some chapters analyze lived experiences within the family and the workplace as well as the sense of belonging felt by Soviet Koreans (*Koryŏ saram*), the former Korean healthcare "guest workers" in Germany, Korean adoptees in the U.S., Korean marriage immigrants to the Philippines, and Asian marriage migrants in Korea. Third, other contributors shed light on the nature of the mobile lifestyle and the aspiration for work and/or for education of *Chosŏnjok* students and young Korean women abroad. Lastly, historical aspects of transnational mobility of Koreans are explored in the case of Korean immigrants to Hawaii in the early 20th century and Korean students in Japan during the colonial period. The range and depth of material in this collection presents a rich body of empirical cases relevant to the so far under-studied field of diasporic people on the move.

Particular focus is put on the complex range of motivational factors behind the pattern of multiple mobilities in and out of Korea to promote a better understanding of contemporary Korean society and Korean diaspora communities outside Korea. Contributors to this collection explore the practices and histories of transnational mobilities which constitute present-day globalized Korea in a positive and critical way.

This volume brings together different mobility-related issues such as gender, media, return migration, and history. Research topics include: gendered migration, the sense of belonging and embodied multiple subjectivities, migrants' socio-cultural engagements in the societies of the countries of destination and origin in historical and contemporary contexts, migrants' work and family, ethnic media consumption in transnational mobility, ethnic return migration, and marriage migration.

These diverse themes of transnational mobility in and out of Korea are investigated from the perspective of various disciplines such as sociology, gender studies, anthropology, geography, history, theater studies, media and communication studies, and Asian studies, covering several geographical regions: one grounded in the study of the texts and traces of the past, and the other based on the analysis of contemporary actors' discourses. Drawing on personal narratives obtained from in-depth interviews, historical and contemporary documents, theater work, or media, authors in this book investigate the conceptual and empirical intersections emerging out of recent and historical patterns of transnational mobility in and out of Korea.

This interdisciplinary approach is advantageous in achieving a fresh perspective on temporary and long-term mobility across various forms of migration, showing the lasting impact it has had across successive generations and highlighting the richness of the related cultural and societal processes.

\* \* \*

In the age of globalization, people are on the move due to a range of motivating factors; employment and education, family reunion in the destination country, homecoming visits, permanent return to the ancestral country, seasonal tourism, accessing healthcare services, or claiming asylum. Thus, the term "mobility" is applied to a broad spectrum of multiple and intersecting population movements for both long- and short-term periods. By contributing to the "mobilities paradigm" (Urry 2000; Sheller and Urry 2006), this edited volume sets out to give an up-to-date overview of diverse forms of complex and multiple mobility that connect people across time and space and to examine its socio-cultural implications in a Korean context.

Transnational mobility is employed as a lens for exploring the ways in which im/migrants both connect to and distance themselves from their ancestral homeland and host-land through inbound and outbound mobility. This edited volume specifically intends to contextualize bi-directional mobility from and to Korea in order to shed light on the complexity of mobile transnational and diasporic lives. Transnational mobility from and to the homeland and host-land, which creates diverse interactions between returnees or migrants and locals in both locations, is explored.

Senses of proximity and connectivity are fused in the age of "time-space compression" (Harvey 1990) and simultaneously imagined. This fuels the growing capacity for high transnational mobility to and from homeland and host-land and constitutes multiple senses of "home." From this perspective, mobility is a resource with which not everyone has an equal relationship (Skeggs 2004, 49).

Therefore, this book attempts to address the rich social and cultural capital associated with im/migrants or returnees and at the same time to raise awareness of their vulnerability throughout their transnational and diasporic lives. This involves paying close attention to the relationship between migrants' individual lives and the wider social structures in which they are enmeshed with an eye to grasping how the migrant-embodied multiple subjectivities are socially or contextually structured in terms of rupture and interconnection, and are furthermore mediated, negotiated, and re/shaped together with their mobility.

Based on the common thread of transnational mobility, the contributors to this volume observe how mobility in and out of Korea has shaped and re-shaped migrants' interconnected social experiences in multiple localities, transforming the sense of belonging and the definition of embodied subjectivity, both at an individual and a collective level.

Contributors to this collection identify the way the Korean diaspora across the globe, as well as foreign-born migrants in Korea, are engaged in a process of constant movement which paradoxically results both in transnational connectivity and disconnectivity. Furthermore, the way in which these people on the move make sense of differences and commonality encountered in their societies of origin and destination, whether in their imagination or in reality, is discussed.

The focus of this volume is not essentializing the Korean diaspora or foreign-born migrants in Korea as a unified group who possess a seamlessly homogeneous identity, but rather it sets out to contextualize the differences and similarities amongst those who have multiple and ambivalent senses of belonging which are constantly shifting and being negotiated in the host country and/or in the ethnic homeland. Another point of differentiation is the existence amongst the Korean diaspora of a hierarchy between those in or from the West and those from Asia/China or the former Soviet Union.

Authors contributing to this collection investigate to what extent a collective cultural identification towards the homeland is either a myth and/or embodied in im/migrants' subjectivity. Both feelings of attachment to and ambivalence about the homeland and host-land by the people on the move have been identified in this volume. Thus, the importance of im/migrants as individuals within host and origin countries is emphasized while reflecting on their collective experiences within the migration regime and gender regime involved in transnational mobility in and out of Korea. In turn, it is hoped that the research featured in this volume can serve as a platform for comparative migration studies with other regions.

## OVERVIEW OF CHAPTERS

This volume consists of four parts subdivided into eleven chapters together with an introduction and a closing section. Part I opens with an examination of transnational mobility and media, investigating the role of the media in the migratory trajectory of migrants, and the representation of Korean adoptees in cultural products.

In chapter 1, Youna Kim aims to achieve an understanding of transnational mobility stemming from educated young Korean women's aspiration for a new lifestyle and a new identity, drawing on detailed biographical accounts of women who have been living and studying in the UK. The author identifies the impact of media consumption on their everyday lives in coping with senses of social exclusion and cultural differences in their transnational lives, and on re/shaping subjectivities in a new light. She plausibly observes that their communicative activities and engagement with the ethnic media space offer significant resources to allow for continued connection to the homeland culture and lives while engaged in the re-making of "home from home." In her concluding remarks, she shows skepticism towards migrants becoming cosmopolitan subjects by reflecting critically on the normative ideal of cosmopolitanism, arguing that transnational mobility conversely enhances national identity through dialectics of inclusion and exclusion which are linked to power disparity and inequality encountered in the destination society.

Chapter 2 by Jieun Lee addresses issues of transnational adoption in theatrical production, focusing on Korean American adoptees' kinship, citizenship and sense of belonging in Korea. The author analyzes Korean American adoptee artist Eric Sharp's *Middle Brother* (2014) based on his semi-autobiographical stories, which investigates the embodiments of the adoptee characters' transnational mobility back and forth between Korea and the United States. Lee argues that the performances of transnational adoption where the adoptees' confrontations and negotiations between family members, nations, and identities are staged is a site of Korean adoptees' interrogation of belonging in the process of reimagining their search and reunion and re-mapping the notions of kinship and citizenship in and out of Korea. In her study, the theatrical production imaginatively shows critical ways in which Korean American adoptees find agency for truth and reconciliation through artistic expression as the audience gains a deeper understanding of adoptees' transnational journey into belonging across temporal and spatial borders.

\* \* \*

Part II of this book examines migratory mobility and gender issues through three cases; Korean migrant nurses in Germany, Asian marriage migrants in Korea, and Korean professional women in Japan. Three contributors (Ahn, Lee, and Lim) strive to re-conceptualize the work and family of migrant workers in the host countries. In this section, gender is considered to play a significant role in the life of migrant women at the intersection of race, gender, migration policy, and governance. Therefore, an effort is made to identify and explain how gender makes a difference in the process and experience of migration for female migrant workers.

In chapter 3, Yonson Ahn focuses on the issue of transnational nurse migration from Korea to the former West Germany (hereafter Germany) as "guest workers" between the late 1950s and the 1970s, which was part of the global outsourcing of healthcare work. The interplay of Korean healthcare workers and the local populace is analyzed in terms of a "contact zone" (Pratt 1992). The migrant-local interaction emerging from their co-presence in social spaces occurred over a prolonged period of time in the context of delivering nursing care. The healthcare workers' personal narratives obtained from multiple in-depth interviews with former Korean nurses who settled in Germany represent the material for a micro level examination of the nursing care practices through which the host culture and the migrants' cultures meet, clash, and are negotiated and/or dropped. The social space of the face-to-face encounters between the migrant caregivers and the local populace, especially co-workers and care recipients, is contextualized in the framework of a "contact zone" with particular consideration given to the intersection of gender and ethnicity. A focus is put on the German social construction of stereotypi-cal Korean femininity as kind, gentle, smiling, non-confrontational, or sub-missive that was prevalent in Germany at that time (Ahn 2014). The ways in which the Korean healthcare workers complied with, negotiated, and/or re-sisted such attributions through migrant-local interaction are addressed.

Chapter 4 by Seonok Lee opens by examining transnational mobility into Korea focusing on the two groups of marriage im/migrants in Korea: migrant brides and migrant husbands from South and Southeast Asian countries. The author begins with the question of why the Korean government mainly sup-ports the integration of foreign brides but not foreign husbands, even though both have different racial and ethnic backgrounds. Migrant foreign women are expected to integrate into the existing socio-cultural system so that they reproduce and transfer markers of "Koreanness" to their offspring. Converse-ly, foreign husbands' state of "otherness" based on racial differences is main-tained and integration is delayed. The author refers to these specific gendered rules within racial hierarchies as "patriarchal racialization," a process in which patriarchy and racialization are co-created by the state, community, and family members. Consequently, through the examination of both migrant women and men's everyday experiences of difference and hierarchy in the micro-space of the household and in the community, she argues that children of a Korean father and a foreign mother are seen as racially closer to Koreans than the children of a foreign father and a Korean mother. Patriarchal racial-ization creates a link between the belief in paternal blood lineage and the idea of race.

In the following chapter, Dukin Lim explores highly skilled Korean wom-en migrants' re/building of their careers through entrepreneurship in Japan. She begins with considering how the women's various individual aspirations shape their mobility whether for education, tourism, or conducting business in Japan. This is followed by reviewing settlement processes with reference to setting up their businesses.

Although their initial transnational mobility to Japan was for a short-term period as transient visitors, it subsequently shifted to permanent settlement as their career became more established and/or they entered into marriage. De-spite their high level of education and rich work experiences, these migrant women tend to fall into categories of either "unemployed" or "low-skilled," which contributes to their "invisibility" as migrant workers in Japan. The contributor argues that Korean immigrant women act as socio-economic bridges, linking the ethnic networks and communities in and between Korean and Japanese societies. Lee concludes that their contributions in job creation, resource mobilization, and enhancement of the business cycle in Japan (as well as their self-reliance and resilience to overcome the Japanese labor market barriers) deserve better social recognition.

* * *

Return migratory trajectories are featured in part III of this book, which contains empirical studies of Korean diaspora's return to the ancestral country of Korea, a prominent feature of identity and mobility in and out of Korea in their migratory trajectory. Three authors (Suh, Wei and Song) unfold the lived experiences of Korean Americans, *Chosŏnjok*, and *Koryŏ saram* as diasporic returnees to the ancestral homeland.

Part III begins with chapter 6 by Stephen Cho Suh who examines the phenomenon of ancestral homeland migration through the perspective of the second-generation Korean American "returnees." Using Yen Le Espiritu's (2003) definition of "differential inclusion," the author explores the young Korean Americans' ambivalent position within their "homeland" society—not entirely excluded but partially included—in being integral to the state only because of their marginalized or transient status within the "homeland." He contests assumptions about them holding a relatively privileged position as presented in preexisting literature and draws attention to the way the Korean American "returnees" reconcile socio-legal barriers they encounter to integrate into Korean society. It is concluded that their ambiguous position falling between co-ethnic insider and non-citizen foreigner—but not quite foreign enough—has created a paradoxical predicament for them in society.

The largest group of ethnic return migrants amongst other Korean diaspora returnees are ethnic Korean Chinese whose number in Korea in 2019 has reached 731,452 (Ministry of Justice 2019, 42). While preexisting literature on ethnic Korean Chinese returnees primarily focuses on the marriage migrants and unskilled laborers among them, Ruixin Wei's chapter 7 examines the third generation of educated young Korean Chinese, an under-explored field of the Korean Chinese transnational migration flows and trends. Since the young Korean Chinese are embedded within a transnational space largely created by cross-border connections between China and Korea since childhood, she investigates their connections and disconnections with the two societies. By analyzing the narratives of a group of Korean Chinese students in Korea, the author delineates their identity negotiation by uncovering how the students exploit their agency of being Korean Chinese in both the public and private spheres. In the public sphere, they are fitting in well in Korea but do not necessarily feel a sense of belonging to the society. In the private sphere, they attach great importance to their perceived Korean Chinese cultural heritage while developing their own understanding of being Korean Chinese. In conclusion, she notes the aspiration and probability of the third generation of young Korean Chinese to become "global elites" in the future through utilizing their particular cultural capabilities.

Another case study of remigration of ethnic Koreans, called *Koryŏ saram*, from the former Soviet Union is presented by Changzoo Song. He investigates how *Koryŏ saram* diasporic returnees to their ethnic homeland, Korea, after having lived in their host countries as diaspora for two or more generations, construct their diasporic identity in their ancestral homeland. Song highlights how coming from the former Soviet Union republics such as Uzbekistan and Russia, and also having lost their mother tongue, along with the traumatic forced migration experience in the former Soviet Union, means that *Koryŏ saram* manifest substantial differences from their Chinese Korean counterparts in terms of their relationship with their co-ethnics and as well as their ethno-national identities. Based on interviews carried out with members of the *Koryŏ saram* community in Korea, the author explores the identification of the ethnic returnees in Korea and the ethnic hierarchy among the various Koreans in their ethnic homeland.

\* \* \*

Since transnational mobility is not only a contemporary but also a historic phenomenon, part IV places Korean diaspora in a historical perspective by examining outbound transnational mobility of Koreans. This includes the Korean sugar plantation workers in early 20th-century Hawaii, Korean students in Japan between the 1910s and 1920s, and Korean women who married Filipinos during the Korean War (1950–1953), drawing on historical documents, journals, and interview narratives. Although contemporary migration can in many ways be regarded as unprecedented, the legacies of the earlier colonial and Korean War periods, and contemporary demographic shifts continue to influence migrants' mobility in the present day. Adopting a historical perspective on the Korean diasporic populations is insightful when examining the patterns, routes, and issues of contemporary migration.

Wayne Peterson's chapter 9 concerns the influence of Japanese imperialism in hindering Korean immigration to Hawaii. The author focuses on Japan's exertion of pressure on—and colonial policy toward—Korea as evidenced by banning the emigration of Koreans to Hawaii to work on sugar plantations in the early 20th century. In this period, Hawaiian sugar planters had started to bring in Koreans as strike-breakers against the Japanese. He identifies this colonial policy as arising from the country's efforts to protect its own interests and to preserve its prestigious image as an empire. Drawing on historical documents, Patterson highlights the background to the policy of stopping Korean immigration to Hawaii which was intended to raise the wages for Japanese workers on Hawaiian sugar plantations and thus to reduce the flow of Japanese from Hawaii to California where the wages were much higher than on the island. This intention was related to efforts at rendering a Japanese Exclusion Act in the early 20th century in the U.S. unnecessary. As the act was viewed as tarnishing the image of the empire, the Japanese government was determined to prevent Koreans from moving to the United States so that its own nationals would not be excluded. He concludes that this is evidence of Japan's effort to maintain its national prestige.

Another aspect of transnational mobility during the colonial period is student border-crossing to Japan. Chapter 10 by Dolf-Alexander Neuhaus traces the transnational mobility of Korean activists, students, and intellectuals and the contributions of Korean students' activism against Japan's colonialism in Japan during the 1910s and 1920s together with the role of Taiwanese activists in shaping the history of interwar pan-Asianism from below. Examining colonial period journals published by Korean students and independence activists, including the *Asia Kunglun* (*Asia Kongnon* in Korean), the author observes anti-imperial critiques, shared "Asian" values, and Asian solidarity represented in the journals. He notes that the transnational intellectual space created by the student mobility and intellectual interaction amongst East Asian students and independence activists served as a platform for those seeking national liberation by envisioning a unity of Asia that transcends national and imperial boundaries.

Moving toward the 1950s, the next chapter by Minjung Kim looks at how the war-migration-marriage nexus created a special case in the history of war by investigating Korean marriage im/migrants from the Korean War period (1950–1953) in the Philippines, who are a rather invisible group among overseas Koreans. Drawing on the life stories of Korean women married to Filipinos, the author demonstrates their contribution to building the early Korean community and their own independent network building in the Philippines to provide mutual support. She addresses how the connection to their birth country reinforces the women's ethnic identities while embracing their intermarried status that distinguishes them from other Koreans in both Korea and in the Philippines. Her work centers on these marriage immigrants' ethnic identity and their agency in their migratory trajectory.

\* \* \*

The closing section by Brenda S.A. Yeoh expands the discussion of transnational mobility beyond Korea to the wider context of Asia, focusing on how family and work are shaped and reshaped through transnational migration, through which intimacies and identities across borders are negotiated. She suggests a highly mobile life is characteristic not only of permanent forms of migration, but also of temporary modes of migration as a broad range of people in Asia are on the move at any given time, and examines the way in which im/migration and mobility shape migrant-led complex diversifications in places of reception such as new practices of coexistence, cosmopolitanism, and bridge-building.

## NOTE

1. The total population of South Korea consists of 51,709,098 in July 2019 (Korean Statistical Information Service 2019, Ch'ugye in'gu).

# REFERENCES

Ahn, Yonson. 2014. "Gendering Migration: Koreanische Arbeitsmigrantinnen im Pflegesektor in Deutschland." In *Unbekannte Vielfalt: Einblicke in die koreanische Migrationsgeschichte in Deutschland*, edited by Young-Seoun Chang-Gusko et al., 166–187. Berlin: DOMiD.

Espiritu, Yen Le. 2003. *Home Bound: Filipino American Lives across Cultures, Communities and Countries*. Berkeley: University of California Press.

Harvey, David. 1990. *The Condition of Postmodernity: An Enquiry into the Origins of Cultural Change*. Oxford: Blackwell.

Korean Statistical Information Service. 2019. "Ch'ugye in'gu." http://kosis.kr/index/index.do.

Ministry of Foreign Affairs. 2017. "Chaeoe tongp'o hyŏnhwang 2017." http://www.mofa.go.kr/www/wpge/m_21507/contents.do.

Ministry of Justice. 2019. "2019nyŏn 5wŏrho ch'uripkuk oegugin chŏngch'aek t'onggye wŏlbo." http://www.moj.go.kr/bbs/immigration/227/502500/artclview.do.

Pratt, Mary Louise. 1992. *Imperial Eyes. Travel Writing and Transculturation*. London and New York: Routledge.

Sheller, Mimi, and John Urry. 2006. "The New Mobilities Paradigm." *Environment and Planning A* 38(2): 207–226.

Skeggs, Beverley. 2004. *Class, Self and Culture*. London: Routledge.

Urry, John. 2000. *Sociology Beyond Societies: Mobilities for the Twenty-First Century*. London: Routledge.

*Part I*

# Transnational Mobility and Media

*Chapter One*

# Media and Transnational Mobility of Korean Women

## Youna Kim

From the mid-1980s onward there has been a rising trend of Korean women leaving their country to experience life overseas either as tourists or students, eventually surpassing the number of men engaging in foreign travel (Kim 2011). These new generations of women, who depart from the usual track of marriage, are markers of contemporary transnational mobility, constituting a new kind of diaspora—a knowledge diaspora. This phenomenon is part of a larger trend described as the feminization of migration, yet there remains a striking lack of analysis both on the gender dimension and on the role of the media in this migratory process. Why do women move? Starting with this question, this chapter explores the unstudied nature of diaspora among young Korean women living and studying in the West. What are the actual conditions of their transnational lives? How do they make sense of their transnational lives through the experience of the media? Are they becoming cosmopolitan subjects? This study documents and analyzes the highly visible, fast-growing, yet little-studied phenomenon of women's transnational mobility and its relationship to the impact of media consumption in everyday life. Questions of identity are refigured in flows of desire that now operate transnationally, enacted by Korea's economic growth and integration into globalization that have enabled new generations of women to experience and then create a different life trajectory. This study brings forth a deepened understanding of the consequences of transnational mobility and the role of the media, providing detailed empirical data on the nature of the women's diaspora. Today's proliferation of the media, with new imaginations, new choices and contradictions, generates a critical condition for reflexivity, engaging everyday people to have a resource for the learning of self, culture, and society in a new light (Kim 2005, 2008, and 2011). As the study will argue, this plausibly powerful capacity of the media, deeply ingrained in what people take for granted, should be recognized in any attempt to understand the present phenomenon of transnational mobility.

This contemporary manifestation of transnational mobility has been facilitated by the proliferation of new media communications, digital technologies, and the deregulation in the 1990s creating multi-vocal, multimedia, and multi-directional flows, such as the "Korean Wave" media culture (Kim 2013), thereby making transnational networks and relations available with much greater frequency and regularity, as well as creating new meanings of being in the world. The choice of study abroad is not just a legitimate channel for physical mobility and displacement, but importantly involves the very nature of identity itself emerging as an increasingly popular do-it-yourself "reflexive biography," a self-determined yet highly precarious biographical strategy that is driven by imagined futures of individualization (Kim 2011 and 2012). A generalization about women's decisions to move can be grounded in an understanding of the transnationally dispersed sites, instances, and cultures of female individualization. Educated women have a strong interest in the idea of individualization, autonomous choice, and the aspiration for self-actualization; however, interest in individualization is a growing response not to the successful actualization of that aspiration, but to the frustrated desire for subjective autonomy that is increasingly felt in the "no choice" situation. This study intends to draw attention to the rise and the problematic issue of female individualization among young Korean women in the context of transnational mobility, while making a case for a more interrogatory approach towards gender and social change in the male-stream debate about individualization. The individualization of life experiences has become one of the central claims of contemporary social theory (Giddens 1991; Beck 1992; Bauman 2001; Beck and Beck-Gernsheim 2002). Education and career opportunities are generally regarded as the driving force behind the individualization of people's lives and social mobility. It is suggested that labor market positions now are constituted less by determinants such as gender, class, age, and place, but more by self-design, self-creation, and individual performance. There is a tendency to emphasize the increased fluidity of contemporary social life, as well as the mobile reflexive individual and his or her freedom of movement along with a consequence of personal choice. This individualization process is characterized by a growing reflexivity, self-monitoring, and awareness, and an expansion of dis-embedding mechanisms (Giddens 1991), including global flows of the media that lift social interactions out of the individuals' local context and allow them to relocate themselves in a transnationally dispersed culture. A shared ground and possibility of individualization is predicated on the labor market—finding work and achieving equality as well as success in education. This study will argue that the claim that education encourages work freedom, economic power, and the enlargement of choice can be illusory for educated women in Korea, where gendered socio-economic and cultural conditions persist and continue to structure labor market outcomes and lifestyles. Whose individualization? A contradiction lies at the heart of female individualization. The individualization of life experiences may reflect a discursive shift in the ways women today "imagine" and "talk" about their lives, rather than a substantive change in actual life conditions, regulative dimensions of gender and social structure which continue to shape available opportunities and constrain personal choice and freedom.

Against this social context, this study will consider a pull-effect of the media; that is, women's mediated symbolic encounter with the West that generates imaginations of alternative lifestyles and work (Kim 2005 and 2011). People seem to imagine routinely the possibility that they will live and work in places other than where they were born, and their plans are affected by a mass-mediated imaginary that frequently transcends national space (Appadurai 1996). Those who wish to move and those who have moved rarely formulate their plans outside the sphere of the media. It is mass mediation, the expanding scale, circulation and impact of media consumption, which distinguishes the present transnational mobility from migration of the past. Under social controls that deny women the ability to act on their own, the chances for individualization become smaller, and individualization can be sought in ever greater participation in media cultural consumption, the complex symbolic project women engage with (Kim 2012). Media consumption can be understood as a key cultural mechanism creating the emergence of individualized identities, both imagined and enacted. Transnational mobility needs to be understood with multi-faceted insights, considering some of the key macro factors affecting women's decisions to move and the micro processes of the ways in which women experience the mediated world of everyday culture, while reflecting the interconnection of these seemingly opposite and contradictory levels of push-and-pull elements within the particular socio-economic and cultural contexts in which women live their everyday lives (Kim 2011).

In the contemporary discussion of transnational mobility, there is a tendency to romanticize all forms of mobility as themselves intrinsically progressive, and this meaning has become celebrated as a transgressive and liberating departure from living-as-usual. Physical mobility is seen as the basis of emancipatory practice, and diaspora as the site of contingency *par excellence* because it generates stasis-disrupting forms of cultural displacement (Clifford 1994). It is further related to the possibility for endless hybrid self-creation, since it involves a translational sense of culture in new in-between spaces to initiate innovative, anti-essentialist signs of identity (Bhabha 1994). In the extreme "beautification of the nomad in Western epistemology" (Peters 1999), transnational Korean women on the move may appear to be new signifiers of change or self-expressive icons of hybridity with endless possibilities for self-creation, and their mobility may be seen as not only physical but also intellectual, liberating thinking from localism and breaking out towards a rootless life with transgressive power. However, this study will suggest that the tendency to celebrate transnational mobility is often separated from mundane reality and obscures actual conditions and experiences; that is, the complex ways in which it is experienced by women within diasporic lives in larger relations to the social contexts of the world, which do not necessarily involve progressive dimensions. Embedded in the liberal West or "liquid individualized society," where individuals must plan, produce, and accomplish their biographies themselves (Bauman 2001), women experience new burdens of choice and dilemmas of personal responsibility alongside increased personal freedoms, as well as global structures of domination and unspeakable inequality of racial relations (Kim 2011).

To avoid romanticization of transnational mobility *per se*, this study will analyze how the diaspora is lived and experienced in the everyday, and importantly what resources women adopt in their efforts to make sense of their transnational lives. The media in a digital age are among the integral resources that shape diasporic experiences and identities (Kim 2011 and 2017). The Internet and television create key spaces where people are variously invited to construct a sense of self—whether as "us" and "them," "insider" and "outsider," "citizen" and "foreigner," "normal" and "deviant," "the West" and "the rest" (Cottle 2000). Displaced from their homelands, diasporic subjects attempt to re-create their own imaginative or mythical space of home and connectivity by developing transnational communications networks which use a variety of information and communication technologies, while negotiating cultural difference and identity between home and host countries (Gillespie 1995; Cunningham and Sinclair 2001; Karim 2003). Diasporic media space is a transnational site of contestation in which nation, race, gender, class, culture, and language continuously interrelate to produce complex identities. New kinds of transnational mobility and media flow are creating unpredictable patterns of identification, as well as insecurities and uncertainties about being and belonging in the world.

Diaspora is a place of identity, living with, living through difference, and the diasporic are always producing themselves anew and differently, finding ways of being the same as and at the same time different from, the others amongst whom they live. Identity is a "production" that is never complete, always in process, always constituted within, not outside, representation, and it must be negotiated (Hall 1990). If the women's identity is in the process of production in the new contexts of transnational encounters, what would that identity be like? If transnational mobility leads to the inner mobility of an individual's own life or to the "globalization of biography" (Beck 2000), precisely what does that globalization of biography mean to the young Korean women on the move? This study will argue that transnational mobility does not necessarily diminish but rather enhances national identity. Women's experience of social exclusion in the lived reality produces paradoxical consequences for media use and new identity positions. While engagement with the Western media back home once had a powerful influence on women to imagine new ways of being and create a new desire to be mobile (Kim 2005 and 2008), such engagement decreases dramatically after moving to a Western destination; in this different context women's ethnic media become of more importance as their ethnic media affirm a sense of belonging, self-esteem, and confidence (Kim 2011). Diasporic nationalism emerges as reactionary ethno-nationalism within global knowledge diasporas of those who appear to be bilingual cross-cultural negotiators moving regularly between different cultures and participating in exchanges across national borders. While the significance of nationalism in a transnational context, or long-distance nationalism, has been recognized (Anderson 1992; Smith 1995), the focus of this study is on a relatively less explored phenomenon of women's transnational mobility and its unique nature—the syndrome of young Korean women, who are highly educated mobile transnationals "willing to go anywhere for a while," is something quite new, in part enabled by the transnational Internet. Transnational practices do not necessarily evoke higher levels of identification with transnationalism or a multiple sense of belonging to more than one nation, but can cause a turn towards nationalism, thus challenging the post-national assumption—the de-centering and decline of the nation as a result of the increase in transnational connections (Hannerz 1996; Beck 2000). Serious concerns can be raised about the use of the popular term transnationalism or cosmopolitanism, mostly prompted by an exaggerated characterization of transnational mobility today.

In the current debate of transnational mobility, cosmopolitanism has become the privileged, prime term of analysis for characterizing qualities in people and their identities. Transnational groups are figured as the bearers of de-territorialized cosmopolitanism, as "always already cosmopolitan," which goes beyond the grip of any individual state. Their cultures are characterized as worldly, productive sites of crossing and as exemplary instances of active resistance to national cultures and localism (Clifford 1992; Bhabha 1994). The recent re-vitalization of cosmopolitanism has been in fashion since the 1990s, amid intensifying globalization of late liberalism, capital, mobility, and the media. Greater frequency of travel and transnational media cultural flows create a zone in which emergent global forms of cosmopolitanism are brought into a conflictual relationship with nationalist forms of culture (Appadurai 1996). Cosmopolitanism suggests a more outward-looking disposition, a mode of engaging with the world and such experiential openness and willingness towards divergent cultural experiences (Hannerz 1990). Invoked as a moral and ethical ideal, cosmopolitanism means learning from each other's differences through conversation and taking an interest in the practices and beliefs that lend them significance (Appiah 2006). It represents a normative philosophy transcending all identities—a universal identification that does not place love/loyalty of country ahead of love of mankind, universal humanity (Nussbaum 1997), assuming that extensive learning of human diversity will lead to a finding of common human qualities and purposes. This emergent form of cosmopolitanism has come to be cast as a potentially liberatory space, a locus of progressive politics and rejection of parochial nationalist positions. But who is it that experiences cosmopolitanism? The question here is, how exactly they are cosmopolitan subjects, in what ways, and whether they construct for themselves a cosmopolitan position. The social reality of cosmopolitanism is much more ambiguous, marked by global structures of power and inequality, exclusion and inclusion governing one's relationship to Others and the world (Kim 2011 and 2017). This study will foreground the tensions and struggles at the heart of the cosmopolitan subject in a hierarchically defined world of the West, where Korean women strive to negotiate their status transnationally.

In order to explore the nature of women's transnational mobility, media, and identity, this ethnographic project undertook a two-stage approach to data collection; personal in-depth interviews and diaries. Interviews were conducted with 20 Korean women who had been living and studying in the UK/London for 3 to 7 years. The women's ages were between 26 and 33 years, and they were single women of middle-class and upper-class positions. They were recruited by the snowball method of sampling, based on friendship networks of the participants, and several snowballs were used to ensure that interviews were conducted with women from different universities. Interviews were open-ended and unstructured, supplemented by some fixed questioning on the social and cultural backgrounds of the participants. Each interview lasted between 1.5 and 2 hours, with 4 to 5 follow-up interviews on average to ensure a maximum flow of relevant data. Their longing to tell stories or the evocation of travelling narratives from the marginal spaces of diaspora, as manifested in the interviewing context, mutually led to another method of conversation: email diaries. A panel of 10 diarists were recruited from the women interviewed; they were asked to write/email diaries about their experiences and to express in detail key issues raised by the interviews. This method was designed to generate biographical material accounts from the women and incorporate a reflexive biographical analysis. The women willingly participated in this study on the condition of anonymity and confidentiality. Throughout the text below, all names of the women in this study have been withheld to protect their identity and vulnerability.

# FEMALE INDIVIDUALIZATION, MEDIA, AND REFLEXIVITY

Education guarantees nothing. In Korea, the more women are educated, the more we would find it difficult to get a job. Not just any kind of job that doesn't need a university degree or just a low-paid secretary. . . .
There was no job future, no hope to make my own life. It's the only exit.

I am doing another MA degree (in the UK), moving from this country to another country, until I find a solution. Don't know if another degree will give me a better job in Korea, or the same job, or a jobless life. . . . I don't think higher education in Korea gives a good job opportunity. I also don't believe higher education overseas will necessarily promise a better job opportunity, but I will give it a try anyway as there seems no other choice.

If work life is not fulfilling, mothers' generation would choose marriage. We try to find an alternative, such as studying abroad, hoping to find better work. Work comes first, marriage later.

"Education without a guarantee" is illustrated in gendered Korea, where the dualistic labor market, with non-regular workers accounting for a third of employment, and the under-employment of women remain labor market challenges (KWDI 2009; OECD 2014; Kim 2016). The low female employment rate (53.5%, the 10th lowest in the OECD) in contrast to women's high level of tertiary education (64%, the second highest in the OECD), and the gender gap in female earnings (64%, the largest gap in the OECD) reflect Korea's under-utilization of its human capital, the high share of women in non-regular jobs, and the far lower share of women in management leadership positions. Many women are employed in traditional female tracks, non-managerial and secretarial positions unrelated to their educational qualifications. A contradiction of female individualization lies in the gap between the growing expectations of education and the reality of work inequality. With the experience of frequent temporary employment, long-term unemployment, and the pervasive culture of uncertainty or scepticism about employment, some middle-class women have been discouraged from seeking work or have given up the search for work. There has been a remarkably impressive increase in educational attainment for middle-class women in Korea, and with universal access to education historically being regarded as a crucial means of national development and upward social mobility, gender inequality is generally thought to be diminished or non-existent at the educational level of the middle class. However, women equipped with work knowledge and marketable skills are often confronted with male privilege that has been perpetuated within the domestic labor market system and organizational corporate culture, from the processes of recruitment to job assignments, promotion, rewards, work identity, and satisfaction. Work identity is a central feature of women's lives. The workplace can be a distinctive site for the construction of identity, and work satisfaction can build a renewed sense of self;

however, little of this seems necessarily available to women. Nevertheless, the self is sought in work biography, the working-self. While marriage is not repudiated but postponed temporarily, women's socio-economic status has not been improved enough to operate individualization through work (Kim 2011 and 2012).

By choosing different ways of living and being in the world, young Korean women desire to take total charge of their own lives and constitute themselves as a designer of their own biography and identity. The emerging trend towards individualization—delaying marriage temporarily yet not completely repudiating marriage, aspiring work participation in the domestic or the international job market, pursuing personal freedom yet manifesting itself in close ties with the family—has become almost a constant focus of the women moving away from Korea (Kim 2011). Despite the fact that younger generations of Korean women have attained as much education as their male counterparts and are relatively free to compete and excel in the domain of education, women's achievement in higher education does not necessarily lead to the viability of individualization—better job prospects, economic and social rewards, enlarged freedom and choice. The educated person does not necessarily or eventually become the producer of her own labor situation, and in this way, of her own social biography. Women's willpower, performative agency, and education alone cannot be an effective transformative force in the identity politics of individualization.

This disjuncture between education and labor market conditions, the persistence of gender inequality, and the women's desire to plan a more self-determined life politics are some of the main forces that have led to growing transnational mobility. "It's the only exit." This indicates a deep dissatisfaction with the systematic contradictions that make Korean women feel that there is little they can do to change the "no choice" situation. Women are frustrated in varying degrees by the way they find themselves disempowered in social conditions that limit work possibilities and lifestyle choices. The lack of fit between the role of education in opening up the possibility of mobility and female individualization, and women's unemployment and under-employment propel them to move away from Korea, which may be an expression not only of their own hopes, but also of their rage against the unproductive consequences of education and the determinacy of structure. The seemingly unachievable idea of individualization is endlessly played out in women's "imagination" and "media talk" and thus remains an unresolved identity in everyday life (Kim 2005, 2011 and 2012).

> I don't like marriage pressure from the whole family, "When will you get married?" Everybody interferes in my life.

In Western society, people choose any kind of life they want. The more I see it on the media, the more I think. If I go there, wouldn't life be free? I imagined such a possibility.

My job might be OK, my life might be OK compared to my mother's. But I didn't feel happy, couldn't be satisfied with just that! I have bigger desires. . . . The more I got to know bigger things through the media, the more I thought about them. I asked myself, am I having a happy life? Why can't I live like that?

"The more I see it on the media, the more I think." The media are implicated in the imaginative pull towards mobility and the emergence of fledgling individualized identities within women's socio-cultural landscape, where the multitude of quotidian constraints and expressions for a not-yet-realized self take place in their lack of choice and control. While Korean society does not encourage women to pursue different ways of being, notions of a new self, an individualized individual, are effectively discovered and articulated within their mediated experience. Although young women strongly desire to be unleashed from traditional norms and expectations, to escape the quotidian constraints of their provincial existence, and to create a self-determining identity of their own, it usually turns out to be the case that the freely chosen game of identity is played out often within the women's imagination and media talk. A yearning for a new identity and a new mode of life is continually expanding in the increasingly globalizing, mediated world of everyday life, which stimulates a high degree of reflexivity in close relation to lived experience and further interweaves its relevance structure into an ongoing process of the self (Kim 2005, 2008 and 2011).

This mediated experience becomes articulated self-reflexively in terms of the changing socio-economic shifts expected by educated Korean women, and these very expectations in light of consuming the symbolic West have led to more complex dilemmas and contradictions. Young Korean women appear to have more choices and capacities in life, higher education, more knowledge, and better material provisions compared to past generations, yet this does not necessarily translate into greater happiness. Expectations of satisfaction have risen, affected by what other people have or an insatiable endless desire to have, which occurs through the intrusion of global cultural Others into everyday consciousness via the global media and has the consequence of causing both rising expectations and rising frustrations. The knowing individual's self-conscious engagement with, and symbolic exploration through, the media develops resources for self-imagining as an everyday social project that has a potential to transform everyday discourse of subjectivity and to mobilize the imagined self in actuality. This imaginative social practice as mediated by the everyday cultural consumption is grounded in deliberate agency and lived experience, generating multiple points of everyday reflexivity, self-monitoring, self-confrontation and self-analysis. ("Am I having a happy life?") Younger generations of educated women today, more knowledgeable than previous generations, can be characterized by a growing reflexivity and the imagining of more choices or a "choice biography against a normal biography" (Giddens 1991), constantly choosing, changing, competing, and constructing an identity, albeit predicated upon structural constraints, thereby a sense of happiness is heavily driven by the situation of imagined global Others and a "heightened desire to keep up with other people" (Layard 2005).

Young Korean women become increasingly aware of differences and changes in the socio-cultural position of women elsewhere in a wider world, while at the same time the process of their self-reflexive imagination in mediated popular culture can cause a sense of unhappiness and a prolonged decision to act upon. Such self-reflexive imagination in an increasingly mediated world may not always present or lead to immediate action, but it is a historically accumulated quality through long-term exposure to the everyday media that can potentially form a powerful yet taken-for-granted staging ground for the conduct of physical movement or a very firm orientation towards mobility. Significantly, media consumption is constitutive of the process of transnational mobility, female individualization, and identity work, not to be seen as an entirely determining force but to be understood as a mediating cultural experience within an imaginative, seductive, yet highly selective and intentional, everyday social project of the self (Kim 2011 and 2012).

## BANAL RACISM

Migrant women may use a transnational space as a rare and effective way to avoid conformity to normative gender roles and regulatory obstacles to their individualization, in an effort to create self-identity without the shackles of home traditions in an extended process of reflexivity and a seemingly open and seductive culture of a world city. Dis-embedded from the everyday regulatory practices, migrant women try to negotiate their way around or out of the initial familial and social position, and hope to find opportunities for a more self-fulfilling and independent lifestyle. Diasporic consciousness develops a new capacity to consider many little cultural differences in everyday encounters and to reflect on who they are in relation to cultural Others, while the increasingly self-steered phenomenon produces the disproportionate cost making them remain vulnerable to the unpredictable and constraining aspects of diasporic conditions. The world city of the multiplicity of Others is a place that is "open to everyone who has their own caravan and money to pay the rent" (Bauman 2001), but also a highly ambiguous place where every decision becomes a personal risk and the state of transnational existence is far from liberating.

> I will be always a foreigner, though having lived here (in London) for 7 years. . . . I often moved room because of fleas, noisy neighbor, water leakage, blocked toilet that never got fixed. Nobody cares. . . . People think moving is a good thing, freedom. But why bother to move if life is so good? I cannot articulate this repressive feeling but feel clearly. . . . It's the everyday little things that matter. Racism is not like hitting but staring or just ignoring. Is it because we are Korean, Asian? We imagined England would be a country of gentlemen.
>
> I feel confused about racism, superiority over Asians. I cannot express but feel clearly. They rarely say "sorry" even though things are clearly their fault. The city space is beautiful if we don't have to deal with people. . . . Life here in London is vulnerable and lonely, not colorful. When a problem (verbal assault) happened in a shop, I wanted to call somebody for help but suddenly realized I don't even have a close friend to call here.
>
> It's like proud B&B culture—people will always come to the city of Buckingham Palace and leave. It signals to foreigners, "If you don't like it, go back to your country." I will never belong. . . . I do all on my own, feel so alone. It's inevitable to invent a life as an observer. While living here, I am physically close but mentally distant.

Korean women's transnational lives are often described in terms of a struggle for articulation as a tool for progressive practice and emancipatory politics. This experiential lack of articulation with the yet-to-be-heard voices precludes the deeply felt tensions, while repressing a complex and many-sided translation of how the banal experience of the everyday, thoughts and sentiments shape and define the meaning of marginal discourses, different conditions of being and becoming. Ambiguous and subliminal forms of everyday racism ("not like hitting but staring or just ignoring"), inferiorization, and alienation at an interpersonal level can be shocking when England was imagined to be different, cultivated ("country of gentlemen"). Racism is a sign of rejection that one will never belong. In a changing Europe, built on economic models of mobility and integration, mobile transnationals appear not to face discrimination; however, seductive world cities like London are also national capitals, which exclude even the most privileged of foreigners on the "human dimension" (Favell 2008). Diasporic space is not primarily a sociable space to valorize, connect, and exchange with Others, but a space of struggle to deal with societal insecurity and a tacit acceptance of individuated practice ("all on my own"). An observational and indifferent predisposition ("physically close but mentally distant") emerges within lived and mediated experience at a symbolic level.

Confusions, struggles, and painful silences continue to operate in the lack of articulation and social support. Reflection upon the subjective ethnic experiences of migration and displacement in ambiguous social situations of eve-ryday life manifestly present unresolved tensions in conflict with banal racism ("everyday little things"), implicitly violent communication and adversity, disrespect, isolation, and loneliness ("feel so alone"). Racism in its multiple forms of discrimination is a very personal and profoundly affective experience in diasporic everyday life, intersected with emotionally charged moments that are felt with sharp clarity but often defy description and legitimate representation ("cannot express but feel clearly"). The prevailing national cultures of the host societies marked by mundane "banal nationalism" (Billig 1995), alongside institutionalized racism and government-sponsored policy interventions, can affect processes of global mobility and the extents of willing integration or resisting non-integration in different ways. These powerful modalities can simultaneously create myriad and subtle forms of social exclusion, and crucially set "internalized limits on the vision and imagination of potentially mobile subjects" (Smith and Favell 2006).

The experiences of new migrant communities today, including those of the highly educated and skilled, relatively empowered, global knowledge diasporas, continue to demonstrate that racism is still endemic and systemic, not only problematically a thing of the powerful colonial past. Global inequalities and the exclusionary workings of race and ethnicity apparently concern and affect the relatively less disadvantaged migration of the higher social classes, even the most hyper-mobile transnational elites of the upper and the middle classes. Their privileged social class position and higher knowledge level does not necessarily prevent exclusion, vulnerability, and precariousness in other ways since they can still be easily racialized or ethni-cized negatively. The emergence of new racisms, subtle yet pervasive, and of new racialized identities in a multicultural world city of Europe with some form of imperialist history, such as London, is often a reflection of and perhaps a result of "fear of the unknown" that may be outrightly and unreasonably hostile to foreigners of any description (Menski 2002).

As a consequence, the sojourning attitude as a perpetual foreigner ("will be always a foreigner") is very common among these migrant women in this study in their mundane experience of social exclusion, with distinctive challenges more than opportunities for interaction with, and willing incorporation into, the mainstream of host society or even the self-claimed multicultural cosmopolitan city, since diasporic individuals and ethnic minorities are frequently reminded of their non-belonging status. Racial discrimination makes subordinate groups withdraw to their ethnic enclaves in order to avoid hostility from the white dominant groups of the mainstream society, or come to engage in social and symbolic closure that may further lead to sustained and durable inequality in racial relations. The consequence of the lived experience of exclusionary practices in diasporic existence often means self-conscious distancing themselves from the mainstream society, and instead, ordering their own lives on their own terms with their own communication channels, mediated networks, and cultural resources as a self-conscious choice of a coping strategy, while simultaneously producing new identity positions on the organization of the self that may paradoxically reinforce self-exclusion (Kim 2011 and 2017).

## DIASPORIC NATIONALISM

In the first year I watched television to know this (British) society. Now (after 3 years) don't watch. The more I watch, the more I feel alienated. . . . There's no connection. It's too British. I liked the British accent before (in Korea) because it sounded posh, but now that accent feels alienating too.

Now (after 4 years) I don't even turn on TV. It's ordinary, stagnant life, no representation of people like us (Koreans).

My room is small, the UK television is in my closet. It's just not interesting. . . . Why try to know them when they don't try to know us (Koreans)? While living abroad we look for something better.

With a deeply emotional and existential doubt about belonging in their experiences of the ambiguous and subliminal forms of banal racism, Korean women's understanding of their social position further resonates in the symbolic realm of confrontation, disengagement, or withdrawal. Everyday UK television and ethos, "very national in its orientation" with distinctive modes of address, humanly pleasing care structures, and the inflexion of a voice, may work naturally on "those for whom it is made" (Scannell 1996); however, it is experienced differently by these Korean women, or not even there-to-be-found ("the UK television is in my closet"). Its defining character and image are often viewed as "too British," "not interesting," "alienating," "no connection" within the national symbolic space, which makes foreign subjects feel disengaged. The degree of disengagement is suggestive not merely of indifference, but also of a small act of resistance and strategy to regulate the tension of belonging and avoid the unexpected surprise that disturbs the diasporic yearning ("something better"). This mediated experience, discontinuous with their feeling, reflecting, and behaving, orients them towards a diasporic media space that is close to a deep and enduring relevance of experience. Engagement with the ethnic media and communicative activities is a logical choice and determining resource that "suddenly" gains a special meaning.

I am suddenly addicted to our Korean media. I rarely watched TV in Korea as my social life was busy, colorful. . . . Through website Naver I get all information, how to make food, kim-chi, do everything myself as everything in London is expensive.

It's all there! Through the Internet I watch Korean dramas, download movies, music every night. I keep in touch with friends, express what I am doing, how I feel, what made me angry today. . . . I cried while watching Korean dramas alone. Perhaps the first time I cried while living abroad, never cried over any hardship. It suddenly evoked a repressed feeling and made me realize home.

Displaced subjects can find social ontological security in their own communication channels and become attached, or even more ("suddenly addicted"), to the inclusive mediated community, while becoming less interested in or connected to the host society. The new connection to the ethnic media from the national homeland and its substantial impact can promote disengagement and further distance from the mainstream. New ways of being and feeling at home are created and sustained by means of virtual engagement. The "Korean Wave" media culture in a digital age (Kim 2013) and variegated ritualistic links—via Korean social networking websites, infotainment online portals, food, drama, film, music as a constant background—are established in the structure of everyday life. This mediated experience away from home has multiple purposes; it is a response to the loss of belonging, a self-determined need to seek symbolic inclusion, a desire to connect with significant others back home, and a pleasure to expand the space for self-expression, understanding, and articulation in the language of home. The habits and strategies for experiencing home in the routines of diasporic lives develop into the Internet resources. But what is significant here is not just the sheer availability of the Internet now, but also the self-determination of users and the consequences of how they use it. They affirm a sense of continuity, self-esteem, and deliberate nationalism that is emotively marked and powerful.

Keeping my distinct Korean identity enhances self-esteem when experiencing disrespect towards minorities. I am always a foreigner. . . . Change me depending upon who they are. Be cool, formal, less smile to the majority to keep respect for who we are. Although we like personal freedom here (in London) that is limited in Korea, there are essential differences between us and them.

Watching TV back home I imagined life here, but living here I become indifferent. Never felt my essential self as Korean so strongly before. I become more Korean, unique while living abroad. . . . I don't fit quite here or quite there. I can live anywhere in the world if there is a good job and the Internet connection for all Korean stuff.

For the Korean women who are acutely aware of the reality of foreignness and how much they differ from the majority, their transnational lives do not easily result in emancipation. Navigating and code-switching ("depending upon who they are") is a life necessity but not a straight choice. A paradox evident is that the more physically close, the more they try to remain different, distinct. The search for uniqueness becomes intense and dependent on the ethnic media space where the symbolic construction of internal and external boundaries is regularly sustained. Although some aspect of lifestyle change can make Korean women feel incompatible with lives back home, there is a strong denial of association or influence from the West host society, finding themselves located neither "quite here" nor "quite there"; indeed, neither place is desirable any longer. To resist a Western influence is a quality that manifests itself in lived relations of difference, often as a reaction to the hegemonic racial order and denigration, as a conscious way of reclaiming status ("respect for who we are"). Diasporic nationalism emerges within a larger transnational framework, reinstating a territorial space for revitalized national perspectives and reifying the taken-for-grantedness of essentialist identities. Ironically, the choice to live in the world does not necessarily lead to an expanded world view or enlargement of self, but rather a constrictive one that is an inevitable consequence of the lived experience of social closure.

When the dominant meaning system of a new culture in a new environment is seen as a constant source of irritation or a daily reminder of non-belonging, some migrants may deal with it in a direct and confrontational way, whereas many other migrants, including these Korean women, may decide to retreat into an ethnic enclave, physically, psychologically, and symbolically. Transnational migrants and ethnic minorities, when feeling pushed aside and excluded from the mainstream of host society, may spend significant parts of their everyday lives on their own communication channels and mediated networks in order to carve out imaginative spaces of control and of highly selective social interaction, or as an effort to seek to express the common experiences of social exclusion and marginality in their own national language and thus counteract dominant discourses in the present (Kim 2011 and 2017). Regular engagement with the online, Internet-enabled, ethnic media space enables Korean migrant women to retain connections to the homeland culture by means of virtual, imaginary, and ritualistic re-creations of home, which can be routinely established in their mediated experience and sustain a more inclusive, sometimes pleasurable and ontologically secure ("comfort zone"), primary diasporic contact zone. This can be seen as part of strategies or everyday tactical activities that lie hidden behind, much less visible, but that routinely make such mediated experience "habitable" in their mind and potentially "negotiate the unfamiliar in the sphere of familiarity" (De Certeau 1984). An increasingly significant channel for the construction of the habitable sphere of familiarity is through the Internet symbolic realm, in which the lived experience of the diaspora is being re-organized and managed in the every day, and in which necessary cultural resources and frameworks for symbolic inclusion and a subjective sense of belonging are being formed in the margin. The ethnic media space, as the necessary cultural resources and tactical arts of living, can often be appropriated and developed as defensive mechanisms among diasporas in everyday life (Kim 2011 and 2017).

This defensive sense of inclusion, self-enclosing engagement with or retreat into an ethnic enclave and the imaginative spatialization of belonging, as enabled by the ethnic media space, is usually strategic and creative but also highly contradictory in its consequences. Self-exclusion, by choice or not, may be operating on a daily basis, when globally mobile migrants choose to engage with alternative spaces of belonging through their own ethnic media as coping mechanisms, not merely to cope with loneliness but also to stay out of the subtle social exclusion in operation and of the local social structures of the host society, which they had chosen to migrate to and inhabit. Migrants caught up in this contradictory situation may remain ethnically distinct, socially constrained, and perpetually excluded, while constituting and inhabiting a new imaginary symbolic home that is mythical yet meaningful temporarily across cultural boundaries. Their lived experience of transnational lives does not easily generate or automatically imply a much greater diversification of life; but rather, diasporic nationalism emerges as an expressive marker of the self, even as Korean women were so eager to stay away from the national home for its gendered socio-economic and cultural constraints and they were often trapped in secondary status in relation to the gendered modalities of power (Kim 2011). This unintended shifting and seemingly contradictory enactment of the national self ("becoming more Korean while living abroad") should be understood in wider relational contexts; the ways in which the global structures and dialectics of inclusion and exclusion operate within the hegemonic politics of difference and identity that is intrinsically linked to differential power and inequality.

## WHOSE COSMOPOLITANISM?

They [British] have no interest in us [Koreans]. Whether inside school life or outside, depending on whom we meet, depending on the luck! Generally they don't bother to know about us.

I don't feel connection in human interactions [in London]. I come to realize, why try to know them when they don't try to know us?

We hear people in the classroom talk about cosmopolitanism. We just listen. Whatever that means, it is their idea. We never invented cosmopolitanism. If that means following them, losing our own identity, it is meaningless to desire that.

"They have no interest in us." Much of the motivation and possibility of becoming cosmopolitan subjects depends on the contexts, discursive and communicative encounters, and common existential experiences. Any possible viability of cosmopolitan identity formation is seen to be a relative one ("depending on whom we meet"), hence, a matter of luck and contingency, more than a matter of choice; one cannot freely choose and operate its potentiality in one's own agency. Cosmopolitanism should be understood by situated and relational experience. It is a dialogic formation in the specific contexts encountered, wherein the meaning of identity operates from its interaction with a system of differences and the inequitable exercise of power shapes the extent of one's belonging, or non-belonging, to the world as a whole. A resulting response by the excluded ethnic minorities is often a feeling of rejection and self-doubt, a reflexive distantiation and potentially subversive resistance, or a self-determined withdrawal from the cosmopolitan openness ("Why try to know them when they don't try to know us?") in the hidden contestation of asymmetrical knowledge and asymmetrical ignorance.

"We never invented cosmopolitanism." A strong disassociation or repudiation from the concept of cosmopolitanism as a Western invention, as well as its situated reason, can be underpinned by the marginalizing experiences of the unequal, West-centric contexts and sometimes antagonistic human interactions. This affective and lived dimension of displacement can reinforce non-cosmopolitanism, and even more, anti-cosmopolitanism. A discussion of diversity in the Western academy, with its unreflexive celebration of cultural difference, is inadequate without an engagement with the asymmetrical postcolonial flows of power in racial imaginations, and difference whose existence may escape such maps of imagination (Shome 2006). Social exclusion and discrimination have been part of the process of constructing Europe that is rooted in nationality not residence. Ethnic minorities are often excluded from Britain's national cultural life with its longstanding racialization of belonging; paradoxically, what a culture of liberty, or the vernacular cosmopolitanism of European capital cities such as London, cannot deliver is a sense of belonging and certainty (Stevenson 2003). An increasing awareness of global connectivity through the media and imagined cosmopolitanism back home may project an inclusive world of strangers that openly receives them, yet the actual experience of inhabiting the world is often devoid of social affiliation and can be unbearably lonely.

Cosmopolitanism, as a lived human experience and as an existential thesis, could stand strongly opposed to, and feel far from, an idealist sentiment of the concept that considerably obscures and de-emphasizes, whether unwittingly or not, the significance of the constraining social structures, the enduring asymmetries of power and domination, inequalities and uneven dialogic relations, in which everyday transnational lives and practices are embedded, operate, and sometimes even reproduce and perpetuate such constraint. Cosmopolitanism as a normative, moral, and philosophical ideal means "learning from each other's differences through conversation" (Appiah 2006), or "overcoming national identity as an ideological or naturalized constraint"

(Beck 2006) and transcending all identities by "a universal identification that does not place love/loyalty of country ahead of universal humanity" (Nussbaum 1997). However, this overwhelmingly normative ideal of cosmopolitanism, and its abstract formulation, or its utopian and automatic cosmopolitan vision, can be seen as merely celebrating cultural differences and human diversity, uncritically assuming an inclusiveness and engagement with differences, and also assuming an unconditionally motivating attitude towards all human beings across national borders and cultural boundaries.

National identity becomes an emotionally charged, ambiguously empowered constitutive narrative of self-understanding that penetrates deep into diasporic thoughts and feelings when there are confusions and doubts about belonging (Kim 2011 and 2017). Actual conditions of transnational lives can underline the new construction of boundaries and essentialized differences while stressing "the nation's uniqueness as an indispensable legitimizing principle" (Conversi 2000). It is suggested that there is a tendency among Asian students to perceive a sense of solidarity and connection with other Asian students in the presence of European students in English-speaking countries (Kobayashi 2010). Although such a tendency is also the case with Korean women in this study, the formation of this context-bound cosmopolitan relationship prompted by unequal power relations of Asia/Europe broadly is also marked by, and limited within, their recognition of, and conscious search for, nationalizing differentiation and the national uniqueness of subjectivity within these shared communities of Asia. Transnational mobility and interaction does not easily generate a cosmopolitanizing experience of the world, a fluid and extended sense of belonging beyond national boundaries, but rather presents concrete manifestations of nationalism and the limits of imagined cosmopolitanism in the motivations of act.

This chapter is a revised version of my book *Transnational Migration, Media and Identity of Asian Women: Diasporic Daughters* (Routledge, 2011) and appears here with the permission of the publisher.

# REFERENCES

Anderson, Benedict. 1992. *Long-Distance Nationalism*. Berkeley, CA: Center for German and European Studies.
Appadurai, Arjun. 1996. *Modernity at Large*. Minneapolis: University of Minnesota Press.
Appiah, Kwame Anthony. 2006. *Cosmopolitanism: Ethics in a World of Strangers*. New York: Norton.
Bauman, Zygmunt. 2001. *The Individualized Society*. Cambridge: Polity.
Beck, Ulrich. 1992. *Risk Society: Towards a New Modernity*. London: Sage.
———. 2000. *What Is Globalization?* Cambridge: Polity.
———. 2006. *Cosmopolitan Vision*. Cambridge: Polity.
Beck, Ulrich, and Elisabeth Beck-Gernsheim. 2002. *Individualization*. London: Sage.
Bhabha, Homi. 1994. *The Location of Culture*. New York: Routledge.
Billig, Michael. 1995. *Banal Nationalism*. London: Sage.

Clifford, James. 1992. "Travelling Cultures." In *Cultural Studies*, edited by Lawrence Grossberg, Cary Nelson, and Paula Treichler, 96–116. New York: Routledge.

———. 1994. "Diasporas." *Current Anthropology* 9: 302–38.

Conversi, Daniele. 2000. "Cosmopolitanism and Nationalism." In *Encyclopedia of Nationalism*, edited by Atheba Leoussi and Anthony Smith, 48–52. London: Transaction.

Cottle, Simon. 2000. *Ethnic Minorities and the Media*. Buckingham, PA: Open University Press.

Cunningham, Stuart, and John Sinclair. 2001. *Floating Lives: The Media and Asian Diaspora*. Lanham, MD: Rowman & Littlefield.

De Certeau, Michel. 1984. *The Practice of Everyday Life*. Berkeley: University of California Press.

Favell, Adrian. 2008. *Eurostars and Eurocities*. Oxford: Blackwell.

Giddens, Anthony. 1991. *Modernity and Self-identity: Self and Society in the Late Modern Age*. Cambridge: Polity.

Gillespie, Marie. 1995. *Television, Ethnicity and Cultural Change*. London: Routledge.

Hall, Stuart. 1990. "Cultural Identity and Diaspora." In *Identity: Community, Culture, Difference*, edited by Jonathan Rutherford, 222–237. London: Lawrence & Wishart.

Hannerz, Ulf. 1990. "Cosmopolitans and Locals in World Culture." In *Global Culture: Nationalism, Globalization and Modernity*, edited by Mike Featherstone, 237–252. London: Sage.

———. 1996. *Transnational Connections: Culture, People, Places*. London: Routledge.

Karim, Karim. 2003. *The Media of Diaspora*. London: Routledge.

Kim, Youna. 2005. *Women, Television and Everyday Life in Korea: Journeys of Hope*. London: Routledge.

———. 2008. *Media Consumption and Everyday Life in Asia*. London: Routledge.

———. 2011. *Transnational Migration, Media and Identity of Asian Women: Diasporic Daughters*. London: Routledge.

———. 2012. *Women and the Media in Asia: The Precarious Self*. London: Palgrave Macmillan.

———. 2013. *The Korean Wave: Korean Media Go Global*. London: Routledge.

———. 2016. *Routledge Handbook of Korean Culture and Society*. London: Routledge.

———. 2017. *Childcare Workers, Global Migration and Digital Media*. London: Routledge.

Kobayashi, Yoko. 2010. "Discriminatory Attitudes toward Intercultural Communication in Domestic and Overseas Contexts." *Higher Education* 59: 323–33.

KWDI (Korean Women's Development Institute). 2009. *Statistical Yearbook on Women*. Seoul: Korean Women's Development Institute.

Layard, Richard. 2005. *Happiness: Lessons from a New Science*. London: Penguin.

Menski, Werner. 2002. "Immigration and Multiculturalism in Britain." A paper presented at Osaka University of Foreign Studies, July 2002.

Nussbaum, Martha. 1997. *Cultivating Humanity*. Cambridge: Harvard University Press.

OECD. 2014. *OECD Economic Surveys: Korea 2014*. Paris: OECD Publishing.

Peters, John Durham. 1999. "Exile, Nomadism and Diaspora." In *Home, Homeland, Exile*, edited by Hamid Naficy, 17–44. New York: Routledge.

Scannell, Paddy. 1996. *Radio, Television and Modern Life*. Oxford: Blackwell.

Shome, Raka. 2006. "Challenges of International Women of Color in the United States." In *Social Justice and Communication Scholarship*, edited by Omar Swartz, 105–126. Mahwah, NJ: Lawrence Erlbaum.

Smith, Anthony. 1995. *Nations and Nationalism in a Global Era*. Cambridge: Polity.

Smith, Michael, and Adrian Favell. 2006. *The Human Face of Global Mobility*. New Brunswick, NJ: Transaction Press.

Stevenson, Nick. 2003. "Cosmopolitan Britain or the Politics of Fear?" Speech at Common Threads: An Agenda for Active Citizenship. London, February 2003.

*Chapter Two*

# Transnational Journey into Belonging

*Korean American Adoptee's Birth Search and Reunion in Eric Sharp's* Middle Brother

Jieun Lee

Since the inception of the practice of Korean transnational adoption in 1953, approximately 200,000 South Korean adoptees have been sent to adoptive families overseas as South Korea (hereafter Korea) maintained its position as one of the top sending countries. Starting from the end of the 1990s, the Korean government invited Korean overseas adoptees "as cultural 'ambassadors' and economic 'bridges,'" yet for adoptees themselves—whose lives have been split across two nations, two families and two histories—the cultural capital necessary to realize their transnational potential seems to have already been forfeited" (E. Kim 2007, 497). This forfeit is precisely what Korean American adoptee actor and playwright Eric Sharp reveals in his first full-length play, *Middle Brother*, in which he also acted as the main character, Billy, a Korean adoptee. *Middle Brother* premiered in Minneapolis/Saint Paul at Theater Mu (Mu) in September 2014 directed by Robert Rosen (Theater Mu, n.d.). Drawing on Sharp's play, I argue that the performance of Korean adoptees' birth search and reunion is an investigation on the process of configuring belonging by revisiting the trajectory of transnational adoption practices. I further argue that performing birth search and reunion reassesses the in-betweenness of kinship and citizenship and discloses how belonging becomes a disciplinary force that demarcates the body and language of adoptees both in Korea and the United States. While contemporary transnational mobility offers adoptees the opportunity of connecting and re-connecting with kindred, it does not necessarily entail their acquisition of a trans-cultural sense of belonging. Through Sharp's *Middle Brother*, this chapter examines the politics of identity which are too complex to merely be solved by an invitation for Korean overseas adoptees to reclaim their Korean-ness as cultural ambassadors or economic bridges. In doing so, this examination of the dramatic representation of transnational adoption unfolds the complex entanglements of being a transnational adoptee in the U.S. and a non-Korean-speaking overseas returnee in contemporary Korea.

In the last two decades, several adult Korean adoptees have started to depict their birth search and reunion experiences by examining transnational adoption through different artistic medium, such as filmmaker Deann Borshay Liem, writer Jane Jeong Trenka, and media artist Jane Jin Kaisen. Kim Park Nelson (2016) writes that "the difficulty and frustration that adoptees experience with their agencies when looking for their birth and adoption histories has been well documented in Korean adoptee memoirs and documentaries. For adoptees like these writers and filmmakers, birth search and reunion with Korean family becomes a central part of their adoptee identities" (158). In the process of formulating their identity through their birth search and reunion, adoptee artists have addressed as part of their artistic endeavors unforeseen issues that they have encountered. For instance, in the field of theatrical art, contemporary Korean American adoptee performing artists Marissa Lichwick and Sun Mee Chomet created autobiographical solo performances that address matters of race and gender in the U.S. and Korea, raising questions of social issues and human rights in their birth search and reunion narratives (Lee 2017, 60–80). By analyzing Sharp's semi-autobiographical play *Middle Brother*, this chapter brings forth questions of kinship, citizenship, and belonging that are transnationally imagined and contested, seen through his own experience of birth search and reunion. Furthermore, this chapter also scrutinizes the significance of creating a theatrical work about transnational adoption which intersects with the concept of artivism and the formation of Asian America.

Eric Sharp is a Minneapolis-based actor and playwright who has largely worked with Mu but has also performed at numerous other theatrical venues such as the Alliance Theater in Atlanta and the Guthrie Theater in Minneapolis. Developed through Mu and the Jerome Foundation New Performance Program, *Middle Brother* follows the narrative of the character Billy, a Korean adoptee in Waterloo, Iowa, since the age of seven, who, in his late twenties, decides to move to Seoul to live. Once in Korea, he discovers he has a biological brother, Young-Nam (also called Hyung in the play). Billy's story incorporates that of his two brothers: in Korea, Young-Nam, who spent eleven years in an orphanage, and in Iowa, Gabe, Billy's adoptive younger brother (though not biologically related), whose own biological parents are unknown to him. The title of the play refers to Billy who thus becomes a middle brother as the consequence of his birth search and reunion, reflecting Sharp's experiences in the course of reuniting with his own biological family. Sharp renders his story in a highly imaginative way, interweaving the present time of the play in the 2010s with flashbacks to the 1980s when Billy was a young boy in Korea and a young adoptee in the U.S. Sharp also incorporates an additional setting in Billy's imagination of what he believes is the Joseon Dynasty (1392–1910), situating himself as the Queen's second son in the royal court. Whenever confronted with unanswerable questions on his journey to self-discovery, Billy falls into these flights of fantasy sequences to attempt to fill in the holes in his life. For instance, in order to understand why he was relinquished for adoption in his real life, Billy imagines himself in the Joseon Dynasty where his mother, the Queen, has him sent away to study so as not to be a potential threat to his older brother's right to the crown. In the production, Sharp purposely mixes Billy's Joseon Dynasty fantasies and the early 1980s and 2010s to depict when the playwright himself went from becoming an orphan to an adoptee and his later transnational journey to Korea from his adoptive country as he navigates between the U.S. and Korea, present and past, the real and the imagined.

## MAPPING SPATIOTEMPORAL FLEXIBILITY AND DEMARCATED BELONGING IN *MIDDLE BROTHER*

In *Flexible Citizenship: The Cultural Logics of Transnationality*, Aiwha Ong (1999) conceptualizes that due to advances in technology and transportation, transnational connection has increased in flexible mobility and nationhood. Throughout *Middle Brother*, the choices of theatricalizing the spaces where Billy's experiences occur in the course of moving in between Korea and the United States expose the transnational connection and its flexibility. In the 2014 production, this trans-pacific mobility was actualized through an open spatial configuration of the set. At the beginning of the play, the letters "한국 (Korea), 아이오와 (Iowa), and 태평양 (Pacific Ocean)" are drawn on the floor with white chalk by members of a chorus consisting of heavily accented Korean men and women dressed in *jjimjil-bang* outfits. A *jjimjil-bang* is a Korean sauna designed as a multiplex entertainment space where people can enjoy a bath, sauna, and health fitness services; play games; eat foods; and even sleep overnight for a low fee, wearing a specific cotton t-shirt and pants outfit. Using a cart-like chariot, actors and actresses dramatize the flexible mobility on the newly created cartography of the stage to illustrate how Billy and the chorus easily move back and forth between the two countries marked on the stage floor. When Billy goes to Korea, the chorus brings the cart over to his side of the Pacific in Iowa (stage left) and wheels him over to the Korean side (center stage and stage right). In one scene, Billy in the U.S. summons the chorus in Korea. The chorus members wheel over a small bridge, crawl on top of it, and cross over the Pacific Ocean from Korea to

Iowa. This staged mapping of trans-pacific movements renders Billy's birth search and reunion across borders imaginable for audience members.

*Middle Brother* also adds an element of temporal flexible mobility by aligning Billy's current birth search and reunion with an imagined story of the Joseon Dynasty's ascending royal lineage. When he arrives in Korea, Billy sings a song in a *norae-bang*, a Korean private singing room where people go to sing songs and have fun. The popular cultural experiences such as *norae-bang* that Billy encounters in Korean urban areas contrast with the fictionalized story of pre-modern Korean history. In the following scene, this contemporary cultural site is quickly transformed into an imagined historical setting of Joseon period Korea with traditional music and royal family characters wearing *hanbok*. The *hanbok* costumes in this play are intentionally designed to suggest a historical sense of temporality, not an accurate representation of Joseon period attire, and, as such, function as an imagined signifier of Korean tradition, culture, history, and royal lineage. To signify their presence at the royal court, performers also embody theatricalized gestures such as bowing to the Queen and using florid honorific speech, revealing the historical imagination through the difference in its mannerism and language. The scene then rapidly changes back to Billy in contemporary time. These quick-change scenes blur the line between Billy's imagination of a past and his present-day reality that the play draws to evoke a fragile temporality. Thus, imaginary spatial and temporal flexibility disrupts the spatial stability and temporal linearity as Billy searches for belonging across time and space.

Billy's birth search and reunion story not only maps the transnational spatial mobility and the temporal fluidity on stage, but also discloses the complexity of kinship and citizenship demarcations that are reinstated to confirm what it means to be a Korean adoptee both in Korea and in the U.S. Situated between the dichotomy of Korea and America, Korean American adoptees are subject to the expectation to assimilate to one of the two cultures. Across time and space, Billy experiences this compulsory force that attempts to shape his identity to be either American or Korean. *Middle Brother* shows the oppressive difficulties and complexities of this bifurcated cultural configuration through which adoptees confront their in-between position that generates confusion and isolation.

The opening scene shows Billy in his apartment practicing speaking basic Korean. Billy tells the chorus that his plan to return to Korea is simple: "Find an apartment. . . . Get a job. . . . Eat Korean barbecue. . . . Apply for a visa, learn Korean, then walk around and blend into society" (Sharp 2014, 7). The chorus responds by mocking him, marking the first time that Billy's issue of belonging is put forward. One of the chorus members mimics him and sarcastically says: "Oh look at me, I am Billy and I'm blending in to Korean society" (7). By ridiculing Billy's naïve belief that his forthcoming assimilation into Korean society will be trouble-free, the chorus also sends a warning that Billy's un-belonging to Korean cultures will make his integration impossible. Billy, who sees himself as Korean, is subject to mockery by "real" Koreans who understand the experiences of Korean American adoptees returning to Korea only to find the hard reality that they are viewed as "Korean foreigners" within Korea, as Park Nelson (2016) conceptualized in *Invisible Asians: Korean American Adoptees, Asian American Experiences, and Racial Exceptionalism* (177).

The chorus also brings up the matter of citizenship, telling Billy that in order to apply for a long-term visa he must bring his U.S. citizenship naturalization documents to prove that he, in fact, is *not* Korean and that his name is no longer on the *hojuk*:

BILLY: Hojuk, hojuk. . . . Okay, what's a hojuk?

CHORUS 3: Korean family registry. You no longer part of family. You no longer Korean person. You now American person. Please prove that you are not Korean person. (Sharp 2014, 7)

The information given by the chorus is significant in that in order for Korean children to become legally adoptable in terms of U.S. immigration law, they must first gain "orphan status," as Eleana J. Kim (2007) writes: "For adoptees, an 'orphan *hojuk*,' or orphan registry, served to render the child as a legible, free-standing subject of the state in preparation for adoption and erasure as a Korean Citizen" (521). Kim continues by stating that when some adoptees decided to apply for "the overseas Koreans visa" they were told they had never been taken out of their birth family registry and "in order to qualify for the visa, they must complete their own erasure from the registry and cancel their Korean citizenship" (521). In other words, returning adoptees' affirmation of their legal recognition by the Korean government is juxtaposed with the negation of Koreanness represented by the family registry. Moreover, for adoptees, *hojuk* thus serves as a decision-making marker whether to belong or not to belong to Korea as a Korean citizen and in a Korean family, just as U.S. Naturalization papers are the stamp of a Korean adoptee who is endorsed as "American." As for both Korean and U.S. authorities, kinship and citizenship are mutually connected; this entangled identification is a contested site of belonging for adoptees that requires strictly demarcated confirmation by an arbitrary bureaucracy. In *Middle Brother*, the dramatization of this reality facing a transnational adoptee who decides to stay in Korea debunks the romanticized image of flexible mobility that adoptees are often associated with. In addition, Billy's liminal condition accentuates a sense of statelessness that adds to his increasing insecurity as the story progresses.

As a result of his birth search and reunion, Billy becomes a builder of an in-between brotherhood in which he is both an older brother in the U.S. and a younger brother in Korea, and his mobility across time and space functions as an act of re-configuring a compositional kinship. The in-betweenness of belonging in relation to adoptees' kinship formation is foregrounded in the play through the mirrored struggling lives of Billy's two brothers, Gabe in the U.S. and Young-Nam in Korea. Billy and Gabe grew up together as adoptive brothers but, unlike Billy's optimistic disposition, Gabe took on a pessimistic outlook on life. From quitting or getting fired from dead-end jobs to drinking at bars, Gabe, who used to be a good student until sixth grade, just gave up. Billy's biological brother, Young-Nam, suffered temporary memory loss from a bicycle accident as a child and was sent to a boy's home, where he is forced to make "shoes every day for eleven years" (Sharp 2014, 37). In Korea, even though Young-Nam as an adult has reconnected with his biological parents, he still has difficulty holding jobs and sustaining relationships, and spends his time drinking and smoking. When Billy goes back to Korea for the second time, Young-Nam has lost his apartment and ends up living in a *jjimjil-bang*.

In a bar scene, Sharp's specific stage directions dramatize the interim relationship of navigating between the two brothers cross-nationally. Gabe and Young-Nam share the stage but in different bars, one in Waterloo, Iowa, and the other in Hanam, Korea. When Gabe is drinking and speaking in the Iowa bar, Young-Nam plays the part of the bartender but faces upstage. When Gabe stops talking, he switches places with Young-Nam, who drinks while Gabe plays the bartender facing upstage. Both brothers separately narrate a story about Billy. Gabe enviously talks about Billy's intelligence and reminisces about their childhood while Young-Nam imagines Billy's possible struggles living in the middle of a predominantly white population in Iowa and wishes that they will reunite in Korea in the near future. The production's dark lighting and isolated staging of the bar scene accentuate the deep-rooted effects of transnational adoption. Separation and a sense of loss felt by the mirrored characters of both Gabe and Young-Nam make audiences consider the emotional dimension of transnational adoption and adoptee's kinship from both the adoptive and biological family sides. In *Middle Brother*, while the in-betweenness of belonging is theatricalized through the demarcated formation of kinship and citizenship, disciplining adoptees' body and language also becomes a dramatic strategy to reveal how belonging is constructed and contested.

## THE MAKINGS OF ADOPTEES' BELONGING
## THROUGH BODY AND LANGUAGE

Examining the mechanisms of making an unwanted Korean orphan into a desirable adoptee, ingrained into U.S. militarism and neocolonial power in the framework of transnational adoption, SooJin Pate (2014) argues that "the orphan's body was subjected to different methods of biopower—techniques and procedures that governed life and subjugated bodies and that worked to protect the health and appearance of incoming orphans so that they may be made useful [that is, adoptable]" (103). Echoing this Foucauldian analysis, I argue that for adoptees biopower, as seen in the play through body and language, is the means of indoctrination to be re-Koreanized and de-Koreanized into a sense of belonging, thus subjugating adoptees' bodies and "tongues" under scrutiny to be disciplined into each hegemonic culture.

In using Billy's body as a spatial and temporal travelling spectacle, *Middle Brother* displays Billy's bodily transformation under these disciplinary guidelines. In a Korean Air flight scene that Billy dreams about, both his and Gabe's bodies become an exhibition of discipline, complying with the Korean flight attendants' specific series of instructions of how to be "Korean." The two flight attendants, sporting epitomized Korean Air flight attendant perfect outfits and impeccable mannerisms, "extend a special greeting to Billy and Gabe," on behalf of the captain (Sharp 2014, 51). While Billy and Gabe talk to one another, the two attendants perform a "ritual dance in lieu of going through the various safety features verbally" (52). The two women then interrupt Billy and Gabe to train them with "special" verbal instructions for when they meet their biological family in Korea:

> Your seat cushion can be used as a weapon to suffocate your family members. . . . Korean Airlines would like to remind you that Hanguk mal [Korean] is the official language of your home country. By speaking English, you are causing your ancestors pain. . . . In the unlikely event you know two shits about your culture, you would realize that your older brother should be referred to as hyung-nim as a sign of respect. (51–53)

The attendants then take a hold of Billy and in a dance-like ritual, give him more "special" instructions for when he reunites with his biological father. "When the abbeoji [father] light is illuminated, please bow in that very specific way that you were never taught to bow. Helpful hint: If you think you're low enough to the ground—go even lower" (54). One of the attendants physically forces him to bow almost to the ground. "It is against Korean federal regulations to drink soju in front of your abbeoji. Please turn you [*sic*] red face away while getting drunk with family members" (54). The two attendants use their hands to force Billy's face away. This ritual dance forcing Billy's body to morph into Korean cultural standards which he is not familiar with, is a reflection of his anxiety of reuniting with his biological family, having to accustom himself to Korean culture and undergo cultural regulations in his birth land in order to be accepted and belong. Just as in *Adopted Territory: Transnational Korean Adoptees and the Politics of Belonging*, Kim (2010) points out that many adoptees who think about returning to Korea suffer from anguish about their return journey due to the "fear of experiencing a second rejection" (186), this ritual dance is a somatic expression of Billy's fear of possible rejection and failure to be Koreanized in time for his reunion with his biological family.

Biopower as a means of cultural indoctrination is further disclosed as Sharp reveals to his audience members how an adoptee "becomes a person with the barest of social identities, and in the context of Korean cultural norms, . . . lacks the basic requirements of social personhood—namely, family lineage and genealogical history" (E. Kim 2007, 521). In the play, language serves as the practice of shaping adoptees' "barest of social identities" by being usurped in the process of differentiating between Korean orphans and de-Koreanized adoptees in early childhood. In a flashback scene, the chorus rushes in and violently strips off Billy's *hanbok*, a symbol of his royal family lineage in his imagination of the past, revealing a faded orphanage uniform. After Billy has been stripped of his traditional Korean clothing, he is quickly transported to 1980s Waterloo, Iowa, where he meets a young Gabe for the first time. The chorus then puts a large white placard around his neck with his written Korean name, 안영재, crossed out in red marker and his new given American name, Billy, written underneath. Gabe wears similar orphanage garb and also holds his new name placard around his neck. Naming is a way of sculpting one's identity and through this language practice people bond with or separate themselves from others, generating various types of "me" and "you" such as family, community, society, culture, history, and nation. This interpellation is a defining moment in the identity of one's life and the repetition of the name reinforces the formation of one's identity in the Althusserian sense (Althusser 2001, 85–126). In the scene, the visualized name as a written form that represents an adoptee's identity, memory, and family lineage becomes a performative interpellation for adoptees to inscribe upon themselves their new adoptive culture and customs; however, involuntarily losing one's birth name and heritage only renders belonging even more unattainable.

Moreover, Billy realizes even though he and Gabe are not blood related, since they have been adopted together they have become brothers. He tells his younger adoptive brother a secret: given that adoptive parents usually prefer adoptees that are young and healthy babies, their situation must be "special" because they are already older. Billy's fear of relinquishment and non-belonging make him desperate to be accepted, and he instructs Gabe to give up speaking Korean, only speak English, and eat any foods they are given, even if bland in taste. Here, in order to assimilate in the U.S. as a "good" adoptee, Billy and Gabe must negate all that which summons language, taste, and memories of Korea, thus self-disciplining in their new environment. The integration into North American culture and a new given home is also mirrored by Billy's yearning for English. When Gabe calls Billy by his Korean name, Billy hastily hushes him up as if Gabe said a taboo word. Along with the practice of naming, learning either verbal or non-verbal language is a way of attaining a cultural and communicative apparatus to produce, reproduce, and develop one's selfhood and identity in a literate society. However, this act of being obligated to acquire a language skill for one's identification can be read as compulsory force against adoptees' tongues to endow them with a brand new label: Americanness. Billy internalizes this unavoidable need to become American and constrains his Korean adoptive brother to abandon not only his Korean language but also his desire for Korean food. The survival strategy for "successful" belonging as "good" Korean adoptees in the U.S. in this scene expresses how the mother tongue and the actual palatal tongue related to Koreanness are relegated to the Americanness of the English language and "tasteless" American food.

Eventually, Billy successfully adapts into Americanness, but this accomplishment proves to be disadvantageous when he returns to Korea and his re-Koreanization in the form of acculturation through language proves to be a failure. In a market scene in Korea, chorus members playing street vendors tell Billy that he is not blending in because after having lived in Korea for one year, he still does not know how to speak the language, not "even make one sentence in Korean" (Sharp 2014, 28). Billy's inability to communicate and blend in comes to a destructive climax toward the end of the play when the Queen in the Joseon Dynasty setting tells Billy that if he recounts the entire tale of his journey he will be able to take the throne; but Billy is unable to because he cannot speak Korean. Billy, who had self-disciplined into learning English as a young boy, failed to retain his birth country's language and thus loses his proper lineage to the royal family. As Billy's lack of speaking Korean engenders the punishment of losing his familial rights to the throne in the imagined royal court setting, another punishment is inflicted upon him in the present time when his biological brother Young-Nam refuses to talk to him about the past. Billy asks: "I don't get it, Hyung. We spent all this time catching up with abbeoji [father], but the past is still off limits. When can I ask the big questions?" (55). Young-Nam answers: "There are things I can only tell you when we speak the same language" (55). Billy's deficiency in Korean language skills exacts the penalty of exclusion from answers, exclusion from his family, and exclusion from the truth and memories, thus illustrating how disciplining and punishing through language becomes an exclusionary act for adoptees' sense of belonging.

# TRANSNATIONAL ADOPTION ON STAGE:
## ASIAN AMERICAN ARTIVISM

In an interview, Sharp states that his goal for *Middle Brother* is to have people gain "an understanding of what it's like to be separated from your flesh and blood when that's not your choice [and] to give voice to this feeling of confusion that adoptees have when they go back to Korea [where] you keep getting reminders over and over every day that you don't belong here" (Sharp 2015). Not only does *Middle Brother* invite audiences to be and think together about what it means to be a returning adoptee, but the performance also conveys the need to view Korean transnational adoption as a personal as well as a political issue. Kim Stoker (2006) envisions the mutuality between art and activism in the expression of transnational adoption by adoptee artists (223–248). Stoker stresses the "artivist" feature of adoptees' artistic expression of transnational adoption as connected to social transformation and sensitivity about adoption (223–248). *Middle Brother* does not explicitly exhibit a political message or an intention to raise awareness about sensitive issues surrounding adoption practices and its historical correlation between Korea and the U.S.; however, the play undeniably implies a veiled politicity through which audiences feel Billy's ever growing frustration and anguish about his and his brother's loss and how he seeks a sense of justice. This politicity is unveiled in the repetition of a specific question Billy asks three times in three different scenes. When Billy reunites with his biological brother in Korea for the first time, he asks him: "Why didn't you look for me?" (Sharp 2014, 31). At the end of the flashback scene when Billy's Korean brother is just found and transported to a boy's home, Billy asks the chorus: "Why didn't our parents look for him?" And in the following imaginary Joseon period scene when the royal court figures realize that the older brother is missing, a physically present but indiscernible Billy yells out to them like an invisible witness: "Why didn't you look for him? . . . He's in Saint Andrew Kim's Boys Home. It's just one town over. Why didn't you look for him? Why didn't you look for me?" (40). This reiteration of why nobody tried to find the missing boys puts forth the issue of Korea's lack of a social safety system for children and Korean society's acceptance to relinquish "lost" children to orphanages as waiting stations for possible transnational adoption, a practice unquestioned in the 1980s. In this sense, the cloaked politicity implied through this recurrence of the questions evokes in audiences the sorrow of Korean families, and of the nation as a whole, as the entire decade of the 1980s witnessed the peak in transnational adoptions from Korea, according to Arissa H. Oh (2015, 202). As a way of seeking a remedy to cure the wounded past of Billy and his brother, Sharp repeats these questions to give a feeling of urgency to audiences and the need for an answer for justice to rise.

In the telling of these adoption stories, and in their identification with Asian America, Korean adoptees as theater artists gain agency through the content of their own narratives. According to Wendy Marie Laybourn (2018), the history of Asian immigration to the U.S. had excluded the narratives of Korean adoptees and consequently an "appropriate corrective must also incorporate an inclusion of Korean adoptees in how we think about *contemporary* Asian American community and identity" (35). A case in point, *Middle Brother* was performed by all pan-Asian cast members of Mu which, since its foundation in 1992, has been the largest Asian American performing arts organization in the Midwest, producing "great performances born of arts, equality, and justice from the heart of the Asian American experience" (Theater Mu, n.d.). In an interview, Sharp points out the special role that Mu held in creating *Middle Brother*: "We have a very special Midwestern Asian American aesthetic here that Mu is really responsible for and I feel so thankful to them . . . the community, in terms of inspiration for how we worked on the play" (Sharp 2015). As a hub for Asian American theatrical art, Mu has a twenty-year-long history of producing adoption theater starting with *Mask Dance* (1993) and *Mask Dance* 2 (1996) both by Rick A. Shiomi and *The Walleye Kid* and its musical version (1998 and 2005) by Rick A. Shiomi and Sundraya Kase, to Katie Hae Leo's *Four Destinies* (2011). *Middle Brother* fits perfectly in Mu's trajectory of exploring the theatrical world of transnational adoption in the U.S., intersecting Korean adoptees' experiences of their diasporic life stories through Asian American artistic engagement and enlivening their mutual solidarity.

In addition, to offer background information for audiences, the playbill for *Middle Brother*'s 2014 premiere features the timeline of Korean adoption written by critical adoption studies scholar Kim Park Nelson and a glossary of Korean words that the characters in the play often use. Also included in the playbill is a personal quote by Korean adoptee playwright and performing artist Katie Hae Leo, who writes about her experience of growing up adopted and Asian in the 1980s Midwest and states the importance of Mu in the lives of adoptees through its "commitment to producing plays for and by adoptees [and] recognizes the power of seeing oneself represented through art for so many Minnesota adoptees and their families" (7). The playbill's substantial information about Korean transnational adoption shows Sharp and Mu's respectful pledge to situate Korean adoptees' own experiences at the center of generating theater arts. Most importantly, these experiences are not utilized for a simplistic and exploitative one-way storytelling centered on adoptive parents' point of view or told through a melodramatic depiction of adoption as a humanitarian act of rescue. This commitment to adoptees' voices in theater ensures the possibility of contextualizing the complexity of transnational adoption practices beyond those of Korea and promoting the scope of diverse experiences such as adoptee citizenship activism, racialized sexism, and queer identities within and beyond the U.S. borders.

Sharp's own strategy envisions how adoptees can create artistic works in which audiences can be entertained and think about adoption without being overly preoccupied by the rigid dualistic identifications between being an adoptee and an artist, between an actor and a playwright, and, thus between Billy and Sharp. Through the artivist imagination of his play and collaboration with the Asian American theater community, Sharp brings to audience members an empathetic understanding of the Korean American transnational adoption experience and the complications that adoptees encounter during their birth search and reunion for belonging across temporal and spatial borders.

## CONCLUSION

In an era of globalization in which the global and local seamlessly intermingle through greater flexible mobility, belonging loses its sense of permanence and thus security. As Billy moves along on his journey of birth search and reunion in *Middle Brother*, the intricacies of belonging become bound to the affective aspects of his identity. Every piece of information he uncovers places him one step closer toward the reconstruction of the puzzle of his childhood, but each new discovery also brings with it a sense of loss and injustice. Sara Ahmed (2004) emphasizes that "justice involves feelings, which move us across the surfaces of the world, creating ripples in the intimate contours of our lives. Where we go, with these feelings, remains an open question" (202). At the very end of the play, Young-Nam tells Billy that none of their family members ever told him that Billy had been relinquished, and that they destroyed all traces of him: "All your pictures. All your clothes. Vanished" (Sharp 2014, 68). In this trans-pacific-scape between Korea and the United States imagined on stage, the ending of the play does not give a satisfying answer about Billy's questions on his past and vanished memories, and justice is not achieved. This lingering feeling of loss and incertitude leaves audiences with open questions about Billy's and other adoptees' past, present, and future birth search and reunion with their biological families. Albeit all traces of Billy have been erased, Sharp, by mapping Billy's imagination across time and space, brings the sense of belonging ever closer within reach as we become travelling companions to, and witnesses of, Billy's transnational journey into belonging.

## REFERENCES

Ahmed, Sara. 2004. *The Cultural Politics of Emotion*. New York: Routledge.

Althusser, Louis, Fredric Jameson, and Ben Brewster. 2001. "Ideology and Ideological State Apparatuses (Notes towards an Investigation)." *Lenin and Philosophy and Other Essays*, 85–126. New York: NYU Press.

Foucault, Michel. 1990. *The History of Sexuality: An Introduction.* Vol. 1. Translated by Robert Hurley. New York: Vintage Books.

Kim, Eleana J. 2007. "Our Adoptee, Our Alien: Transnational Adoptees as Specters of Foreignness and Family in South Korea." *Anthropological Quarterly* 80, no. 2 (Spring): 497–531. https://doi.org/10.1353/anq.2007.0027.

———. 2010. *Adopted Territory: Transnational Korean Adoptees and the Politics of Belonging.* Durham, NC: Duke University Press.

Laybourn, Wendy Marie. 2018."Being a Transnational Korean Adoptee, Becoming Asian American." *Contexts* 17, no. 4 (November): 30–35. https://doi.org/10.1177/1536504218812866.

Lee, Jieun. 2017. "Performing Transnational Adoption: Korean American Women Adoptees' Autobiographical Solo Performances." *Theatre Annual* 70 (Fall): 60–80.

Leo, Katie Hae. 2014. Playbill of *Middle Brother.*

Oh, Arissa H. 2015. *To Save the Children of Korea: The Cold War Origins of International Adoption.* Stanford, CA: Stanford University Press.

Ong, Aiwha. 1999. *Flexible Citizenship: The Cultural Logics of Transnationality.* Durham, NC: Duke University Press.

Park Nelson, Kim. 2016. *Invisible Asians: Korean American Adoptees, Asian American Experiences, and Racial Exceptionalism.* New Brunswick, NJ: Rutgers University Press.

Pate, SooJin. 2014. *From Orphan to Adoptee: U.S. Empire and Genealogies of Korean Adoption.* Minneapolis: University of Minnesota Press.

Sharp, Eric. 2014. *Middle Brother.* Unpublished manuscript, 09/05/14.

———. Interview by author, tape recording. Minneapolis, May 19, 2015.

Stoker, Kim. 2005. "Beyond Identity: Activism in Korean Adoptee Art." *Duksung Women's University Journal* 34: 223–248.

Theater Mu. n.d. "Mission." Accessed December 9, 2018. http://www.muperformingarts.org/mission.

*Part II*

# Migratory Mobility and Gender

*Chapter Three*

# Nursing Care in Contact Zones

*Korean Healthcare "Guest Workers" in Germany*

Yonson Ahn

Since the mid-20th century, transnational migration has played a central role in the provision of healthcare in post-industrial countries. Caregiving tasks are increasingly assigned to, and fulfilled by, female migrant workers.[1] One example of the global outsourcing of care work can be seen in the more than 11,000 nurses and nurse assistants who moved from South Korea (hereafter Korea) to former West Germany (hereafter Germany) as "guest workers" between the late 1950s and the 1970s. At the time, demands on healthcare in Germany were increasing due to an aging population, the growing rates of female participation in the labor force, and the low appeal of care jobs to the German workforce. The "guest worker" program for healthcare workers represented a way to mitigate this nursing care burden and temporarily bridge the labor shortage gap by recruiting Korean healthcare "guest workers" to work in medical or nursing institutions such as hospitals, sanitariums, and nursing homes, or as hospice nurses in Germany. Caring for a range of people from infants to the elderly, the disabled and the handicapped, the injured and the dying, these "guest workers" became integral service providers in the German healthcare system.

The earliest recruits found their way to Germany through individual agents or religious organizations, and later a state agent, *Haeoe Kaebal Kongsa* (the Korean Foreign Development Corporation, KFDC) which orchestrated the German recruitment of healthcare workers from Korea. The Korean healthcare workers' contracts initially granted rotating, temporary three-year contracts, but some workers stayed beyond the duration of their initial contracts and acquired permanent residence or became naturalized citizens. In general, the migratory trajectories of these former "guest workers" vary. Some re-migrated to Korea, while others settled down in Germany or migrated to a third country such as the U.S. or Canada.

The majority of existing literature on "guest workers" in Germany focuses on Turkish migrants (Hunn 2005; Rauer 2008; Amelina and Faist 2008) and only a few studies addressing the Korean "guest workers" in Germany have been published (Roberts 2012). Furthermore, there are even fewer works on female "guest workers" (Ahn 2014). The present work explores this under-researched field and seeks to shed light on the social dynamics of the interactions of Korean women "guest workers" with their host society. It examines the ways in which socio-cultural differences between Korean healthcare workers and their local patients or co-workers were generated, experienced and managed, by drawing on personal accounts from former female Korean healthcare "guest workers" who migrated to Germany during this period and settled in the destination country.

The social space of the face-to-face encounters between the migrant caregivers and the local citizens, especially co-workers and care recipients, are contextualized within the framework of a "contact zone" (Pratt 1992) with consideration given to the intersection of gender and race/ethnicity. The research focus will be on a micro-level examination of the individual nursing care practices and positions through which the cultures, customs, and values of the hosts and migrants met, clashed, and/or were negotiated. Special attention is paid to the (German) stereotype of Korean femininity (represented by traits such as kindness, gentleness, and a smiling, non-confrontational, or submissive demeanor) and the ways in which the Korean healthcare workers complied with, negotiated, and/or resisted such gender attributions.

Towards this end, multiple in-depth interviews with twenty-nine former Korean healthcare workers were conducted in Korean, and one interview with a former German male nurse was conducted in German. Interviews took place in Korea, Germany, and Canada from 2011 to 2018. This particular work cites ten interviews conducted in Germany. All narratives have been translated into English by the author, but German words used in the Korean speaking respondents' accounts have been left untranslated in order to record the usage of hybridized language. All names used here are pseudonyms.

## NURSING CARE AS A "CONTACT ZONE"

Care theorists such as Nel Noddings (1984, 103), Joan Tronto (1993), Bridget Anderson, and Isabel Shutes (2014, 218) draw attention to the fact that the delivery of care is relational, and that human interactions with the people in need of care form an integral part of nursing. Sara Ruddick views care not only as labor but also as relationship, positing that "caring labor is intrinsically relational. The work is constituted in and through the relation of those who give and receive care" (Ruddick 1998, 13–14). Similarly, this interpersonal aspect of care leads Tronto (1993) to define "good" care work as requiring the attentive responsiveness of a care provider to the physical and emotional wellbeing of the person s/he cares for.

This relational nature of nursing practices makes the encounters between migrant healthcare workers and non-migrant care recipients worthy of exploration. In order to illuminate the contexts in which micro-level interpersonal connections are formed through healthcare activities, encounters between the Korean "guest workers" and those they cared for are conceptualized with reference to the idea of a "contact zone" as defined by Mary Louise Pratt (1992). In her analysis of travel writing by Europeans in Latin America and Africa since the eighteenth century, Pratt defines contact zones as "social spaces where disparate cultures meet, clash and grapple with each other, often in highly asymmetrical relations of domination and subordination— like colonialism, slavery, or their aftermaths as they are lived across the globe today" (Pratt 1992, 4).

This notion of contact zone has previously been employed in analyses of domestic work. For example, in their seminal studies on migrant domestic workers Yeoh and Huang (1999) and Gutiérrez-Rodríguez (2010) discuss domestic work as occurring within a contact zone. Similarly, borrowing Pratt's definition, the current study uses the term "contact zone" to refer to the social spaces in which Korean healthcare workers interact with their local co-workers and care recipients in providing nursing care.[2] Within this contact zone, *disparate* cultures not only met and clashed but also were *negotiated*. Particularly during the initial period following the earliest "guest worker" arrivals, the Korean "guest workers" and the citizenry of Germany knew little to nothing about each other's cultures—a fact which resulted in a limited amount of apprehension and misunderstanding. Most of the Korean nurse respondents interviewed recall that their patients and German colleagues often expressed curiosity by asking about the unknown country of Korea. One interview participant, Na, refers to the mutual cultural ignorance present at the time: "As an Asian, honestly Germany was an almost unknown world to me. I had learned very little about Germany at school. And it seemed that Germans had barely any *Ahnung* (idea) about Korea, almost nothing. So surely it must have been difficult for them to understand us" (Na, former theater nurse). When groups of Korean healthcare workers began arriving in Germany, especially in small German towns between the 1950s and 1970s, the locals must have been interested in the changes to their previously homogeneous townscapes and curious about the newcomers.

The novelty of the arrival of Korean healthcare workers is clear from a 1966 German newspaper headline implying interest in what was likely the first cross-cultural contact for most members of both groups: "Encounter with the Far East [Begegnung mit dem Fernen Osten]" (*Neue Presse* 16

August 1966, quoted in Roberts 2012, 71). Other German newspapers from the 1960s ran headlines such as "Charming Korea in Höchst [Reizvolles Korea in Höchst]" (*Deutschlandausgabe* 17 April 1967, quoted in Roberts 2012, 66). Such phrases demonstrate that the Korean nurses were not viewed individually, but as collectively representing Korea as a nation or more broadly representing East Asia as a region. Such ideas were upheld by the nurses themselves. Na also states: "We tried to be nice to patients and colleagues at work. Thinking a bit more broadly, we thought ourselves to represent Korea. I was concerned about giving a negative impression of Korea if we didn't do well." The women who considered themselves to have been representing the homeland might have shared a collective sense of belonging in relation to the host culture. In fact, the nurses often use the subject pronoun "we" in their interview narratives. Therefore, the contact zone represents a site of interaction not only for unfamiliar individuals, but for the cultures and nation-states they understand each other to represent.

## "SOFT AND EXOTIC ANGELS"

Many care theorists explain care as "embodied labor" (Anderson and Shutes 2014, 217) in the form of both "a practice and a disposition" (Tronto 1993, 104). Nursing care is a professional labor of skill, but also one romanticized as a labor of love, and is imagined in terms of familial relations (Anderson and Shutes 2014, 217). This understanding of nursing is especially prominent in media portrayals of the Korean caregivers, where their ability to provide nursing care is seen not only as a skill set but also as an inherent feature of their disposition in accordance with the imagined Korean femininity. Social and workplace media usually depicted Korean healthcare workers as kind, smiling, gentle, charming, naturally friendly, and helpful. Numerous descriptions can be found of "charming nurses [charmante Schwestern]" (*Offenbacher Rundschau* 1 July 1966) with "an ever friendly smile [Das gleichbleibend freundliche Lächeln]" (*source unknown* 21 August 1971, quoted in Roberts 2012, 73) or "soft angels [sanfte Engel]" (*Schwäbisches Tageblatt* 8 March 1991, quoted in Roberts 2012, 85). A caring image was assigned to the Korean nurses, with slogans such as "Korean nurses for Frankfurt . . . under their caring hands [Koreanische Schwestern für Frankfurt . . . unter ihren pflegenden Händen]" (*Neue Presse* 1 February 1966, quoted in Roberts 2012, 67), and this caring behavior is confirmed by the Korean nurses as well: "Whether it was giving a bath [to my patients] or whatever it was, I treated them as they were my own parents, brothers or sisters" (Han, former nurse).

Korean nurses' caring and gentle manner at work was even viewed as an embodied capacity by the women themselves:

During the night shift I had some time available to chat with the patients whom I looked after and tried to give them some comfort. When I passed *Schlaftabletten* [sleeping pills] to those who needed them, some told me personal stories, sometimes scary or painful. Other patients asked me what the doctor had said after checking them. They would not dare to ask the doctor directly. They asked us afterwards because they knew we [Korean nurses] were *nett* [kind]. Germans [nurses] usually didn't respond like us. (Hwang, former nurse)

Such accounts bear witness to social correlations of femininity with nursing care as practiced by the Korean nurses.

German local media depicted the women as "always only smiling [immer nur lächeln]" (*Bildzeitung* 14 February 1966, quoted in Roberts 2012, 68) and for patients in particular, the image of smiling Korean nurses was often presented. For the women, smiling was a way of expressing kindness and politeness, and also a means of negotiating a linguistic barrier. Some, like Kang, found that smiling allowed her to communicate with her patients and co-workers until she had gained linguistic proficiency in German: "As I didn't understand all that was said [in German at the clinic where I worked], I felt at least I should respond with a smile. Our nicknames were all smiling girl" (Kang, nurse assistant).

It is clear that some "guest workers" attempted to reduce the possible tensions and/or distance caused by a linguistic barrier in their interactions by smiling. However, sometimes this tactic was ineffective. One interviewee recalls the frustration of not being accepted by some of her patients: "Sometimes when I responded to a call [when a patient rang the bell to call a nurse in charge for help], he would want to have somebody else [another nurse]. Most likely he didn't trust me, as he thought we could not understand each other" (Kim, former nurse). Thus, the ability to understand the language of the host society was seen not only as a secondary skill, but at times as a fundamental measure of one's competence as a nurse or even of one's maturity. This view demonstrates highly asymmetrical social relations across the linguistic gap, as the language barrier created a hierarchy in the women's encounters with the host society.

The language barrier and the "smiling" image of the women also played into contemporaneous German media portrayals from the 1960s and the 1970s which infantilized the women (Roberts 2012, 66). For example, they were often depicted as sweet, little, or pretty girls: "little In Ja [die kleine In Ja]" (*Main-Taunus-Rundschau* 20 May 1970), "the girls [die Mädchen]" (*Main-Taunus-Rundschau* 20 May 1970), or "graceful, pretty Korean women [die grazilen, hübschen Koreanerinnen]" (*Frankfurter Rundschau* 29 April 1969, quoted in Roberts 2012, 63). Such portrayals by the dominant group were reinforced by the women's own feelings, in that they often felt themselves to be like children when faced with challenges communicating in the local language upon arrival in Germany: "I had just one month of German lessons [before I left Korea]. I didn't even know when I had to say 'yes' or 'no.' I felt dumb and like a child who knew nothing. . . . It was like standing in front of a high wall understanding nothing. I felt like that. [At that time] I wasn't sure how I could survive here" (Kim, former nurse).

The language of the dominant culture is the norm for migrants to learn in order to function as a fully grown adult in society. Smiling provided a means of expression in situations where communication through vernacular expression was difficult or impossible, and is therefore best understood as a means to overcome incomprehension, rather than an expression of innate amiability.

However, the public discourse on Korean womanhood which prevailed in the German media included descriptors such as "innate lovability [angeborene Liebenswürdigkeit]" (*Deutschlandausgabe* 17 April 1967, quoted in Roberts 2012, 66), implying kindness as an inherent attribute of the Korean healthcare workers. Such discursive practice shaped the social construction of the stereotypical notion of Korean womanhood as perceived in Germany, and the migrant healthcare "guest workers" adapted this social code in their behavior, thereby reinforcing concepts of the feminine and caring image of Korean nurses and nurse assistants. These discursive practices are shaped and reproduced by the social script of Asian womanhood at various levels— individuals, social practices, and institutions.

In German media depictions, Korean healthcare workers constituted a discursively homogenized group whose characteristics can be understood as extensions of racial and cultural stereotypes of "Asian" women. In the course of cross-cultural encounters occurring within the context of the greater local community where the migrant workers resided and worked, for the most part, the Korean female nurses were viewed as "exotic." German local media during the 1960s and the 1970s presented the Korean nurse "guest workers" in this way on the basis of physical appearance, describing "nurses with exotic facial features [Schwestern mit den exotischen Gesichtszügen]" (*Frankfurter Allgemeine Zeitung* 17 February 1966, quoted in Roberts 2012, 63), or as exotic "charming lotus flowers [charmante Lotosblumen]" (source unknown, 12/13 January 1974). Other media portrayals of the Korean nurses include descriptions of "soft hands and almond eyes [Zarte Hand und Mandelaugen]" (*Allgemeine Zeitung* 29 April 1966) or "a face with slanted eyes, an almond gaze and black tresses [ein Gesicht mit schrägen Augen, Mandelblick und schwarzen Locken]" (*Bildzeitung* 14 February 1966, quoted in Roberts 2012, 63). The Korean guest workers' "otherness" as represented in these media portrayals is based on ideas of racial distinctiveness which went hand in hand with stereotypes of gender and culture.

The media portrayals and stereotypes discussed above had direct consequences for the women in their daily work and lives, particularly in small towns. Local communities demonstrated reactions to the Korean migrants' culture, customs, ideas, and values which ranged from enthusiasm and curiosity, to indifference, ignorance, and prejudice. Neumann, one of my interviewees who worked with Korean female nurses in a small town (C) in the 1960s, talks about the local population's reaction towards the women:

> It was not necessarily negative [toward the Korean nurses], I think, rather curiosity. No Asians lived in the area [where I worked] before they came. The women [the 19 Korean nurses] look very different from other people they [the local people] had seen [in that area] and they [the women] were simply exotic for the people there. (Neumann, male nurse assistant)

"Otherness" as described in the media drew further attention to the women by racializing and gendering them as exotic. The exoticizing gaze nurtured the local population's image of Asian/Korean femininity and often led to unpleasant levels of inquisitiveness from the local population, along with a sense of isolation and a general lack of privacy for the women. Encounters in the social spaces of small towns could be particularly uncomfortable, leading many healthcare workers, like Nam, to depart provincial areas following the end of their first employment contract: "After I had done my three years [work] there, I found another job and moved to a bigger city even though the clinic offered me renewal of my contract. Since then I have always lived in a rather big city, no more in a small town where dialects are spoken."

In general, metropolitan cities offer more diasporic space to practice and engage with one's own ethnic culture and customs, which can lessen migrants' feelings of isolation and loneliness. In fact, most of the women I interviewed chose to move to larger cities at some stage of their life for this exact reason. For them, foreign and homogeneous local towns were perceived as places from which to exit, searching for a location where they could feel a sense of "belonging" and an alternative community where they could feel as if they were at home, enjoying an associated element of emotional security.

In terms of relations with the host society, the Korean "guest workers" doubly identified themselves as both migrants and women. Their responses to the gendered and "exoticized" features of womanhood to which behaviors such as kindness, smiling, or acquiescence were attributed varied from acceptance to resistance. Though the women may have tactfully played upon images of themselves widespread within the German media, they did not represent themselves solely in these terms, but also strove to negotiate their own images.

Some healthcare workers were attached to the social code and public image of Asian women, while others distanced themselves from it. Some, like Han, acceded to the stereotype: "Surely Asian women are soft and friendly, and we are supposed to be like that. This is a strong point of Korean women. So those German men who didn't like a strong type of German woman were attracted to Korean nurses and married them" (Han, former nurse).

Han regards the code of Asian/Korean femininity as a form of social capital which might be utilized as an asset in the destination society. What were deemed to be normative Asian feminine practices were therefore sometimes reproduced and sustained in cross-cultural encounters by the women themselves. A local newspaper in the 1970s romanticized the German men's perspective on the Korean women as "desired wives" and even commodified them in phrasing such as: "they sell like hotcakes [Sie gehen weg wie warme Semmeln]" (*Der Abend* 16 July 1970, quoted in Roberts 2012, 76). Such phrases highlight the host society's racialized cultural translation of the social values of ideal womanhood and social expectations regarding women's roles as wives.

Others put little effort into adhering to the cultural code of normative Korean femininity:

> When I worked at a private clinic in 1976, one of the patients made a comment that I didn't look like a typical Korean woman. All the Korean women he knew were quiet and shy. I responded that nursing is a profession where one cannot do a good job if one is shy. Why should I have fit myself into the frame [for Korean women] that he had made? (Son, former nurse)

Her refusal to act out society's racialized, gendered script can be interpreted as deconstructing stereotypical Korean womanhood. Son even received a similar comment from her supervisor: "When I complained, the head of nursing department at the clinic where I worked asked me whether all Koreans were impolite like me. She said she thought Asians were easy to work with, but doubted Koreans" (Son, former nurse).

Son's resistance towards the social and normative code of Korean womanhood thus resulted in expressions of doubt towards the concept of a polite "Koreanness," which all Koreans were presupposed to demonstrate. As noted in this section, the women have conformed to, negotiated, or contested in various ways the gendered and racialized media portrayals and stereotypes imposed on them.

## INCLUSION

Cross-cultural interactions between the migrants and non-migrants involved prejudice and boundaries, but could also be sites of camaraderie, appreciation, and social inclusion. Positive relationships developed over time, growing from the attentiveness and sympathy expressed by the Korean caregivers towards the local care recipients. "Patients waiting for operations in the theater usually get anxious, and I tried to comfort them, sometimes patting their arm and saying everything should be fine" (Lee, former nurse). Choe said she always made efforts to amuse younger patients before giving them injections or taking blood samples to divert their attention and calm their anxiety. Bedside nurses were usually responsible for helping patients whose physical mobility was limited, or who might be living in conditions of dependency and vulnerability. In return, care recipients often expressed gratitude towards the caregivers. Most of the healthcare workers who participated in interviews with me shared the development of positive interpersonal relationships with their patients, including attaining recognition, compliments, gifts, or invitations for meals or coffee from patients whom they had cared for. Positive feelings about the Korean nurses can be seen in some patients' preference for being attended to by Korean nurses, and also in media coverage. Neumann, who worked with Korean nurses, recalls: "They [my Korean colleagues] were acknowledged [at the clinic]. Many of them were invited for meals by their recovered patients or the patients' families" (Neumann, former male nurse assistant). In this way, the "guest workers" came to attain visibility and recognition within the host society.

The reality that the Korean nurses' caring work, commitment, and perseverance in supporting and responding to the needs of patients were viewed positively is a fact supported by several German newspapers. *Der Tagesspiegel*, on June 22, 1977, reports that they were "popular among the patients for their gentle, friendly character [and] valued among their colleagues for patient diligence" (*Der Tagesspiegel* June 22, 1977, quoted in Roberts 2012, 79). German media descriptions like these represent the positive reception and recognition of Korean nurses and their professional competence in nursing practices in the contact zone. Therefore, care giving and receiving can be understood to have allowed for positive cultural mediation in cross-cultural exchanges between the Korean nurses and the German populace.

The Korean "guest workers'" professional competency as nurses allowed them to frequently feel a sense of inclusion, power, and agency even within the host society's hierarchies of gender and ethnicity. Hwang talks about her competency as a theater nurse, a skill which provided her with subtle power she could use to exercise and protect herself from potential discrimination:

Of course I have felt discrimination because I am an *Ausländer* [foreigner]. But those with whom I worked, whether nurse or doctor, didn't treat me like that [like a foreigner]. How on earth? We [Korean nurses] worked so hard and indeed we were good at our job, and we could even have some influence over the doctors [we worked with]. They couldn't afford to behave arrogantly towards us. (Hwang, former nurse)

Hwang's inclusion in the workplace was achieved via her professional skills. Her competence and diligence as a theater nurse could not go unnoticed by her co-workers, and over time co-workers and doctors came to respect and depend on her, generating some sense of power and inclusion in the workplace.

Reciprocal appreciation occurred in this contact zone as the "guest workers" also experienced a sense of caring from their co-workers. Hwang still appreciates the support she received from her co-workers when she gave birth:

> They [my colleagues] collected things I needed for my baby like a *Kinderwagen* [pram], clothes and other stuff, and often asked me how my baby daughter was doing. When my daughter got sick and I had to stay at home to look after her, some of them didn't mind covering my shift at work and swapping theirs. It was a really warm atmosphere and my feelings of homesickness were gone. (Hwang, former nurse)

The sense of proximity and interconnectedness Hwang experienced was not a superficial contact, but based on meaningful interactions which provided her with a sense of being home-from-home in the host country through social reception and acceptance. As a consequence, a contact zone could be transformed into an "intimate zone" with familial type relations. Furthermore, a sense of solidarity was heightened when some of the local populace, including their co-workers, supported the Korean nurses' right to stay in Germany when they were forced to leave after the recruitment of foreign migrant healthcare workers was stopped in the late 1970s. The Korean healthcare workers were employed in a specialized line of work that allowed for prolonged interactions, especially with patients who might be in vulnerable positions, thereby increasing their chances of acceptance by the dominant society.

However, it is important to note that rather than forming part of their natural disposition, in reality the women's embodied caring and kindness, as well as their work ethic, were often learned and/or performed as coping strategies for dealing with "othering" within their country of destination as discussed earlier. These strategies represented a way to maneuver the dominant culture within the contact zone as migrant "guest workers": "Here is Germany, not Korea, and we are *Ausländer* [foreigners] here forever. . . . In order not to give a bad impression of *Ausländer* like us, I worked *fleißig* [hard] and treated them [the local people] nicely . . ." (Hwang).

In Hwang's accounts, and many others', personal commitment to high standards of performance and carrying out one's work in a spirit of goodwill were seen as helping to prevent prejudice against foreign migrant workers. In media coverage, the work ethic of the Korean nurses was referred to with terms such as hardworking, diligent, "always ready to help" [immer hilfsbereit] (*Frankfurter Allgemeine* 17 February 1966, quoted in Roberts 2012, 63), or "a helping and healing hand from the Far East [die helfenden und pflegenden Hände aus Fernost]" (Radio Interview with Barbara John 2003, quoted in Roberts 2012, 89). In this way, work was also linked to the women's constant awareness of their "foreignness" and to their desire for inclusion and recognition as "model guest workers" in the dominant society.

## DISCORD: CULTURAL DISTINCTIONS IN DAILY LIFE

The spatial and temporal co-presence of the migrants and the "native" demonstrates both positive and negative aspects. This section examines tension and cultural disparity and the types of clash experienced in the contact zone. The linguistic gap discussed earlier enhanced the women's "foreignness" in relation to the local population. For example, Korean names were deemed difficult to pronounce, and as a consequence, a substantial number of the Korean "guest workers" were given German names upon arriving at their workplaces: "Each of us was given a German name there, as it was difficult for them [to say our Korean names]. Nina was mine and Maria, Sonja, Marion something like that for others . . ." (Min, former nurse).

Here it will be worth reflecting on the power of naming. Andrea Dworkin writes: "This power of naming enables men to define experience, to articulate boundaries and values, to designate to each thing its realm and qualities, to determine what can and cannot be expressed, to control perception itself" (Dworkin 1981, 26). Renaming migrants with German or Western European names within a healthcare institution might be seen as stemming from practicality on the supervisor's side, but on a deeper level the power of naming, as discussed by Dworkin, is being enacted in this practice. Dworkin makes the above point in the context of men's power over naming women's experiences, but her approach can be applied to the context of migrant experiences as well. A name given by one's family at birth is a significant marker of personal and ethnic identity. According to Korean custom, the belief exists that a name determines the life of those who carry it, therefore parents generally take the task of seeking a good name for their newborn child very seriously. However, asymmetric power relations in contact zones frequently enable and legitimize the renaming of migrants, rendering the values of other culture's names as invalid. Renaming can thus be an imposition of assimilation through the everyday routine of using a name from the dominant culture and involuntarily losing one's own. This process might have had an impact on the embodied identities of the migrant women.

The local population's reactions to aspects of the women's "foreign" culture, like the Korean language, demonstrate views of the migrants as "exotic" others. These views can be observed in one of the major German newspapers, *Frankfurter Allgemeine,* in 1966. The Korean language as spoken by the nurses is depicted as "peculiar conversation [eigenartige Konversation]" that alleviated the patients' boredom (*Frankfurter Allgemeine* 17 February 1966, quoted in Roberts 2012, 66).

Culinary culture was another marker of ethnicity and an everyday practice over which migrants and the local populace sometimes clashed. Food is often regarded as defining people, as apparent from well-known adages such as "you are what you eat." In Germany, certain foods are even used to stereotype entire minority groups. "*Knoblauchfresser*," a derogatory term for garlic eater is used to refer to Turkish, "Oriental," or Balkan people, while "*Zwiebelfresser*," a derogatory term for onion eater is used to refer to Russians. As made clear by the existence of gastronomically based derogatory terms in German, these markers of ethnic culture and identity are the sites of cultural clashes within a contact zone. Ethnic food, like personal names, can be a source of distinctive emotions and memories of the homeland and can be a determining factor in social inclusion and exclusion.

With the exception of garlic, the majority of my interviewees received positive feedback upon introducing Korean cuisine to their co-workers and friends. Some local German patients or colleagues with whom they interacted on a daily basis at work complained about "garlic breath" from the Korean nurses after consuming their ethnic cuisine. Almost all of my interviewees narrated at least one such situation revolving around garlic in interactions with locals. Chin reports once having a fairly serious argument over the consumption of garlic:

> I avoided having *Knoblauch* [garlic] for the first several years since the patients I had to deal with made so much fuss about the *Knoblauch* smell [on my breath]. In the 1990s, when I rekindled my contact with the Korean community here, I enjoyed having garlic again. But one of my co-workers asked me almost every morning "*Hast du Knoblauch gegessen*? [Did you have garlic?]," which drove me mad, so one day I hit back by saying "If I stopped having garlic, there wouldn't be any smell from me, but you were born with odor and don't you think it bothers me?" (Chin, nurse assistant)

The recurring, loaded question from Chin's colleague can be considered to have been based in part on an essentialist approach to "race" and ethnicity which offended Chin. From Chin's retort to her co-worker, it can be seen that the idea of racialization associated with a distinctive body type was also expressed by the migrants towards the majority population. Whether in the form of body odor or unpleasant breath from food, odor may reinforce an uncomfortable feeling of "otherness" on both sides, and is thus often a sign of irreconcilable differences. This represents a tense moment of intercultural friction in the contact zone, and is linked to the migrants' embedded experiences of social exclusion and mutually racializing cultural disparity. While the essentialist tone of her remark may appear to suggest belief in a fundamental racialized difference, rather it represents a perception of "otherness" arising from the embodied daily experiences she had to cope with as shown in the tensions over different culinary culture.

As the consumption of ethnic cuisine gave rise to constant tension, most of the Korean healthcare workers often reduced their intake of Korean food, to avoid complaints about its strong aroma: "For the days I was on duty I didn't have *Kimch'i*, because of garlic breath. And also no bean paste soup was cooked at home. My neighbors might knock on my door to complain about the strong smell. So I didn't cook it. It was a difficult time for me to be concerned about many things" (Lee, a former nurse). Lee's account marks the migrants' burden of coping with the disparate culinary culture in daily life. The Korean healthcare workers' experiences of negotiation with ethnic food are constructed in time and space. Some, like Na and Han, married local German men and adapted by preparing local German cuisine at home for their non-migrant spouses and children:

> For 20 years after my marriage not a single piece of *Kimch'i* touched my lips because Germans don't like the smell of *Kimch'i*. I thought that my children shouldn't have the *Knoblauch* [garlic] breath when they were out and mingling with friends. Probably I myself was biased [about Korean food]. I cooked only German or Western style food for my children. When my children were grown and had moved out of the home, I resumed making *Kimch'i* at home. (Han, former nurse)

For Han, preparing German food was a way of circumventing and negotiating culinary disparity in the intimate space of the home which became a contact zone through inter-marriage between a migrant and a non-migrant citizen. In her case, the major concern seems to have been ensuring that her children were not ostracized as a consequence of consuming Korean food.

Different attitudes towards sharing food can be observed from the interviews as well. Kim felt her co-workers demarcated a clear boundary of ownership between the personal and the shared, while she viewed offering or sharing food as a simple matter of politeness and kindness: "I was really surprised that my [local] co-workers did not share the food they brought with others. It is like you eat yours and I eat mine. But I always asked and offered them to try mine. This is just my habit, or our custom. Then many did try and even some enjoyed it, but they didn't offer theirs to others" (Kim, former nurse). Food is thus not only a source of physical nourishment, but a signifier of collective culture. Hence, when different cultures come into contact, their food practices may create social boundaries.

Cultural differences were mutually experienced between the German and the migrant healthcare workers carrying out nursing activities. Neumann, who worked with Korean nurses, compares the different attitudes of the German and Korean nurses towards their patients: "The cultural difference was a rather big deal. German nurses are somehow stricter. That was a difference [from the Korean nurses]. The Koreans were not so hard on their patients. The German nurses told their patients off again and again if they [the patients] didn't do what they were supposed to do" (Neumann, former male nurse).

A Korean nurse, Na, observes a different emphasis on work style: "The most important thing for my German colleagues was *Sauberkeit* [cleanliness] while for us it is giving good nursing care" (Na, former nurse). Na considers the work style of the German nurses to have been focused on cleanliness and efficiency without much emotional engagement, while she defines the Korean nurses' work as being centered on demonstrating care and emotion. While such concepts fed the image of caring and gentle Korean nurses shared by local patients and the German media, they also demonstrate personal feelings that culturally distinct patterns of thought and behavior existed, especially in the delivery of nursing care. Such perceived and experienced differences in daily interactions lead people to draw distinct boundaries. A sense of cultural distinctiveness, shaped and confirmed through daily encounters with the dominant group, reinforces a sense of migrants' ethnic identity in contact zone exchanges.

As noted earlier, the nature of care activity is highly interpersonal. Both migrant caregivers and local care receivers or colleagues at work in the host country meet in person and develop positive and negative emotions and attitudes towards one another during their interactions in the contact zone. Prejudicial attitudes on the part of the patients towards the Korean nurses are recounted in experiences like those of Pang, a former nurse assistant, who still remembers a rude patient telling her to "go back to where you came from" when she made a mistake. In this articulation of exclusion, the politics of space and the position of "host" and "guest" without residency rights in this space are clearly expressed. Space is not only physical, but an ongoing process of drawing and redrawing a metaphorical boundary between the self and the other. This boundary connects, limits, and separates the people inhabiting it, and is therefore entangled with power relationships (Lefèbvre 1991; Löw 2008).

In summary, the Korean nurses experienced both inclusion and exclusion from the host society, especially in their relationships with the patients they cared for and colleagues they worked with. Ample narratives from my interview participants demonstrate a complex set of interactions, ranging from prejudice, friction, contempt, appreciation, kindness, empathy, and/or inclusion in the contact zone throughout the process of delivering and receiving nursing care.

## TRANSCULTURATION

This concluding section examines the way in which socio-cultural differences are managed in constituting transcultural subjects. Mary Louise Pratt (1992, 4) uses the term "transculturation" to describe processes through which members of marginal groups selectively borrow cultural characteristics from a predominant culture. "Transculturation" is a term that thus resonates with the migrants' navigation of their positions within the contact zone. Son shares her experience of selectively adapting from the host culture: "What I like here [in Germany] is their consideration not to bother others and paying attention to not breaching regulations and laws. Also, things need to be done in a precise, not sloppy, way. These observations are what I have learned from my time here. But what is missing here is warmth towards others."

Son points out the local values and work ethic she has adopted and other features of which she disapproves. Such selective adoption and appropriation of the dominant culture's lifestyles, customs, and values by the Korean "guest workers" served to support their transculturation and settlement in the host society. In the process, some amount of cultural distinction between the migrants and the non-migrants was negotiated and reduced.

Transculturation was not always a mutual affair and, more often than not, was achieved through the migrants' dropping or "overcoming" of their own culture or habits in favor of those of the dominant culture. Cross-cultural encounters, often taking place through prolonged interactions over several decades, exist within asymmetrical and hierarchical relations of the "host" and the "guest." However, the existence of a power imbalance did not mean that the "highly asymmetrical relations of domination and subordination" (Pratt 1992, 4) in the contact zone were intact at all times. The power flow was not always unilaterally in favor of the "host," while the "guest workers" exercised agency in both subtle and direct ways. As noted in various narratives of the healthcare workers, gendered and racialized boundaries of "self" and "other" could be transgressed and/or contested through prolonged interaction with members of the local populace.

New power configurations that took shape over time in contact zones were complex. In the context of nursing care, the migrant workers were able to both express vulnerability and to witness it from patients in conditions of dependency, illness, or immobility. The interactions in this contact zone took place within the particular context of nursing care and resulted in complex relationships between care givers and care recipients. As witnessed in their narratives, the Korean healthcare "guest workers" themselves experienced a complex range of emotions in their cross-cultural interactions—receiving warmth but also being distanced at times, and experiencing hospitality/hostility, inclusion/exclusion, refusal/recognition, or ignorance/comprehension.

Na, who worked as a nurse for over 30 years in Germany, discusses withstanding the challenges of interacting with a distinct culture in a contact zone and her life of "in-betweenness":

> We have been living in between two cultures. The Korean one did not disappear [in me]. I don't intend to get rid of this part [Korean culture] of me. [I] want to keep what I have cherished since my childhood, and also adopt German culture like food and language and get on well with it. I think I have managed living in between [two cultures] well and I worked hard here [in Germany] till I became *Rentner* [pensioner]. Well, I actually put up with [work] till the end, it was not always easy though.

In the healthcare workers' lived experiences of "in-betweenness" and existing across two cultural spheres, they never completely assimilated into the dominant culture, but at the same time remained somewhat at a distance from the ethnic culture of their country of origin. In the course of their prolonged interactions with members of the host society, the Korean healthcare workers developed their own coping mechanisms for negotiating the racialized and gendered cultural script of "Koreanness." The Korean healthcare workers can be neatly fit neither into the prescribed category of "typical German" nor into that of "typical Korean women." The women's practice of transculturation can thus be understood as a conscious effort to transcend the cultural binary in which the women lived through the selective utilization of German culture, customs, and values.

Contact zones are places of intersection where different parties observe each other's values, attitudes, and lifestyles, and decide what aspects to embrace, negotiate, or negate. In the current work, the face-to-face encounters between the Korean healthcare "guest workers" and the local population (especially their co-workers and the patients they looked after) are understood as the site of a contact zone. These cross-cultural encounters might be uncomfortable but remain inevitable as a consequence of dissimilar cultures meeting in the social space of the contact zone. Through cross-cultural interactions, two different cultures clashed and converged to shape a transcultural lived experience for the migrant nurses. While competing cultural boundaries were not entirely lifted, proximity was created through interactions in the dynamic contact zone. In the course of these interactions, the migrants appropriated and reshaped aspects of the dominant culture, without giving up ethnic cultural practices, in order to assimilate. Thus, their lived experiences can be defined in the context of transculturation, which is not a fixed state but a constant and dynamic process of making and remaking.

# NOTES

1. My sincerest thanks are due to the former Korean healthcare workers in Germany who participated in interviews for this project and who shared their life histories with me.
2. Though the current work focuses on interactions between Korean migrant workers and their local German co-workers, it bears mentioning that respondents share that, while working in Germany in the 1960s and the 1970s, they also had co-workers from Eastern Europe and other parts of Asia including India and the Philippines.

# REFERENCES

Ahn, Yonson. 2014. "Gendering Migration: Koreanische Arbeitsmigrantinnen im Pflegesektor in Deutschland." In *Unbekannte Vielfalt: Einblicke in die koreanische Migrationsgeschichte in Deutschland*, edited by Young-Seoun Chang-Gusko et al., 166–187. Berlin: DOMiD.
*Allgemeine Zeitung.* 1966. "Zarte Hand und Mandelaugen." 29 April 1966.
Amelina, Anna, and Thomas Faist. "Turkish Migrant Associations in Germany: Between Integration Pressure and Transnational Linkages. 2008." *Revue Européenne des Migrations Internationales* 24(2): 91–120.
Anderson, Bridget, and Isabel Shutes. 2014. "Conclusion." In *Migration and Care Labour: Theory, Policy and Politics*, edited by Bridget Anderson and Isabel Shutes, 213–224. Hampshire: Palgrave MacMillan.
Dworkin, Andrea. 1981. *Pornography: Men Possessing Women.* London: Women's Press.
Gutiérrez-Rodríguez, Encarnación. 2010. *Migration, Domestic Work and Affect: A Decolonial Approach on Value and the Feminization of Labor.* New York and London: Routledge.
Hunn, Karin. 2005. *"Nächstes Jahr kehren wir zurück . . .": Die Geschichte der türkischen "Gastarbeiter" in der Bundesrepublik.* Göttingen: Wallstein Verlag.
Lefèbvre, Henri. 1991. *The Production of Space.* Translated by Nicholson-Smith. Oxford: Blackwell.
Löw, Martina. 2008. "The Constitution of Space. The Structuration of Spaces through the Simultaneity of Effect and Perception." *European Journal of Social Theory* 11(1): 25–49.
*Main-Taunus-Rundschau.* 1970. "Schwestern aus Indien und Korea: Etwas einsam in der Klinik." 20 May 1970.
Noddings, Nel. 1984. *Caring: A Feminine Approach to Ethics and Morals Education.* Berkeley: University of California Press.
*Offenbacher Rundschau.* 1966. "Charmante Schwestern." 1 July 1966.
Pratt, Mary Louise. 1992. *Imperial Eyes: Travel Writing and Transculturation.* London and New York: Routledge.
Rauer, Valentin. 2008. *Die öffentliche Dimension der Integration: Migrationspolitische Diskurse türkischer Dachverbände in Deutschland.* Bielefeld: Transcript Verlag.
Roberts, Suin. 2012. *Language of Migration: Self- and Other-Representation of Korean Migrants in Germany.* New York: Peter Lang.
Ruddick, Sara. 1998. "Care as Labor and Relationship." In *Norms and Values: Essays on the Work of Virginia Held*, edited by Mark S. Halfon and Joram C. Haber, 3–25. Lanham, MD: Rowman & Littlefield.
Tronto, Joan. 1993. *Moral Boundaries: A Political Argument for an Ethic of Care.* New York, London: Routledge.
Yeoh, Brenda S.A., and Shirlena Huang. 1999. "Singapore Women and Foreign Domestic Workers." In *Gender, Migration and Domestic Service*, edited by Janet Henshall Momsen, 273–296. London and New York: Routledge.

*Chapter Four*

# Patriarchal Racialization

*Gendered and Racialized Integration of Foreign Brides and Foreign Husbands in South Korea*

## Seonok Lee

South Korea has long referred to itself as *tanil minjok kukka*—"the single ethnic nation state."[1] Until recently, enhancing pride in being a single ethnic nation and emphasizing the importance of maintaining "Korean blood" were popular themes of public education in South Korea. Therefore, the majority of Koreans still believe that maintaining *tanil minjok* (the single ethnic nation) is essential to Korean identity. However, since the mid-1990s a rapidly growing marriage migrant and foreign migrant worker population has led to an increased awareness that South Korea is becoming more ethnically and racially diverse (Jung 2007; Lee 2008; Hong and Kim 2010; Jo 2011; M. Kim 2014; H. Kim 2014).

Due to declining birth rates, the South Korean government began recruiting marriage migrants from neighboring Asian countries, such as China, Vietnam, Philippines, Cambodia, Thailand and Mongolia. Since 2005, in response to the dramatically growing numbers of marriage migrants, the South Korean government has actively supported multicultural integration programs for marriage migrants through multicultural family support centers. These centers provide free Korean language classes, Korean culture classes, Korean cooking classes, parenting seminars, speech clinics for children, legal aid, translation services (usually in Chinese, Vietnamese, and Tagalog), and basic job training programs. Particularly popular amongst new marriage migrants are the Korean language and culture classes, because these courses provide the participant with an exemption from the written and oral tests for acquiring permanent residency or citizenship. There is no doubt that multicultural family support centers and their integration programs greatly assist marriage migrants in adapting to Korean culture and society. In fact, many couples of international marriages even try to find housing near such centers.

Yet a closer look at who these multicultural activities are created for, and what they actually entail, reveals that the South Korean government mainly supports the integration of foreign brides rather than foreign husbands. This raises a number of questions: Why, despite strong undercurrents of ethno-nationalism and the myth of ethnic homogeneity, is the South Korean government attempting to integrate foreign brides from different racial and ethnic backgrounds? At the same time, why is the South Korean government not attempting to integrate foreign husbands?

Drawing upon ethnographic research on marriage migrants, their Korean family members, and neighbors in South Korea, I argue that racial logics play a central role in reproducing patriarchal family structures and that to do so, these logics operate in opposing ways for foreign brides and foreign husbands. I call this active process *patriarchal racialization*. Patriarchal racialization is a gendered racialization process whereby patriarchal gender roles are emphasized to minimize racial differences for certain groups that need to be integrated into the existing socio-cultural system. At the same time, the racial differences of other groups are maximized to amplify their "foreignness," which delay their integration into the society. Patriarchal racialization involves multiple actors, such as the state, community, and family members in the microsphere of the household. The outcome of patriarchal racialization involves both the production of a new racial category and the inscribing of specific gendered rules within racial hierarchies. Patriarchal racialization is problematic because it justifies the unequal distribution of access to resources such as work and education, as well as social, economic, and political power. The co-formation of patriarchy and racialization can be broadly observed even though the actual cases may appear differently in historically and locally specific contexts. Therefore South Korea offers a prime example for studying how economic migration interacts with global systems of gender and racial inequality.

This chapter is organized as follows: I begin by weaving connections between the literature on patriarchy and racialization in race and gender studies. I then turn to my empirical study of foreign brides and foreign husbands living in South Korea. This involves analysis of the role of the South Korean state in gendered marriage recruitment, settlement services, and citizenship policies. I also examine both migrant women and men's everyday experiences of difference and hierarchy in the micro-space of the household and in the community. I conclude by exploring patriarchal racialization, which reproduces patriarchy as a system of gender domination and subordination by facilitating racial logics.

# THEORETICAL BACKGROUND FOR
# PATRIARCHAL RACIALIZATION

As one specific way of Othering, racialization imposes otherness on a certain group of people. According to Omi and Winant (1994, 64), the category of race is an outcome of a racialization process, which involves "the extension of racial meaning to a previously racially un-classified relationship, social practice or group." Similar to Omi and Winant's definition of racialization, Miles and Brown (2003, 102) define racialization as "a dialectical process by which meaning is attributed to particular biological features of human beings, as a result of which individuals may be assigned to a general category of persons which reproduces itself biologically." Racialization is problematic because it includes a dialectical process of the conceptualization of the self (in-group) as a superior race, which simultaneously solicits the conceptualization of the other as the inferior race by attributing a negative evaluation to the Other (Miles and Brown 2003). Van Dijk (1993, 20) points out that racism "affect[s] other people primarily because they are thought to belong to another group, that is, as group members and not as individuals." This means that a specific ethnic group is seen as "alike and interchangeable" (Ibid., 20). This process inscribes racial meanings to specific ethnic groups and individuals within the existing ethno-racial hierarchy, which influence social mobility, access to societal rewards and resources, and overall quality of life (McDonnell and de Lourenco 2009).

Building upon Omi and Winant's (1994) racial formation theory, Kandaswamy (2012, 12) argues that "racial formation is fundamentally a gendered and sexualized process." In this view, gender and race do not exist and create inequalities in isolation. Rather gender and race—as mutually constitutive powers—engage with one another in the distribution of uneven power and the creation of social inequalities. However, despite increasing recognition of the intersectional relations between gender and racialization, patriarchy as a social system of organizing gender and of privileging male authority is not typically analyzed in its co-formation with racialization. The role of patriarchy tends to be marginalized from the scholarly discussion of racialization, which overlooks the way various forms of patriarchy have intersected with other forms of inequalities such as racism.

The intimate space of home and family is an important site for reproducing not only gender hierarchies but also racial hierarchies under the patriarchal order (Collins 2001, Stoler 2002). The inseparable relationship between race and gender under patriarchal domination can be easily traced back to the 19th century of European colonial power. For example, Stoler (2002) examines how the management of sexual arrangements was fundamentally structured into the making of racial categories and racial hierarchies in colonial Indonesia by looking at sexual and racial dynamics among white Dutch men, white Dutch women, local Indonesian women, and mixed-race children. While returning to the Netherlands from colonial Indonesia with an Asian wife and mixed-race children was prohibited, Dutch bachelors in Indonesia were encouraged, or at least tolerated, to live with native Indonesian women. Their cohabitation was considered to help colonial development and expansion by stabilizing political order and public colonial health. When Dutch women entered colonial Indonesia, however, the boundary between white Dutch families and native Indonesians, and the hierarchy of the colonizer and the colonized, became much clearer. Mixed-race children of Dutch men and native Indonesian women were located above the local population but below that of the Dutch colonizers. Thus, control over sexual activities, marriage, and reproduction were a crucial colonial apparatus for constructing racial hierarchies between the colonizers and the colonized. As Stoler puts it, "gender-specific sexual sanctions and prohibitions not only demarcated positions of power but also prescribed the personal and public boundaries of race" (Ibid., 42). Along the same line, McClintock (1995, 56) describes a patriarchal racial order in the 19th-century Britain in her book *Imperial Leather*: "The English middle-class male was placed at the pinnacle of evolutionary hierarchy. White English middle class women followed. Domestic workers, female miners and working-class prostitutes were stationed on the threshold between the white and black races."

However, the main literature on racial boundaries under patriarchy is concentrated on 19th-century European colonialism (cf., Stoler 2005; McClintock 1995). There is little literature on the intersections between patriarchy and racialization in relation to contemporary migration in East and Southeast Asia. Therefore, building upon the discussion on gendered racialization shows how patriarchy reproduces racial hierarchy, and racialization reinforces patriarchal order in the context of gendered migration in East Asia.

## ETHNOGRAPHY ON MULTICULTURAL FAMILY

This article is based on ethnographic research conducted in two typical industrial working-class cities in South Korea—Ansan and Siheung—between September 2013 and May 2014. A significant population of immigrants and foreign migrant workers populate these neighboring cities because of the industrial complex located there. In this industrial complex there are more than 10,000 small- and medium-sized factories. I was interested in examining not only "what people say" about race but also "what people actually do" (Waters 2001, 11). While working alongside migrants in several factories, and participating in classes at the migrant centers, I observed everyday interactions and experiences amongst different actors in order to gain insight into the process of patriarchal racialization.

The migration flows toward South Korea are characterized as labor and marriage migration. As female migration between East Asia and Southeast Asian countries has increased, Korean migration scholars place migrant women at the center of marriage migration while paying little attention to migrant men. Most of these men from South and Southeast Asia married Korean women after originally entering Korea as unskilled foreign migrant workers. Therefore, I include migrant men in order to examine the gender and racial dynamics amongst Koreans, and both migrant women and men.

I volunteered as a child minder at the Ansan Multicultural Family Support Center. I also attended some classes offered to female marriage migrants and their families, such as Korean cooking classes, basic job training (cooking certificates and coffee brewing), childcare seminars, and language classes alongside Chinese, Korean-Chinese, Vietnamese, Filipina, Japanese, Mongolian, and Uzbek women. At the center, the majority of programs were intended for migrant women under the official category of "multicultural family" based on the assumption that marriage migrants are women and full-time homemakers. Even though I am a native-born ethnic Korean, I was able to take these classes with other female marriage migrants, because of my "foreigner" husband. Therefore, my family was also officially categorized as a multicultural family. My foreign husband was not in South Korea with me during my field research, but my daughter often accompanied me to the classes whenever I could not arrange child minding for her.

Theoretically, foreign husbands can also use the services and classes in the multicultural family support center. However, they usually do not visit the center because they see the center as a place "for women" but not for them due to its immigrant women–oriented services. Instead, they use the foreign migrant workers' welfare center, which is intended for documented and undocumented foreign workers who enter Korea with a three- to five-year contract for manufacturing and service industries. The foreign migrant workers' welfare center mainly provides labor counseling services on top of computer classes, driver's license classes, martial art training, free medical services, and ethnic group meetings. These centers are open for any foreign migrant workers, but usually young male foreign workers hang out in the lobby more often than female foreign workers. I regularly visited the foreign migrant workers' welfare center to meet male immigrants and foreign migrant workers.

I realized that the neighborhood is also a very important site to capture the interactions between migrants and Koreans. Whenever I traveled by subway or bus with my toddler daughter, I noticed that my daughter always drew very visible attention from people because of her biracial look. Responses differed depending on whether they saw me as an Asian foreign bride with a non-Korean looking child, or whether they saw my daughter as a white *honhyŏl* (mixed blood) from a white father. I also had to deal with inconsiderate comments and curious glances at my child and me, and I learned about my new social category, *tamunhwa* (multicultural family), through social benefits programs that I applied for, and in everyday interactions with people. For example, I learned that my family is *tamunhwa* when I registered my daughter on the wait lists of public daycare centers. The director of the public daycare center told me that my family is in the category of *tamunhwa,* so my daughter could get a priority for the registration, which is the same benefit offered to underprivileged families, such as single parent families, low-income families, and disabled parents families.

Interestingly, my status as the mother of a biracial child offered opportunities to get closer to migrant women. As they found out that I also have a foreign spouse and a biracial child, they invited my daughter and me over to their homes for playdates and family occasions like birthday parties. Sometimes, we went on picnics with our children to the local museum and parks. As part of the ethnographic research, I conducted semi-structured interviews with local Koreans and migrants from Bangladesh, Vietnam, Philippines, Cambodia, Nepal, and China about their feelings about international marriages or their experience living together as a multicultural family.

In the following section, I examine the role of the state by looking at the institutional conditions of marriage immigration and gendered settlement services.

## THE STATE'S INTERVENTION TO GENDERED MIGRATION FLOWS AND SETTLEMENT

In this section, I explore one facet of how patriarchal racialization occurs— the state, which institutionally controls migration flows, settlement process, and membership through the citizenship and settlement policies. In South Korea, almost every city has a multicultural family support center to assist marriage migrants' successful settlement and their families' cultural adjustment to the new relationship. However, these government-installed centers are gender-specific venues. In other words, the center is a place for foreign brides and their children, but not for foreign husbands. For example, Nepalese husband Udaya,[2] who is in his early thirties, did not go to the center near his house. Right after marrying a Korean woman, he visited the center to see if he could use its programs and services. However, he found that there were no programs and services for him. He explained, "it seems mainly foreign ladies go to the center, because they need to learn how to look after their babies, learn how to cook Korean foods, and how to deal with their Korean family-in-law. I heard that their Korean mothers-in-law give them lots of stress." Although the multicultural family support centers offer Korean language classes and some other useful services, foreign husbands still do not feel comfortable going to the multicultural family support center. Perhaps they see it as not for them.

By 2013, there were 211 multicultural family support centers across the country that had been installed under the Multicultural Family Support Act. These centers are supposed to serve any family who is categorized as a multicultural family. However, not everyone can use these centers. The majority of the programs are designed to help foreign brides adapt to their Korean family's culture and for Korean-born children to improve their Korean language proficiency. Thus, they provide Korean language, cooking, child-rearing, and culture classes based on the assumption that visitors to the center are full-time homemakers and primary caregivers. The center also organizes foreign wives as volunteers and connects them to local charity groups in order to enhance their social integration. However, it is rare for these centers to provide services in the evenings or on weekends for foreign husbands who usually work in the factories during weekdays. Therefore, while these centers teach specific gender roles to foreign wives through their settlement programs, the centers neglect foreign husbands from integrating into Korean society institutionally.

This gendered approach to marriage migrants is clear even before foreign brides enter South Korea. Foreign brides are advised to take Korean cultural programs while they are waiting for their visas. There are several overseas Korean culture centers for new brides in the Philippines, Vietnam, and other countries. These overseas Korean culture centers provide an overview of Korean society and Korean culture. In particular, they provide the new brides with information on how to have a successful marriage with a Korean man—for example, how to manage in-law relationships and how to behave properly as a wife and a daughter-in-law.

When we look closely at the citizenship and immigration policies, it is clear that the Korean state plays a critical role in reproducing patriarchal family relations by controlling marriage migrants' gender composition. The state promotes importing foreign brides from lower income countries but restricts the entry of foreign husbands. Accordingly, settlement services are also geared towards foreign brides in order to strengthen the patriarchal family relations which contemporary Korean women are increasingly resisting. South Korean immigration policy is oriented towards female marriage migrants. It is based on two interrelated gender ideologies: blood passing down paternally and a wife being under her husband's control. First, Koreans' belief that blood passes down through a father is important to understanding gendered immigration and citizenship policies which are inclusive of foreign women but exclusive of foreign men. Until 1997, a foreign bride could automatically attain Korean citizenship upon marriage to a Korean husband, but a foreign husband was only allowed to get a temporary visitor visa. In many cases, foreign husbands had to re-enter South Korea every three month to renew their visitor status. Since they were officially tourists, they were not allowed to get jobs in South Korea until 1997. While the children of a foreign bride and Korean man were Korean citizens, the children of a foreign husband and a Korean woman were not recognized as Korean citizens (Jung 2007). They had to register as foreign nationals in their homeland because they had to follow their father's nationality (Ibid.). In 1998, the Korean nationality law was revised, but instead of allowing fast-track citizenship for foreign husbands as well, the South Korean government discontinued automatic citizenship for foreign brides (Lee 2008). Thus, both foreign men and foreign women now have to wait at least two years before applying for Korean citizenship.

Immigration policy and citizenship are crucial tools to define outsiders, insiders, and racial others. Immigration policies have historically made a distinction between the alien and the citizen in order to legitimize a specific group's modern citizenship rights (Ibid.). This is a way of differentiating between who is, and who is not, a member of the national community.

## PERFORMING TRADITIONAL GENDER ROLES: FOREIGN BRIDES' GENDERED INTEGRATION

Having a foreign wife is considered a less-than-ideal situation in South Korea. Having a wife from a lower-income country signals a man's incompetence in the Korean marriage market compared to his middle-class white-collar counterparts and hurts a man's honor and his family's pride (M. Kim 2014). However, symbolically an unmarried man is in some degree infantilized, so to remain unmarried is to be seen as a total failure as a man (Ibid.). He is not seen as the patriarch of his own household or a "respectable family man" (Freeman 2005). The parents of an unmarried man often feel responsibility to make sure their son has a wife in order to continue the family lineage, so it is not rare for parents to initiate international marriage for their sons.

While a Korean wife is ideal, if an international marriage is necessary, a foreign wife's nationality and her homeland's economic status are carefully considered. The relative desirability of a foreign wife depends on her country of origin, whether she comes from a relatively developed country or a less developed country, and what ethnicity or race these countries represent. However, the majority of international marriages are unions of rural farmers or working-class Korean men and foreign women from Southeast Asia and China. Western European or North American wives who reside in South Korea are not common. These Korean husbands of Western European or North American wives are usually professionals—or at least middle class. Therefore, there is a clear class division in the international marriage market along the husbands' privileged class position, and perceived hierarchies of wives' country of origin. Based on this hierarchy, expectations toward foreign wives differ. Wives from Western Europe and North America are treated as bilingual cosmopolitans without much expectation of domesticity (Hong and Kim 2010). This is in sharp contrast to the way that wives from Southeast Asia and China are treated: as obedient wives and good homemakers whose main quality comes from her domesticity. Regardless of the class status of a Korean family, Korean husbands and in-laws believe that they are superior to their foreign wives based on their nation's position in the global economic hierarchy (Abelmann and Kim 2005, M. Kim 2014, H. Kim 2014).

Corresponding to this social expectation, female marriage migrants have to adjust by identifying as "the good wife and mother." As H. Kim (2014) points out, however, female marriage migrants are neither from the past nor intrinsically obedient and traditional. Rather, many of them have previously experienced more gender-equal relationships under socialist regime or matriarchal family culture of their home countries. They, thus, have to adapt to Korean gender roles and perform "the good wife" to integrate into Korean society. Thirty-three-year-old Filipina immigrant Susanne's case illustrates this well.

Susanne and her Korean husband Young-Hoon live on the outskirts of the city, with their children and her Korean mother-in-law. Susanne expressed that she has a good relationship with her Korean mother-in-law. Her neighbors complement her cooking and hard work, saying Susanne is just like a Korean. She seemed well integrated into traditional Korean family culture. However, Susanne recalled that it took years to adapt to the Korean way of interacting. There were lots of arguments and tense situations until she finally adapted her husbands' family culture:

> When I just got married, I could not understand my father-in-law at all. He asked me to serve every little thing, like serving water or coffee whenever he needed it. And my husband asked me to do everything for him too. In the Philippines, all the boys know how to do household work. But Korean men, they asked me to even serve water. I felt that it's very unfair. One day I talked back to my father-in-law. This made him angry and he overthrew the dinner table. It was tense. I was so frustrated and angry because of this culture where women should serve men. Why did they ask me to bring water in the morning? [Laughs.] Now I understand it is just Korean culture. I learned that respecting seniors and listening to them is part of Korean culture. Also I learned cooking and serving meals are a wife's duty.

At first, she protested against traditional gender roles, but she eventually accepted her role in the family. Susanne understood this to be Korean tradition and a cultural difference between the Philippines and South Korea, instead of exploitation of women within the family. Not every foreign bride accepts this traditional gender role though. For example, patriarchal family culture is one of the main complaints of foreign women about their marriage lives and patriarchal expectations often cause family troubles or divorces (Freeman 2005; Yu 2010; Park 2011). However, when a foreign bride adapts to patriarchal gender roles, they tend to have a comparatively peaceful marriage life and decent relationships with their in-laws.

While foreign brides are integrated into Korean society if they accept the role of a good wife, Korean husbands also have to perform the traditional gender role of "the respectable family man" (Freeman 2005). While a Korean husband relegates reproductive and domestic labor to his foreign wife, he is expected to be the main breadwinner and financially support his wife's natal family. However, since the majority of Korean men who chose international marriages are factory workers or rural farmers, being able to financially support a wife's natal family is often quite difficult (H. Kim 2014). Sending remittances to the wife's natal family is also expected even though not every couple is able to send remittances regularly, or at all (Ibid.). Younger generations of Koreans in their 20s and 30s tend to be less patriarchal and more sensitive to gender equality. This means not only that young Korean women challenge their traditional gender roles as a wife, daughter-in-law, and mother, but also that young Korean men do not want to take the full responsibility of being the sole breadwinner. However, Korean patriarchy is still influential in shaping family relations, especially for multicultural families who expect both foreign brides and Korean husbands to perform traditional gender roles, as foreign brides are integrated into Korean society through demonstrating their Korean-ness through the family.

## RACIAL/ETHNIC PREFERENCES OF A FOREIGN WIFE

Koreans are highly perceptive of ethnic and racial differences. Depending on a spouse's skin color and appearance, the family may be able to pass and possibly blend into Korean society, or they may constantly encounter gazes from strangers and discrimination. Thus, Koreans prefer East Asian–looking brides such as Chinese or Vietnamese women to darker skinned brides from the Philippines or Thailand. The following excerpt shows the racial/cultural preferences in choosing a foreign wife. In September 2012, a Korean man posted about his experience of international marriage on an online forum for the benefit of other Korean bachelors. After careful deliberation, he narrowed down his wife-to-be's nationality to Vietnam and Uzbekistan. In the end he chose an Uzbek bride because his parents would not accept a Southeast Asian woman as their daughter-in-law. The following excerpt of his racial/cultural evaluation of foreign brides provides a snapshot of some common cultural and racial stereotypes.

## China

Pros: Similar appearance to Koreans, thus children easily blend into school life.
Cons: High risk of fake marriage or divorce. There are huge cultural differences in terms of caring for in-laws due to socialism.

## The Philippines

Pros: Speak English, so they can teach English to children.
Cons: Thick lips and flat nose. Their darker skin never becomes lighter even after living in Korea. No Confucian culture—huge cultural differences.

## Vietnam

Pros: Have Confucian culture so they can easily accept the Korean family culture; they are obedient. They have a bit darker skin but it turns pale like Koreans after living in Korea.
Cons: None

## Uzbekistan

Pros: Not everyone, but Islamic culture may share some similarities with Confucian culture (support parents, dominance of men over women). Their western appearance may satisfy Korean men's sexual fantasies.
Cons: Too stubborn because of former socialism and nomadic culture.

On the list, two prominent evaluation rubrics are present: racial attributes and cultural characteristics. The cultural characteristics indicate whether a foreign woman's country has a patriarchal culture. This may help the woman accept Korean patriarchal family culture and carry out the traditional role of wife, as is the expectation. On the other hand, the racial attributes describe a foreign women's skin color and facial features. Historically, light and dark colors were associated with class status in traditional agrarian Korean society long before Western racial hierarchies were introduced. Light colors represented ruling class, higher social status, and cultural sophistication, while dark colors represented lower social status, cultural vulgarity, and ignorance. This was because the ruling class had a paler skin tone while peasants and laborers were tanned from working outside. Thus, historically Korean color prejudice was closer to class prejudice rather than ethnic/racial prejudice. However, after racial hierarchies were introduced to Korea after the Korean war in the 1950s, this traditional Korean class-based color prejudice was fused with skin-color distinctions in the making of racial others (Kim 2008). Thus, this classed and racialized color distinction connotes that lighter skin equals superiority and darker skin is an indication of inferiority. A wife's skin color is one of the main considerations when choosing a bride-to-be.

Regardless of the type of marriage—an arranged marriage or a love marriage—a wife's skin color is carefully considered for different reasons. Most families want to avoid unwanted attention and reduce potential discrimination against their family and children. Sometimes, however, a Korean family prefers a very dark-skinned wife with the belief that her unfavorable appearance would reduce her chance of running away and would increase the "pitiful" woman's loyalty to her Korean family because no other Korean man would like to live with her. Therefore, racial/ethnic preferences and expectations that foreign brides from less developed countries will accept patriarchal culture reinforces the gender ideology of the traditional good wife and mother. This makes for an interesting contrast to the situation that foreign husbands face in South Korea. It is to the topic of foreign husbands as "forbidden patriarchs" in Korean society that we now turn.

## FORBIDDEN PATRIARCHS: FOREIGN HUSBANDS

Marriages of Korean women and foreign men tend to be so-called love marriages (*yŏnaegyŏrhon*); however, they usually elicit strong protests from the Korean woman's family members, regardless of the husband's nationality and race. Traditionally a marriage used to be understood as a bride merging into her husband's family culture, and her essential role was to reproduce children, especially sons, who are expected to continue the patrilineage. Traditionally Korean parents showed great hospitality to their son-in-law (*sawi*) in concern of their daughter's comparatively lower position to her new family as a *myŏnŭri*. Even though this traditional meaning of marriage is gradually eroding, it is still problematic for a Korean woman to marry a foreign husband because she is joining an ethnically and racially different family lineage.

Since the majority of foreign husbands are North Americans, Western Europeans, and Japanese men, a Korean woman's international marriage is considered as a form of global "marrying up," and these couples tend to reside in the husbands' home countries. On the other hand, couples who remain in South Korea tend to be unions of Korean women and foreign husbands who initially came to South Korea as foreign migrant workers from China, South Asia, or Southeast Asia. Thus, a white husband is somewhat more acceptable compared to a South or Southeast Asian husband because the white husband, in moving the unit back to his homeland, does not disturb Korean blood lineage.

South and Southeast Asian men are considered an underclass due to their initial entry to Korea as foreign migrant workers, even if they have college or university degrees from their home countries. Thus, the union of a Korean woman and a South or Southeast Asian man is seen as the Korean woman's "marrying down." As a South or Southeast Asian (*tongnama*) man is more likely to stay in South Korea, he may become a financial or social burden to his Korean wife and her family. More critically, Koreans understand a South or Southeast Asian husband and his children as a symbol of contamination of Korean lineage. Therefore, a Korean woman with a *tongnama* husband faces stronger social stigma and protests from the Korean woman's family and from society than a Korean man with a *tongnama* wife.

When a Korean woman marries a South Asian or Southeast Asian man, she struggles to convince her Korean family to accept her husband-to-be as their parents' *sawi*. She often threatens her parents that she will not contact her parents until they acknowledge her partner, or her parents threaten their daughter that they will disown her if she follows through with the marriage. Udaya (age 30), a Nepalese immigrant who came to Korea as a foreign migrant worker, recalls his experience of marrying a Korean woman. His Korean wife is very close to her mother and they talk on the phone several times a week. When she planned to marry him, she told her family "I won't see you anymore if you protest this marriage."

At the same time Korean women dating South or Southeast Asian men also try to reduce protests from the family as much as possible. They sometimes do this by presenting their husband-to-be as a white-collar office worker. This is thought to compensate for the low position of the husband-to-be's home country. Since marrying a South or Southeast Asian man is considered as marrying down in South Korea, Udaya's wife was already concerned about her family's reaction when they started dating. She thus asked him not to tell her family that he was a factory worker when she introduced him. She assumed that her family would never accept Udaya if they found out that Udaya was a foreign migrant worker, on top of his undesirable Nepalese nationality. Accommodating his wife's wish, after their marriage Udaya quit his factory job and moved to the government-funded migrant worker center to take a job as a counselor assistant. Even though the salary is significantly lower than what he received doing factory work, his wife prefers him to be an office worker at the government institute.

As this case demonstrates, couples made up of Korean women and Southeast Asian men have to struggle to get married. Having a foreign spouse is treated as a less-than-ideal marriage in general. However, there are huge differences between marrying a foreign bride and marrying a foreign husband. Although there are prejudices and stereotypes against international marriages, the South Korean government actively recruits foreign brides based on the social consent that importing foreign brides is inevitable in order to maintain the Korean population and to solve the care deficit. Foreign brides are expected to accept Korean culture. While a Korean man's international marriage is understood as a choice made under conditions of necessity, a Korean woman's international marriage is questioned. Nevertheless, there are distinctions within this category as white men from the first world are acceptable, but not South and Southeast Asian men. White men in South Korea are seen as professionals or English teachers who may be financially more stable and culturally more advanced, and who, it is assumed, will eventually return their country with their Korean wives. Thus they are not expected to compete as patriarchs with Korean men, nor form racially different families within Korea.

However, South Asian or Southeast Asian men in South Korea, who are associated with the image of the underclass, will most likely stay in Korea, Koreans generally fear that they may attempt to become substitute patriarchs, and they may even form ethnically and racially distinct families in Korea. Thus, while the marriage of a Korean man and a foreign woman is acceptable and even encouraged, the marriage of a Korean woman and a South and Southeast Asian man is deeply frowned upon.

South and Southeast Asian husbands who initially came to Korea as foreign migrant workers are permanent foreigners, regardless of their current legal and economic status (Jung 2007). While female marriage migrants are considered *myŏnŭri* who are accepted under their Korean husbands' control, foreign husbands are not accepted as members of society because Korean society cannot permit foreigners to rule the family as substitute *sawi*. In terms of degrees of inclusion then, a gendered racial hierarchy is in the process of being constructed in which Korean men are followed by Korean women, who are followed by foreign brides and finally foreign men.

## FOREIGN HUSBAND'S SKIN COLOR AND RACIAL DISTANCE

A foreign husband's ethnic and racial background is one of the reasons why a Korean family may not accept him as the legitimate partner of their daughter. In general, as the foreign population and the mixed-race second-generation population increases, racial discrimination has become a growing social issue. However, foreign husbands' ethnic and racial backgrounds are considered more negatively than those of foreign brides. Koreans regard their skin to be lighter than South and Southeast Asian skin tone. In South Korea, brown or even light brown skin is considered to be closer to black skin than to Korean skin color. As a result, while Koreans consider their skin color to be closer to that of Caucasians, South and Southeast Asians' skin tone is considered closer to black skin. During my field research, I often met interviewees who used the black/white color frame to describe South and Southeast Asians and mixed-race second generations.

Why is brown skin seen as black in South Korea? In order to answer this, we need to take into an account U.S military involvement in Korean modern history. As Nadia Kim (2008) points out, contemporary Korean skin color distinction is influenced by the American black/white binary racial order, which was introduced to South Korea after the Korean War in the 1950s. So-Young (Korean woman, age 40), who is a manager at a publishing company, got married to a Bangladeshi man named Said, who initially came to Korea as a foreign migrant worker. Their case illustrates this point well.

> My dad expected that Said was some sort of Asian, but when he saw the photo of Said, he got a shock. "He is not even Asian. It is such a shock for me. I can't allow this marriage." [Loudly laughs.] For him, Said is not Asian; he is almost black and a very different race. My dad was in the South Korean army, so he saw lots of American soldiers at camp towns. In his words, American *kŏmdungi* [black] harassed Korean girls, to be specific Korean prostitutes. I think his generation has a huge racial trauma about this. Do you remember the American TV drama *Roots*? There is a scene where the main character scrubbed his body very hard to bleach his dark skin. My dad said that was a very sad scene, and he thought being born with black skin meant becoming a being with lots of obstacles and difficulties in life. That being will become my daughter's partner, and your child will be *kŏmdungi*, who will be looked down on and neglected. He wrote in his e-mail that these were the reasons why he could not accept this marriage.

In this interview, So-Young's father opposed her Bangladeshi husband-to-be because his dark skin color reminded him of the racial trauma that the older generation experienced after the Korean War. So-Young's father interpreted this Bangladeshi man's race through the American black/white racial hierarchy that he had learned from the U.S. military camp and from American TV, which was dominant in South Korea until the 1990s.

Until the mid-1980s, many Korean women worked as sex-workers near U.S. military camps. The child of a Korean woman and an American soldier was called a *honhyŏl* (literally "mixed blood"). Scholars point out that Korean men felt emasculated by the U.S. military after the Korean War and *honhyŏl* were a living symbol of Korean men's impotence under the regime of the U.S. military (Choi 2009; Park 2007). Korean society, especially in those days, was very patriarchal, so women were blamed for sleeping with U.S. soldiers. *Honhyŏl* were considered to be byproducts of prostitution with foreign men. Amongst *honhyŏl* children, a racial hierarchy existed according to the father's race. *Honhyŏl* children born to a Korean woman and a black American soldier faced far more discrimination than *honhyŏl* children with white fathers (Park 2007). Koreans internalized the racial hierarchy that was visible within the U.S. military and American media (Moon 1997; Park

2007; Kim 2008). Thus, So-Young's father could not accept her daughter marrying a Bangladeshi man, who is almost black to him.

Therefore, a foreign husband's ethnic and racial background is judged more seriously than a foreign bride's. Since the patriarchal idea of marriage is still influential in shaping family culture, a Korean woman's international marriage to a South and Southeast Asian man is understood not only as marrying down but also as the voluntary formation of an ethnically and racially inferior family whereby the Korean woman's racial/cultural attributes may be absorbed into the foreign husband's. At the same time, the American black/white racial binary is influential in shaping Koreans' understanding of foreign husbands and their location within Korean racial hierarchies. In the making of South and Southeast Asian husbands, therefore, there is a complex intersection of foreign husbands' race and Korean women's gender roles under Korean patriarchy. The intersectionality of race and gender in the racialization process of South and Southeast Asians becomes more prominent when we see how the second generation of multicultural families is understood in Korean society.

## RACIAL PROXIMITY OF THE SECOND GENERATION

In South Korea, there exists a strong sense of ethno-nationalism, often expressed as *hanp'itchul* (one blood) and *tanilminjok* (single ethnic nation). The idea of one blood and of a single ethnic nation arose comparatively recently as a way to mobilize the country as it aimed to achieve modernization after independence from Japanese colonialism (Choi 2009). Ethno-nationalism is so pervasive that non-ethnic Koreans are not fully recognized as Korean citizens even if they acquire legal citizenship status (Lee 2008; Jo 2011). Even though Korea is transforming into a multicultural and multiethnic society, the powerful ideology of "one nation" and "pure blood" reinforces the category of *han'guk saram* (Korean) (Kim 2008). The following conversation with Mrs. Park (Korean woman, age 37) shows this clearly:

Lee: What is the most important thing for Korean identity?

Mrs. Park: I really think father and mother should be ethnic Korean, then the children can be *han'guk saram* (Korean). Living in Korea, and knowing Korean culture is not enough to be *han'guk saram*. Korean father and Korean mother, this is the most important thing for Korean identity.

Like Mrs. Park, for those who believe that sharing Korean ethnicity is the most important ingredient for Korean identity, cultural assimilation into Korean society is not sufficient to be an "authentic Korean." Along the same lines, for them multicultural children (*tamunhwa adong*) are almost but not quite Korean, because one of their parents does not have Korean blood, regardless of the fact that these children were born in South Korea and raised in the Korean culture.

The ideology of ethno-nationalism intersects with patriarchal ideology to ensure that Korean blood passes through the father's line. This creates a symbolic boundary between multicultural children and authentic Korean children. Furthermore, it creates another symbolic boundary among multicultural children, based on who has a Korean father and who does not. Foreign fathers are treated as contaminators of Korea's "pure blood" and "one nation," regardless of their ethnicity. However, relationships between Korean fathers and foreign mothers are acceptable because the child of such a partnership is considered to be more Korean. The following conversations between three Korean women (Mrs. Seo, age 63; Mrs. Choi, age 59; and Mrs. Kim, age 54) and Mr. Han (Korean taxi driver, age 58) illustrates this patriarchal understanding of nationhood and race:

Lee: Well, is a child of a Korean father and a foreign mother Korean?

Mrs. Kim: [Raises voice.] Of course, Korean! That's obvious.

Mrs. Seo: Of course. They have Korean blood.

Mrs. Choi: Because the foreign mother came to Korea.

Lee: Do you consider foreign wives Korean?

Mr. Han: I consider them foreigners. But they speak quite good Korean. Those foreign wives are very nice people.

Lee: Then what about the children of Korean men and foreign women? Do you consider them Korean?

Mr. Han: It depends. Some kids look like Koreans—similar to their fathers. But some kids look like foreigners—similar to their mothers.

Lee: Then, there are foreign men who get married to Korean women, do you consider them Korean or foreigner?

Mr. Han: Yeah, there are some Korean ladies who get married to Filipino Manila hubbies and Bangla hubbies. These guys have a small business, so they have some money, they speak good Korean. But, I still don't feel that they are Korean.

Lee: What do you think of the children between them?

Mr. Han: I don't feel they are Korean, to be honest.

The conversations above show that while foreign wives and foreign husbands are both considered non-Korean, foreign wives are considered "less foreign" than foreign husbands, because they are supposedly under their Korean husbands' control, and therefore they are able to integrate into Korean culture. Moreover, the children of a foreign mother and a Korean father are generally considered to be Korean because Korean people still believe that blood is passed down paternally. Mr. Han nevertheless makes a distinction between children who resemble their Korean fathers and those who take after foreign mothers. However, the children of a Korean mother and a foreign father are considered less Korean despite their looks and their legal status as Korean citizens, for "Korean-ness" is not passed on by the Korean mother. The children of a Korean father and a foreign mother are seen as racially closer to Koreans than the children of a foreign father and Korean mother. Thus, Korean ethno-nationalism and continued belief in paternal blood lineage results in patriarchal racialization, as foreign wives are considered to be culturally and biologically more adaptable than foreign husbands.

## CONCLUSION: PATRIARCHAL RACIALIZATION

This article has explored the inextricable relationship between patriarchy and racialization in the context of marriage migration in South Korea by looking at two categories of marriage migrants: foreign brides and foreign husbands. In contemporary Korea, patriarchy becomes one of the domains through which rural farmers, working-class Korean men, and their families recover their dignity and exercise power in the micro-sphere of the household. They do this by mobilizing foreign brides from Southeast Asia and China. In order to create the perception of Korean culture as conservative and homogenous, reproducing patriarchy depends on structural arrangements (government-sanctioned importation of foreign brides, marriage, immigration law), social activities in the community, and everyday interactions in the family and extended kinships.

Working-class and rural Korean men attempt to reproduce patriarchal family structures through marriage immigration with women from lower-income countries. Reproducing Korean patriarchy as essential and ahistorical requires minimizing the "foreignness" of foreign brides. Thus, parents and husbands emphasize the cultural and racial similarities between specific groups of foreign brides and Korean women. On the other hand, the racial differences of foreign husbands are underlined in order to amplify their "foreignness." Thus, children of a Korean father and a foreign mother are seen as racially closer to Koreans than the children of a foreign father and Korean mother.

In the case of South Korea, patriarchal racialization creates an opportunity for working class and rural Korean men and their family members to exercise their power by re-entrenching patriarchy in the micro-sphere of the family. It offers them a way to maintain their status within the family and the kin circle despite their socially disadvantaged class position. Patriarchal racialization reinforces the continued ethno-racial belief in patriarchal blood lineage—the belief that lineage passes down through the Korean father's line. In this regard, the reconfiguration of racial hierarchies has a very critical role to play in reproducing patriarchy.

Patriarchal racialization involves two processes. The first process is about connecting the ideology of patriarchy to race, which normalizes patriarchal racial hierarchies in family and society at large. The rhetoric of *han'guk saram* (Korean) and racial stereotypes of foreign spouses works to normalize racial hierarchies among Koreans, immigrants, and their children. In particular, the ideology of Korean ethno-nationalism idealizes the blood tie as the natural link connecting family, kin, and the national community. While the Korean national community is still seen as an extended blood tie, a father's blood lineage is considered more dominant and superior than the mother's blood lineage. Therefore, the "foreignness" of foreign brides can be minimized by emphasizing their traditional gender roles, while the racial differences of foreign husbands are maximized to amplify their "foreignness." As a result, a multicultural family with a Korean father is located in a better position than a multicultural family with a Korean mother within the racial hierarchy of multicultural families.

The second process involves gendered racialization. The excerpt from the online forum about the pros and cons of four different groups of female marriage migrants shows how Koreans create bounded understandings of regional/country-specific developmental stereotypes, racial stereotypes, and patriarchal rhetoric of the ideal Korean family. It also illuminates how these stereotypes work to normalize racial and gender hierarchies. Koreans' racial and cultural stereotypes of Southeast Asian women are drawn from Koreans' understanding of what Southeast Asia is, and who Southeast Asian people are. In the process of constructing these racial and cultural differences, very specific and particular images are chosen to delineate the identity of a Southeast Asian.

As a consequence of patriarchal racialization, a gendered racial hierarchy is constructed in which Korean men are followed by Korean women, who are followed by foreign brides and finally foreign husbands. Patriarchal racialization involves multiple actors; such as the state, community, and family members in the microsphere of the household. The outcome of patriarchal racialization involves both the production of a new racial category and the inscribing of specific gendered rules within racial hierarchies. Patriarchal racialization is problematic because it justifies the unequal distribution of access to resources, such as work and education, as well as social, economic, and political power.

## NOTES

1. I thank Jennifer J. Chun, Wendy D. Roth, Robert Prey, and Fazeela Jiwa, who offered valuable comments on this article.
2. Pseudonyms were used for the interviewees.

## REFERENCES

Abelmann, Nancy, and Hyunhee Kim. 2005. "A Failed Attempt at Transnational Marriage: Maternal Citizenship in a Globalizing South Korea." In *Cross-Border Marriages: Gender and Mobility in Transnational Asia*, edited by Nicole Constable, 101–123. Philadelphia: University of Pennsylvania Press.

Chan, Sucheng. 1991. *Asian Americans: An Interpretive History* (Twayne's Immigrant Heritage of America Series). Boston: Twayne.

Choi, Kangmin. 2009. "1950, 60 Nyeondae Hangooksoseole Natanan Hangookingwa Migookinui Gwangyeseong: Damunhwajui Kwanjeomeul Jungsimeuro." *Hangookmunyebipyeong* 29: 131–60.

Collins, Patricia Hill. 2001. "Like One of the Family: Race, Ethnicity, and the Paradox of US National Identity." *Ethnic and Racial Studies* 24(1): 3–28.

Freeman, Caren. 2005. "Marrying Up and Marrying Down: The Paradoxes of Marital Mobility for Chosonjok Brides in South Korea." In *Cross-Border Marriages: Gender and Mobility in Transnational Asia*, edited by Nicole Constable, 80–100. Philadelphia: University of Pennsylvania Press.

Hong, Jia, and Kim Hoonsoon. 2010. "Dainjong Kajŏng Chaehyŏnŭl T'onghaebon Han'guk Sahoeŭi Damunhwa Damnon: TV documentary In'gan'gŭkchangŭl Chungshimŭro." *Ha n'gukpangsonghakpo* 24(5): 544–583.

Jo, Jeongin. 2011. "Nuga Wae Yŏsŏnggyŏrhoniminjadŭlgwa Saengsan'ginŭngjik Kŭnnojadŭrŭi Yuip Chŭnggarŭl Pandaehanŭn'ga." *Han'gukchŏngch'ihak'oebo* 45(2): 281–305.

Jung, Hyeosil, 2007. "Pakistan Ijunodongjawa Kyŏrhonhan Yŏsŏngdŭrŭi iyagi." In *Han'guksahoe Damunhwajuŭi: Hyeonsilgwa Jaengjeom*, edited by Kyoungsuk Oh, 167–196. Seoul: Hanul Press.

Kandaswamy, Priya. 2012. "Gendering Racial Formation." in *Racial Formation in the Twenty-first Century*, edited by HoSang, Daniel Martinez, Oneka LaBennett, and Laura Pulido, 23–43. Berkeley: University of California Press.

Kim, Hyun-Mee, 2014. *Urinŭn Modu Chibŭl Ttŏnanda: Han'gugesŏ Ijujaro Saragagi*. P'aju: Tolbegae.

Kim, Minjeong. 2014. "South Korean Rural Husbands, Compensatory Masculinity, and International Marriage." *Journal of Korean Studies* 19(2): 291–325.

Kim, Nadia Y. 2008. *Imperial Citizens: Koreans and Race from Seoul to LA*. Stanford, CA: Stanford University Press.

Lee, Hye-Kyung. 2008. "International Marriage and the State in South Korea: Focusing on Governmental Policy." *Citizenship Studies* 12(1): 107–123.

McClintock, Anne. 1995. *Imperial Leather: Race, Gender, and Sexuality in the Colonial Contest*. New York: Routledge.

Moon, Katharine H.S. 1997. *Sex among Allies: Military Prostitution in US-Korea Relations*. New York: Columbia University Press.

Omi, Michael, and Howard Winant. 1994. *Racial Formation in the United States: From the 1960s to the 1990s*. New York: Routledge.
Park, Chaekyu. 2011. "Kukchegyŏrhon Yŏsŏngiminjaŭi Kajok'aech'e Wŏnin mit T'ŭksŏng Punsŏk." *Pogŏnsahoeyŏn'gu* 31(3): 104–139.
Park Kyungtae, 2007. *Miguk Kŏju Han'gukkye Honhyŏrin Siltaejosa*. Seoul: Overseas Koreans Foundation.
Stoler, Ann Laura. 2002. *Carnal Knowledge and Imperial Power: Race and the Intimate in Colonial Rule*. Berkeley: University of California Press.
Waters, Mary C. 2009. *Black Identities: West Indian Immigrant Dreams and American Realities*. Cambridge: Harvard University Press.

*Chapter Five*

# Doing Business in Contemporary Japan

*The "New" Wave of Korean Female Immigrants*

## Dukin Lim

Since the 1980s, documenting women's migration has gained academic attention (Asis 2005; Castles and Miller 2009), with a legion of feminist scholars emphasizing the unique motivations and consequences of female migration. Women in Asia, for instance, migrate to seek a safer environment and better options for marriage and family life (Asis 2005). In more recent times, women have been making migration decisions based on a variety of considerations such as education, career, and other personal aspirations.

Japan has become a host to newcomer immigrant women whose mobility is shaped by individual factors such as improved economic status and education compared to the past, when historical and political linkages between countries shaped women's movement. However, extant research has so far concentrated on either marriage migrants (Nakamatsu 2005; Piper 2003) or entertainers (Chung 2015), who tend to use informal or illegal resources and exercise limited individual agency. Hence, earlier research is limited to problematizing the marginalization of Korean immigrants due to their socio-economic class and status, as well as ethnicity associated with the image of oldcomer *(Zainichi)* Koreans. (This will be covered in the following sections.) However, rapid economic globalization has led to an increasing number of women with high education and career experiences coming to Japan recently to seek a variety of jobs available in the labor market. Some of these women have engaged in diverse entrepreneurial activities that made significant contributions to economic development (Verheul, Stel and Thurik 2004), even though their activities are not recognized enough because they have been presumed to be dependent on male (read husband) immigrants. Some studies that looked into "Korean immigrant entrepreneurs" have focused on oldcomer Koreans in Japan (Han 2007, 2012; Lim 2007) and newcomer Korean male entrepreneurs (Lim 2004). As Lee (2016, 78) and Yoon (1997, 64) suggest, Korean immigrants have been more visible in business than other "highly educated" immigrants in contemporary Japan.

This chapter is concerned with the entrepreneurial activities of newcomer Korean immigrant women, or those Korean females who came to Japan after 2000. It looks into the status and characteristics of Korean female immigrant entrepreneurs and how they cope with the challenges of doing business as a foreigner in Japan. This chapter argues that newcomer Korean women's entrepreneurship has become a strategic path for them to participate and integrate into Japanese society.

The chapter is organized as follows: an overview of the immigration of Korean women to Japan, situating their movement to female migration trends and their forms of entrepreneurship in Japan, and the challenges they faced and coping strategies they used in order to succeed and integrate into the host society. Also, this study attempts to address the differences between Korean female migrants who migrated from 1980s to 1990s, and those newcomers since 2000s in terms of their entrepreneurial activities to clarify the new wave of female immigrant entrepreneurship among recent Korean newcomers.

## REVIEW OF THE LITERATURE

### Korean Migration to Japan and Japanese Immigration Policy

According to the Japanese Ministry of Justice, the population of Japanese residents as of June 2018 was 126.52 million, which is 250,000 less than the previous year. On the other hand, the number of foreign residents in Japan is about 2.63 million (Ministry of Justice 2018), which is about 2 percent of the total population, including foreigners categorized in an extensive range of types of migration such as labor, education, and marriage (Japanese Ministry of Justice 2018). Among the registered foreigners, the population of registered Koreans is 452,701 or 17.2 percent of the total registered foreign population, following Chinese residents (28.1 percent). Compared to other nations of immigrants, such as the United States, Canada, and Australia, this number is low. Therefore, Japan is widely considered as a nation of non-immigrants or an ethnically homogeneous nation. The largest groups of foreign residents are Chinese and Koreans, including both North and South Korean nationals.

Although it is difficult to statistically disaggregate Korean newcomers from oldcomers (*Zainichi*), a historical distinction can be made. The latter group arrived before the end of World War II and established Korean communities in Japan as a result of Japanese imperialism during the 20th century. A large number of them are former colonial subjects while their offspring have obtained the category of special permanent resident. On the other hand, the former group has founded the Federation of Korean Associations (在日本韓国人連合会) for Koreans who settled in Japan since 1965 based on the Korea-Japan accord as newcomers to distinguish themselves from Korean oldcomers because they do not share the same historical and political status. Since the liberalization of overseas travel in the late 1980s, the number of newcomer Koreans has been increasing significantly with the rising number of short-term trips, study abroad, business and employment opportunities, and family visits (The Ministry of Justice of Japan 2018). In terms of legal status, while the oldcomer group has special permanent residence status, newcomer Koreans have entered Japan on short-term visas, which they later changed to long-term residence status through work, study, or marriage. In the context of Japan, even though there have been various studies (Lie 2008; Weiner 2003; Chung 2010) on Korean oldcomers about their identity, settlement, and social discrimination, there is not enough attention paid to the role and socio-economic involvement of Korean newcomers in Japan.

Since the 1980s when Japan suffered from a shortage of labor, there has been a rapid increase in the inflow of temporary workers. In more recent years, Japan has been accepting more foreign workers in order to solve the labor shortage. For that, they created a new status of residence for migrants involved in simple (read low-skilled) labor (e.g., construction, agriculture, and nursing care). However, immigration researchers have not evaluated shifts in immigration. Scholars suggest that more research needs to be done on labor immigrants to determine which policies better address Japan's demographic and labor issues (Tsukasaki 2008; Oishi 2012). Takenaka, Nakamuro, and Ishida (2016) reveal that labor immigrants in Japan, for instance, tend to be negatively assimilated to the Japanese labor market due to significant competency and wage disparities. Additionally, studies on skilled immigrants in Japan in particular are relatively few and focus on institutional factors such as existing immigration policies aimed at attracting more foreign labor.

As Weiner (2003) observes, "Japan's initial submission to the Human Rights Committee of the United Nations in 1980 . . . denied the existence of minority populations" (Weiner 2003, xiii). This stems from Japan's pervasive illusion of linguistic and cultural homogeneity as the nation is inhabited by more than 90 percent of Japanese nationals. Thus, Japan is more likely to overlook the rich history of racially and ethnically diverse people living in its midst and contributing to the various facets of its society.

## Female Immigrants in Japan Then and Now

Foreign women who migrated to Japan as laborers since the 1980s have concentrated mainly in the entertainment industry. From the 1990s, many of these women sought partnerships with Japanese men. From the 2000s, parallel to the global trends in women's migration, the patterns of gendered migration in Japan have also changed. First, more women migrate independently instead of following their spouses (UN 2005; Oishi 2005). Second, despite the lack of global-scale analysis of female immigrant's economic participation (Kofman 2000), immigrant women who migrate for their own career development are gradually contributing to the growing number of active participants in the labor force (Ouaked 2002). Third, immigrant women's changing status and roles over time (Piper 2005:154) exert influences in the variety of ways and levels of economic-social participation in the Japanese society. Fourth, women are no longer pursuing temporary migration; instead, they are pursuing a combination of marriage, education, labor, business, and other personal goals through migration. As a result, it becomes complicated to categorize them as either labor or marriage migrants (Piper and Roces 2003).

While its immigration policies may have classified women's mobility through different visa categories, Japan is one of the significant destination countries for working women from Korea. To be specific, Japan became an important migration destination owing to its stable economy and quality standard of living. In reality, the Japanese government deals more with incorporating immigrant women into their society, rather than recognizing their capabilities and potential to do business. On March 1, 2017, the first workshop on the economic and social participation of foreign women in Japan, organized by the Ministry of Foreign Affairs of Japan and the International Organization for Migration (IOM) in Tokyo, was held. It was titled the International Workshop on Acceptance of Foreign Nationals and Their Integration into Japan: Toward an Intercultural Society—Focusing on Life and Active Participation of Foreign Women in Japan. The official purpose of this event was to discuss how foreign women can become contributors in Japanese society by actively participating in the workplace and sharing their experiences as foreign residents. However, most of the panelists emphasized how migrant women assimilated well into Japanese society through learning Japanese language and culture. Other participants openly criticized the workshop for prioritizing migrants over foreigners who have already been in Japan for years. They expressed that it is more important to develop their capacities such as economic development and employment, network, and social capital than providing essential services such as teaching the Japanese language, Japanese traditional ceremonies, and ways to become a good neighbor in the immediate locality. The tension between the goals of the program and the expectations of the participants shows that foreign women, who have already been working, participating in their communities, and forming families in Japan, are still marginalized for being strangers, minorities, and women.

Even though the conditions and prerequisites for becoming an entrepreneur for migrant women and Japanese women are similar except the legal status (visa status), migrant women face more challenges in the process. First, immigrant women face more unexpected difficulties and higher social barriers after migration than male migrants. In particular, as newcomer female immigrants, they may expose themselves to new vulnerabilities resulting from unstable legal status, discrimination, exclusion, and isolation from the host society (Jolly and Reeves 2005). Also, there are further restrictions on immigrant women entrepreneurs, which may be community know-how, language/cultural barriers, and lack of network. Thus, even though female migrants' participation in the labor market has been emphasized, most immigrant men work in finance and science and technology, which are regarded as sectors of highly talented people in Japan, while women are thought to have no knowledge or competency in technology to contribute to the Japanese economy. Second, women tend to strive to balance work and family life more often than men. Instead of considering immigrant women as active social agents who negotiate economic, social, and cultural constraints in the host society, the few studies on the role of migrant women have narrowly focused on those women's role as mothers and their strategies for keeping a balance as mother and wife in their family in Japan (Nakamatsu 2005).

## Korean Entrepreneurship

Korean immigrants in business have been the subject of research since the 1970s in the United States, focusing on the characteristics of Korean business owners and their businesses (Kim 1981; Min 1996; Light and Bonacich 1988 and Yoon 1997). This is due to the increase in the number of Korean immigrants who started small-scale self-employment as a result of the labor market restrictions, language barriers, and cultural restrictions. Much of the existing research on Korean self-employment has been based on the "disadvantage thesis." Its main argument is that Korean Americans have chosen to be self-employed because of the many disadvantages that they face in American society (Min 1996; Yoon 1997). Nonetheless, Korean immigrants who seek to achieve both economic and social mobility through self-employment as a way to survive in the midst of economic adversity have received scholarly attention.

The salience of ethnic networks that is generally defined as a social relationship between people who share ethnicity has been the focus of several studies done in the United States. Ethnic networks are considered as a social resource that must be mobilized in order to overcome the social disadvantages of certain immigrant groups. In addition to the everyday life of Korean immigrants, job-related information is also distributed through ethnic networks. These networks are used in a variety of ways and purposes in business. While Yoon (1997) and Kim (1981) insist on the maintenance of ethnic networks for their immigrant settlement, Light and Bonacich (1988) point out that there is a dual logic that ethnic networks reject other races, or that there are restrictions on the range of activities of the ethnic minorities, from the host society.

Kwon (2014) further adds that Korean churches as a social network play an important role in the Korean community, as they provide a place to secure business resources needed for the economic activities of Korean entrepreneurs. Over time, the role of ethnic churches has changed from maintaining the immigrant's ethnic identity to providing a practical service for settling and establishing contacts.

Another important factor vital to business establishment among Korean entrepreneurs is rotating credit associations (RCA; *Kye* in Korean) (Light et al. 1990; Yoon 1997). RCAs have led immigrants towards being more competitive in the labor market and influence their social mobility (Light et al. 1990). Yoon (1997) also finds that RCAs for Korean entrepreneurs in Atlanta are useful in maintaining and investing in business. The importance of RCAs is also mentioned in the study of Korean female entrepreneurs in Japan (Yoo 2013, 241–259) as a useful capital resource for economic stability of Korean entrepreneurs themselves.

Although extant scholarship states that Korean entrepreneurs are mostly concentrated in self-employed businesses in retail and personal services trades and therefore have established Korean in major Japanese cities (Yoon 2003), the study has still done little work on newcomer as entrepreneurs since they have been regarded as simple labor for fulfilling the labor shortage. Moreover, female immigrants are rarely considered as active participants in the labor market. Therefore, not much is known about immigrant women entrepreneurs in Japan, especially newcomer immigrants, who engage in entrepreneurship as a pathway to socially, culturally, and economically integrate into the host society. Tajima's study (1998, 212–220) on newcomer Korean entrepreneurs in *Shinokubo* in Tokyo reveals that the prosperity of ethnic businesses and corporations is based on ethnic networks centered on ethnic churches.

Although the socio-economic background of Korean immigrants who migrated to the United States and Japan are different, their contribution to the host country's economy as female entrepreneurs is a necessary aspect of future Korean migration and women's migration research.

## METHODOLOGY

The study investigates the situation of Korean female immigrant entrepreneurs in Japan. It examines (1) how their entrepreneurial activities are built, (2) what types of resources they use, and (3) what types of business they engage in. This chapter looks into the factors that influence the establishment and maintenance of immigrant business.

As such, this study is based on semi-structured interviews from 2014 to 2018. To obtain qualitative data, I first used snowball sampling to locate my research participants. To conduct this qualitative research with newcomer Korean female immigrant entrepreneurs who have been living, studying, and working in Japan for at least 10 years, I collected informants as follows. To distinguish my informants from *Zainichi* Koreans, I excluded women who were born and raised in Japan. I avoided finding informants in major Korean residential areas such as *Shin-Ookubo* or *Akasaka* in Tokyo where the population of Korean immigrants is bigger; instead, I concentrated on ethnic businesses or retailers since I want to focus more on various kinds of labor force participation of Korean women.

In total, I conducted interviews with 35 Korean businesswomen who mostly live in Tokyo. The average age of the women was 50 at the time of interview. The youngest informant was 33, while the oldest was 68 years old. They are independent contractors, primary small-business owners, or co-owners of a small business with family members (usually their husband). Regarding legal status, informants have been living in Japan for 21 years on average at the time of interview; the shortest period is 10 years whereas the longest is 38 years. This means that most of them have experienced changing visa status, from student visa, and/or work visa, and/or family visa, and/or dependent spouse visa to their current visa status.

Education is one of the most important means of equipping women with the knowledge, skills, and self-confidence which are indispensable to their broader labor participation. Adapting the OECD concept of highly skilled as someone who has completed university education and work abroad (Chaloff and Lemaitre 2009), the informants in this study are referred to as highly skilled immigrants since they all have attained university or vocational education and either work or own a business in Japan. More specifically, 17 women obtained bachelor's degrees from four-year universities including the learning requirements for general education and liberal arts courses in either Korea or Japan. Fifteen women attended vocational schools (*senmon gakko*) that mostly offered one or two years of specialization programs designed to support students to go directly into their specific career areas after graduating from school in either Japan or Korea. Three women attended graduate school and obtained master's degrees in Japan. Most informants have had direct use of their education in their career and their educational backgrounds became the significant springboard for their career to some extent. Apart from their educational background, women's language skills have a strong influence on their labor market success. While other factors also affect labor participation, the degree of language fluency is a strong predictor for determining employment chances and increased wage levels. Most of them are bilingual.

## MIGRATION MOTIVES

Existing studies tend to homogenize the reasons for the migration of low-skilled and high-skilled immigrants. They are both seeking better economic opportunities and working environments, and challenge themselves in the new environment in the destination countries. In this study, I divided the waves of Korean female migration into two periods based on their different motivations for migration to Japan: 1980–1999 and the 2000s. This periodization helps disaggregate the characteristics of newcomer Korean female immigrant entrepreneurs, and distinguishes them from previous waves of Korean migrants.

During the first period, the Korean women in this study are regarded as goal seekers who are influenced by Japan's economic prosperity. Although they did not migrate through the aid of brokers or agencies, they were introduced by relatives or friends who had already settled in Japan. The newcomer women in this period, meanwhile, often described themselves as life restarters, because they were motivated to overcome their family and business failures back in Korea. During this period, the strong push factors of emigration from South Korea included the growing incidence of poverty, particularly in 1997, which severely affected families. Since the 2000s, the immigrant women have been making migration decisions independent of their Korean natal family. They often rationalize that in order to succeed overseas, they must possess professional knowledge and skills prior to migration. Thus, compared to the previous waves, the most recent Korean migrants arriving in Japan are driven by personal aspirations, characterized by desires for greater educational advancements and more internationalized dispositions.

## BUSINESS DEMOGRAPHICS

This section discusses the different aspects of Korean migrant women's entrepreneurship, beginning with the starting phase of doing business, to identifying the challenges and strategies they use in order to overcome the socioeconomic and cultural barriers in Japan.

## Starting a Business

The more recent Korean female migrants (arriving from the 2000s) have different motivations for quitting their jobs and starting their own businesses from those Korean women who migrated between 1980 and 1999. Economically motivated, women in the earlier decades expressed the need to survive in Japan, having to deal with their husbands' business failures, becoming either widowed or divorced, or facing unstable financial status. They aimed to contribute to the household economy. On the contrary, women in the latter period wanted to regain control over their finances independent of their families. They also sought freedom from the constraints of the Japanese labor force market, like short-term legal status that limited their job choices. As a lot of Japanese companies are reluctant to sponsor visas for new employees, ambivalent status causes anxiety among Korean women.

Second, most women respondents in this study desire flexible time at work in order to fulfill their role of raising children. Jeon (34)[1,2] used to work at a Japanese IT company, but she took a break for a year after giving birth. Although the company promised to absorb her back after a year, they did not keep their promise and hired another employee to replace her. In her words: "If I lived in Korea, my mother or other family members would take care of my child while I worked outside, but here in Japan, we have to do child rearing by ourselves."

Third, apart from gendered obligations in the family, other informants revealed that failure to secure promotion in a company prevented them from keeping their employment in Japan. Chu (46),[3] who worked previously as a consultant for an online shopping company, waited for three years to obtain promotion. She was confident she would receive it after several successful projects she helmed. However, she did not get the same chances as her male colleagues. Her male boss asked her casually during meetings about her plans of either getting married or having a baby. Even though she knew that asking such personal questions was a form of sexual harassment, she ignored them because she wanted to get promoted. In addition to delayed promotion, gendered workplace competition discourages women from staying at their company. Working as a regular employee, they often struggle with work-life balance and gender discrimination at work. To overcome these challenges, Korean women sometimes resolve to become entrepreneurs.

Fourth, many women pointed out that foreigner discrimination in the Japanese labor market is pervasive even though Japan has become more globalized or internationalized recently. Three women cited initial difficulty in finding a job as a foreigner while searching for a part-time job. They could not go further than the interview stage, which made them perceive that companies do not favor hiring foreigners, owing to limited language capability, lack of familiarity with Japanese culture, and lack of networking relationships. They also observed that Japanese employers seemed to be more interested in knowing how much effort they have exerted to be a member of a Japanese company or society. Their inability to identify reasons for being treated as an outsider or as someone perceived to be less capable by coworkers affected them emotionally and psychologically, leading to the decision of establishing their business.

## Types of Business

Tajima (1998) defines ethnic business as a relationship between people sharing ethnic background and migration experience. In reference to Tajima's definition, the ethnic businesses described in this study refer to newcomer Korean women who utilize ethnic resources to provide products and services to the Korean ethnic community in urban Tokyo. Table 5.1 presents the ethnic businesses classified according to the goods and services and the clients of the business. As shown, Korean women set up ethnic groceries, where they sell foods of the home country, and ethnic magazines (Aldrich et al. 1985). They also open beauty salons (hair salon, nail salon, clinic, etc.), fashion shops, and travel agencies that target new immigrants living in Korean-concentrated areas. They tend to hire Korean nationals who are able to communicate easily with them and make the working environment comfortable. They attribute their success in doing ethnic business to their cultural background and Korean networks. Indeed, the emergence of a newcomer Korean community has opened up a space for female Korean migrants to be involved in ethnic business. However, depending on the location and type of business they do, their business expansion is not without limitations. Since similar industries are located in Korean-concentrated areas, competition is high and conflicts with other business owners inevitably ensue.

Other Korean women have found relative success in pursuing businesses that cater to gendered and localized needs, such as cosmetics, educational institutions that offer Korean language classes, and Korean-style massage parlors. They hire mostly Japanese natives and few Korean nationals who are long-term residents and have higher linguistic ability and cultural knowledge. Forty-five percent (16 women) of them have employed Japanese employees. They provide a range of products and services to mostly Japanese residents. In summary, the newcomer Korean women who are in businesses that cater to the needs of Japanese nationals possess the following characteristics. First, they have more than enough Japanese language ability and understanding of the Japanese culture and working environment. Second, they have access to a Japanese network that can help them put up their business without the aid of the Korean ethnic community. The first and second features are related to each other. Since they already had pre-working experiences in the same industry before establishing their businesses, they

**Table 5.1.**

| | | Customers | |
|---|---|---|---|
| | | **Same nationals** | **Not only Same nationals** |
| **Types of goods and services to be provided** | **Ethnic resources** | Grocery shop<br>Korean restaurant<br>Ethnic newspaper<br>Real estate<br>Private institution | Korean restaurant<br>Cosmetics<br>Private institution<br>Massage shop |
| | **Non-ethnic resources** | Esthetic clinic<br>Beauty salon<br>Accessory shop<br>Travel agency | Convenience Store<br>Medical company<br>Elderly house<br>Care work<br>Bar |
| | **Including customers in home country and (sometimes) third country** | Interior<br>IT<br>Design<br>Select shop | Publishing company<br>Media<br>Fashion<br>Interpreting<br>Trade |

have secured the minimum customers and know-how. Third, they strategically establish their business near or within Japanese communities where they also reside with their families so that they can manage their household while running the business. Their major customers are their neighbors with whom they have formed friendships over the years through helping one another with children and family duties.

Another group of newcomer Korean women refers to those running businesses between Korea and Japan. Doing transnational business enables these women to maximize Korean and Japanese resources and tap on to the needs of people in homeland Korea as well as those in the third country. Their foreign status gave them negative experiences while living in Japan and constrained their career goals, there were also notable cases where some women took advantage of transnational networks and linguistic skills to advance their economic and professional aspirations. Gotou (41)[4] was a computer engineer who worked for an IT company for four years in Seoul, Korea. After her marriage to a Korean, she moved to Tokyo, Japan, in 2000 when her company partnered with a Japanese IT company to work on a project. Upon the completion of the project, however, her contract was not renewed and she became a full-time housewife for two years. When her former employer invited her to take another project of developing software to

sell in Japan, she realized that working as a freelancer would give her more
control over options and opportunities. She introduced herself to other IT
companies as an expert engineer who understands Japanese and Korean markets better while working as a freelancer for two years. In 2015, she decided
to establish an IT company to work officially between Japan and Korea by
selling, buying, and re/developing software programs.

## Barriers to Doing Business and Coping Strategies

As partly mentioned in the previous section, newcomer Korean women faced
a great deal of challenges that pushed them towards their determination to
become a business owner: work-life balance and being Korean.

A major barrier to Korean women's socio-economic participation is their
family roles. Motherhood prevents them from entering and climbing the
corporate ladder. A few women in this study endured rejection several times
due to their status as a mother of a young child. Similarly, some women
experienced difficulty in job-hunting due to their family circumstances. The
traditional role of women in Japan that was restricted to taking care of the
household (although Japanese lifestyles and attitudes have changed recently)
gave rise to new opportunities for women to enter the small-scale business
sector. As a result, as shown in the table on the previous page, 60 percent (21
women) in this research are involved in gendered business such as education,
beauty, and care services.

In addition to the burden of being a foreigner raising a family in Japan,
their ethnicity affects Korean female migrants as well. Being Korean can be a
source of discrimination at work due to the existing negative image of Koreans as portrayed in the media, particularly of marriage immigrants or entertainers. Some of them expressed difficulties dealing with their co-workers or
bosses due to these pervasive stereotypes of Korean women. Such interactions made them aware of the low regard for Korean women in Japan. However, as they establish their businesses through their bilingual ability and
ethnic resources, their Korean ethnicity becomes their strength.

Newcomer Korean women's workplace discrimination may be similar to
the cases of other immigrant women or women in general. In her study on
Chinese people working in Japan's transnational economy, Liu-Farrer
(2009), for instance, acknowledges that although there are existing constraints to advancing their careers linked to the tension between occupational
privilege and social and institutional prejudice, their bi/multilingual competencies allow them to access more occupational opportunities. Korean female
entrepreneurs, meanwhile, contend with marginalization associated with
their status as female and Korean. These barriers caused them to seek support
from their family, build multiple social networks, and accumulate greater
human capital through education, language learning, and training.

Relying on one's family for support is vital to newcomer Korean women's success. Through their Japanese husbands, they are able to secure legal status and financial resources. Having a Japanese husband or a Korean husband who is a permanent resident, Korean female migrants become eligible for a "spouse of a Japanese" or a "spouse of permanent resident" visa. Through this status, they can start their own business in a few years. Otherwise the Korean women had to obtain permanent residency through working and living in Japan for at least ten years and must have sufficient savings to establish a company. Seventeen percent (6 women) who hold the status of "study abroad" "work" under categories of "technology/humanities" are not allowed by the government to operate a company. They need to obtain a status of residence called "investor/business management." In order to acquire a business management visa, a foreign resident must engage in a small business, hire at least two full-time employees, and have a minimum of five million yen as starting capital. Thus, securing the legal status through one's husband is the fastest way to venture in business. In terms of financial support, almost half of the women respondents (17 women) received partial financial support from their husbands. Another 15 percent (4 women) received funding from Japanese parents-in-law, 17 percent (6 women) obtained it from their parents in Korea, while the rest of the women launched their business independently. Thus, 60 percent (21 women out of 35) of Korean migrant women in this research started their business in partnership with mostly husbands or friends while the remaining 40 percent established their firms with single ownership. Therefore, unlike the previous studies where immigrant entrepreneurs relied heavily on RCAs, such a pattern cannot be found in the latest group of Korean business owners as they depended on their family for legal and financial resources.

Second, maximizing various networks has also enabled newcomer Korean female migrants to manage their business activities in Japan. As many scholars have pointed out the importance of family and other social network to access resources and information, the Korean women in this study mainly utilize their family and ethnic networks found in Korean ethnic organizations and churches to prepare for their business, increase the number of customers, and gradually widen their business. Some Korean entrepreneurs were able to gain the trust of Japanese neighbors while raising children and participating in community activities. More than half of the Korean women in this study have become more locally involved due to their being permanent residents. On the other hand, most recent immigrant women, or those who migrated since the 2000s, have been more reliant on transnational networks due to the frequent use of social media and online community sites. Eighty percent of the Korean female entrepreneurs (28 women) interviewed have been advertising their business on virtual social spaces.

Third, as they face unstable and marginalized situations, Korean women gradually realize the importance of obtaining more human capital. Unlike women who migrated to Japan between the 1980s and 1990s and learned language through either various institutions (local government programs or private language institutions) or Japanese family, more recent immigrant women have already spent at least half a year learning Japanese while in Korea. Another half of them re-entered a Japanese private language institution upon arrival. Prior to starting up a business, they put utmost effort in improving communication skills as the first step. Obtaining higher or professional education in Japan is another way to learn the Japanese working environment, institutional system, and customer relations, as well as acquire professional certifications. Seven women entered vocational colleges in addition to their bachelor's degree in Korea, while six women pursued higher education. The commonality among these newcomer women is that they all experienced working in a company immediately upon arrival. They started businesses in the same sector that they originally worked in, usually for at least two years. Their previous work experiences made them realize the structural barriers as well their potential for finding success through entrepreneurship in Japan.

## CONCLUSION

This study has examined the phenomenon of newcomer female immigrant entrepreneurship in Japan by looking at their motives, types of business, challenges, and strategies for overcoming barriers in the Japanese workplace. It has identified the characteristics of recent Korean immigrants who have ventured into entrepreneurial activities.

To summarize, their motives for establishing business include economic improvement, flexibility in managing work and career lives, and freedom from the Japanese workplace culture that tends to sideline female career aspirations. Their types of business, which they successfully established through family, ethnic, and Japanese social networks, serve Koreans and Japanese in Japan and Korea. Newcomer Korean women's status as foreign women struggling to balance work and business and being ethnic Koreans sometimes makes it challenging to manage their business. To overcome these barriers and sustain their entrepreneurial activities, they recognize the value of support from their family and multiple social networks and the continuous accumulation of human capital. Newcomer Korean immigrant businesswomen are breaking away from stereotypes and prejudices (both of their gender and social group) associated with the older generations of Koreans in Japan. As owners of businesses, they help overcome the marginalities stemming from the notion that immigrant women are vulnerable subjects and continue to embody pre-conceived images of previous female migrants. At the same time, these women are contributing to the gradual improvement of the positive social representation of female entrepreneurs.

Although the current study validates that gender inequality remains visible among skilled immigrant workers in Japan (e.g., Liu-Farrer 2011), Korean female migrants' situated decision-making enables them to transform their disadvantages into advantages, forming immigrant integration patterns comparable to those of men. I contend that Korean immigrant women are gradually overcoming persistent challenges to their socio-economic integration through becoming entrepreneurs, utilizing a range of gendered and ethnic resources at their disposal. Determining how to better integrate into the host society by accumulating highly gendered and ethnic involvement, they renegotiate their identity to become more closely involved (rather than simply assimilated) in Japanese society.

This study has shown that Korean female migrants are penetrating the business scene in several ways. Even though the pervasive gender inequality in the Japanese labor market manifested through misrecognition of Korean women's high levels of education and competence, the exacerbating marginalization of foreign ethnic minorities at large have informed of the need to seek alternative ways by doing business while attending to family life. Throughout this research, I have argued that it is necessary to take a step further in Japanese society to see immigrant women acting as socio-economic bridges, linking the ethnic networks and communities in and between host and home societies. Their contributions in job creation, resource mobilization, and enhancement of business cycle in Japan, as well as their self-reliance and resilience to overcome the high barriers of the Japanese labor market, deserve social recognition.

The current research is limited to only a small sample of Korean female entrepreneurs living in Tokyo, thus, the findings do not reflect an accurate picture of the majority of Korean immigrants across Japan. Moreover, I acknowledge that interviewing Koreans in rural areas outside metropolitan Tokyo can provide a broader view of Korean migrants in Japan, since many Korean marriage migrants who built their lives in the rural areas may have different motivations for coming to Japan and different views from those in the urban setting. However, as shown in this study, Korean women in the urban areas confront challenges and strategies for adapting to and negotiating with a rapidly changing socio-economic environment. Thus, the urban context also offers methodological convenience and distinct empirical insights.

## NOTES

1. Names of all interviewees are pseudonyms.
2. Jeon (owner, trading company) interview with author, August 18, 2017.

3. Chu (owner, fashion trading company) interview with author, September 6, 2017.
4. Gotou (owner, web shop) interview with author, January 26, 2018.

## REFERENCES

Aldrich, Howard, John Cater, Trevor Jones, David Mc Evoy, and Paul Velleman. 1985. "Ethnic residential concentration and the protected market hypothesis." *Social forces* 63(4): 996–1009.
Asis, Majula M. 2005. "Recent Trends in International Migration in Asia and the Pacific." *Asia-Pacific Population Journal* 20(3): 15–38.
Castle, Stephen, and Mark J. Miller. 2009. *The Age of Migration*, fourth edition. Basingstoke: Palgrave Macmillan.
Chaloff, Jonathan, and Georges Lemaitre. 2009. "Managing Highly Skilled Labour Migration: A Comparative Analysis of Migration Policies and Challenges in OECD Countries," *OECD Social, Employment and Migration Working Papers*, No. 79, OECD Publishing, Paris. http://dx.doi.org/10.1787/225505346577.
Chung, Erin Aeran. 2010. *Immigration and Citizenship in Japan*. Cambridge: Cambridge University Press.
Chung, Haeng-ja. 2015. "Transnational Labor Migration in Japan: The Case of Korean Nightclub Hostesses in Osaka." *Bulletin of the National Museum of Ethnology* 40(1): 101–119.
Han, Jae hyang. 2012. "Zainichikankokujin Chōsen hito bijinesu no dainamizumu to genkai [*Zainichi* Koreans in Japan- Dynamism and limitations of business]." In *Nihon no esunikku bijinesu* [*Ethnic business in Japan*]. Higuchi, Naoto. ed. Kyoto: Sekai Shisōsha.
———. 2007. "Pachinko sangyō to zainichikankoku Chōsen hito kigyō" ["Pachinko industry and Korean company in Japan"]. *Socio-Economic History* 73(4): 377–400.
Jolly, Susie, Hazel Reeves, and Nicola Piper. 2005. "Gender and Migration: Overview Report." *Institute for Development Studies,* Bridge publication. http://www.bdigital.unal.edu.co/39697/1/1858648661%20%282%29.pdf.
Kim, Illsoo. 1981. *New Urban Immigrants: The Korean Community in New York*. Princeton, NJ: Princeton University Press.
Kofman, Eleonore. 2000. "The Invisibility of Skilled Female Migrants and Gender Relations in Studies of Skilled Migration in Europe." *International Journal of Population Geography* 6(1): 45–59.
Kwon, Victoria Hyonchu. 2014. *Entrepreneurship and Religion: Korean Immigrants in Houston, Texas*. Abingdon, UK: Routledge.
Lee, Chan-Haeng. 2016. "'naseong-e gamyeon': loseuaenjelleseu han-ingwa jayeong-eob" ["'Nasŏng-e Kamyŏn': Korean Americans and Small Businesses in Los Angeles." *American Studies Institute, Seoul National University* 39(2): 69–100.
Lie, John. 2008. *Zainichi (Koreans in Japan): Diasporic Nationalism and Postcolonial Identity*, vol. 8. Berkeley: University of California Press.
Light, Ivan, and Edna Bonacich. 1988. *Immigrant Entrepreneurs: Koreans in Los Angeles 1965–1982*. Berkeley: University of California Press.
Light, Ivan, Im Jung Kwuon, and Deng Zhong. 1990. "Korean Rotating Credit Associations in Los Angeles." *Amerasia Journal* 16(2): 35–54.
Lim, Young Eon. 2004. "Kangokujin kigyōya: Nyūkamā no kigyō katei to esunikku shigen" ["Korean entrepreneur: Newcomer's entrepreneurial process and ethnic resoures"]. PhD dissertation, Sophia University.
———. 2007. "Zainichi korian kigyō-ka no keiei katsudō to nettowāku no tenbō" ["Management and network of *Zainichi* Korean entrepreneurs in Japan"]. *Journal of Ohara Institute for Social Research* 588: 44–60.
Liu-Farrer, Gracia. 2009. "Between Privilege and Prejudice: Chinese Immigrants in Corporate Japan's Transnational Economy." *Global Movements in the Asia-Pacific*, 123–145.
———. 2011. *Labour Migration from China to Japan: International Students, Transnational Migrants*. London and New York: Routledge.

Min, Pyong Gap. 1996. *Caught in the Middle: Korean Communities in New York and Los Angeles*. Berkeley: University of California Press.

Ministry of Justice (MOJ). 2018. "Toroku gaikokuji tokei tokeihyo" ["Statistical Table of Statistics on Registered Foreigners"]. http://www.moj.go.jp/housei/toukei/toukei_index2.html (accessed Nov 8, 2018).

Nakamatsu, Tomoko. 2005. "Faces of 'Asian brides': Gender, Race, and Class in the Representations of Immigrant Women in Japan." *Women's Studies International Forum* 28(5): 405–417.

Oishi, Nana. 2005. *Women in Motion: Globalization, State Policies, and Labor Migration in Asia*. Standford, CA: Stanford University Press.

———. 2012. "The Limits of Immigration Policies: The Challenges of Highly Skilled Migration in Japan." *American Behavioral Scientist* 56(8): 1080–1100.

Ouaked, Said. 2002. "Transatlantic Roundtable on High Skilled Migration and Sending Countries Issues." *International Migration* 40(4): 153–166.

Piper, Nicola, and Mina Roces. 2003. "Introduction: Marriage and Migration in an Age of Globalization." In *Wife or Worker? Asian Women and Migration*. Boulder, CO: Rowman & Littlefield.

Piper, Nicola. 2005. "Gender and Migration: Policy Analysis and Research Programme of the Global Commission on International Migration." *Global Commission on International Migration*, 1–54.

Tajima, Junko. 1998. *Sekai toshi Tōkyō no Ajia-kei ijū-sha* [*Asian migrants in world cities*]. Tokyo: Gakubunsya.

Takenaka, Ayumi, Makiko Nakamuro, and Kenji Ishida. 2016. "Negative Assimilation: How Immigrants Experience Economic Mobility in Japan." *International Migration Review* 50(2): 506–533.

Tsukasaki, Yuko. 2008. *Gaikokujin senmonshoku gijutsushoku no koyo mondai* [*The problems and conditions of skilled migrant workers*]. Tokyo: Akashi Shoten.

United Nations. 2005. "Trends in Total Migration Stock, 2005 Revision." *Population Division, Department of Economics and Social Affairs*.

Verheul, Ingrid, André J. van Stel, and A. Roy Thurik. 2004. "Explaining Female and Male Entrepreneurship across 29 Countries." *EIM Business & Policy Research and Scientific Analysis of Entrepreneurship and SMEs*, 1–35.

Weiner, Michael. 2003. "'Self' and 'other' in imperial Japan." In *Japan's Minorities*, edited by Micheal Weiner, 23–42. London and New York: Routledge.

Yoo,Yon-Suk. 2013. *Kankokujin no Kokusaiiidou to jenda- gurobaruka zidai wo ikinuku senryaku* [*Korean female's International migration and gender- strategies of survive in globalization era*]. Tokyo: Akashi publisher.

Yoon, In-Jin. 1997. *On My Own: Korean Businesses and Race Relations in America*. Chicago: University of Chicago Press.

———. 2003. "Korean Diaspora: Migration, Adaptation, and Identity." *Korean Journal of Sociology*. 37(4): 101–142.

*Part III*

# Return Migration

*Chapter Six*

# Living as "Overseas Koreans" in South Korea

*Examining the "Differential Inclusion" of Korean American "Returnees"*

Stephen Cho Suh

This chapter examines the phenomenon of ancestral homeland migration[1] through the perspectives of Korean American "returnees."[2] As ethnic Koreans born and/or raised in the United States, Korean American "returnees" migrate to South Korea as foreign nationals who have weak or fleeting ties to the country. Prior scholarship on ancestral homeland migration to South Korea has detailed the socio-legal barriers faced by Korean ancestral homeland migrants to their social incorporation (Seol & Skrentny 2009; Song 2009; N. Y. Kim 2009; E. Kim 2012). This body of research has provided a comparative account of how societal prejudices, geopolitical factors, and global capitalism impact the "return" trajectories of different ethnic Korean populations of varying origins. Much of this research, however, has focused on the barriers to incorporation faced by Korean migrants from China and the Commonwealth of Independent States (CIS), typically only utilizing "returnees" from the U.S. as a relatively privileged control group to which many of these obstacles do not apply. Conversely, most studies that have examined the adaptation narratives of Korean American "returnees" have been limited in their analytic scope by not considering the broader social and political processes impacting the relocation and adaptation of this migrant population.

This chapter adds to this body of scholarship by (1) detailing the societal barriers faced by Korean American "returnees" as they attempt to integrate into South Korean society and (2) documenting the ways in which Korean American "returnees" negotiate these impediments. Though at first benefiting from the human capital bestowed upon them by their connections to the U.S., this chapter finds that interviewees' status as "returnees" significantly complicates their positioning within South Korean society the longer they reside in it, eventually situating them in a liminal social status that straddles the line between co-ethnic insider and non-citizen foreigner. In particular, I draw attention to the seeming "double-edged" nature of interviewees' "return" experiences in South Korea—where, on the one hand, interviewees (as "overseas Koreans") eventually encounter many of the same socio-legal barriers to societal incorporation as other ethnic Korean and non-citizen migrants in the country, while, on the other hand, their status as ethnic Koreans also disqualifies them from unabashedly embracing or taking advantage of the opportunities afforded to them by their foreign-ness as can certain other American "expat" migrants. Most "returnees" thus find themselves in a somewhat paradoxical predicament where, as Korean Americans living in South Korea, they are at once foreign but not quite foreign enough.

Borrowing from theorization by Yen Le Espiritu (2003), I further contend that the migratory experiences of Korean American "returnees," as well as those of other Korean ancestral homeland migrants, showcase the manner in which they are "differentially included" into South Korean society. Yen Le Espiritu defines "differential inclusion" as the "process whereby a group of people is deemed integral to the nation's economy, culture, identity, and power—but integral only or precisely because of their designated subordinate status" (Espiritu 2003, 47). Though Espiritu's case attends to the migratory pathways and experiences of Filipinos in the U.S., I find her theorization applicable to the sojourns of Korean American "returnees" because of its emphasis not on how migrant populations are excluded but rather on ways that they are "coercively and differentially made a part of the nation" (Espiritu 2003, 47). Though the historical ties shared between Filipinos and the U.S. and Korean Americans and South Korea are undoubtedly different, I maintain that the incorporation of these migrant populations within these respective nation-states has relied upon the perception, not reality, of an equitable and inclusive host society. Within these contexts, these migrant populations are deemed simultaneously of the nation and outside of the nation—for Filipino Americans this status is conferred by their claiming of legal, but not social, citizenship in the U.S., and for Korean Americans this status is appropriated through their shared ethnicity and ancestry with local South Koreans. By extending the concept of "differential inclusion" to Korean American "returnees," I thus contend that they are included and at times even deemed integral to the functioning of the South Korean state and an understanding of embodied "Korean-ness" insofar as they are willing to occupy a liminal or transient position within the country. Ultimately, much like their experiences as "forever foreigners" and "model minorities" in the U.S., Korean American "returnees" are forced to reconcile the limitations inherent to their societal incorporation in South Korea because of their status as non-citizen, "overseas" Koreans.

## LITERATURE REVIEW: SITUATING KOREAN ANCESTRAL HOMELAND MIGRATION WITHIN SOUTH KOREAN IMMIGRATION POLICY

In 1999, during the height of the country's disastrous economic recession, the South Korean government enacted the Overseas Koreans Act and introduced a new F-4 visa classification aimed at attracting the capital and skilled labor of ethnic Koreans residing abroad (Yamashiro 2012). The enactment of the F-4 visa was significant for a few key reasons. First, it was the first time in South Korea's history that the nation-state officially recognized its "overseas" co-ethnic population within its immigration policy, in this case distinguishing between them and other non-Korean foreigners. Second, in a historic period when most other nation-states were becoming more liberal or egalitarian in their immigration policy, South Korea trended toward the opposite, providing immigration preference not only to "overseas" co-ethnics relative to other non-Korean foreigners, but also to "overseas" co-ethnics of higher socioeconomic status who were primarily from wealthy Western nations (Seol & Skrentny 2009; Skrentny et al. 2009; N. H. Kim 2012; Yamashiro 2012). In fact, it was not until the introduction of the Special Work and Residence Visa (H-2) in 2006, as well as the eventual expansion of the F-4 visa to include a larger subset of "overseas Koreans," that South Korea's co-ethnic immigration preference was extended to most if not all of its ancestral "overseas" population, greatly increasing the already substantial rate of ancestral homeland migration into the country.[3]

Despite the enormous success of these new policies in stimulating the "return" of "overseas Koreans," scholars have been critical about South Korea's hierarchical approach to "ethnizenship," or non-citizen ethnonational membership (C. Lee 2012). According to research by Dong-Hoon Seol and John D. Skrentny (2009) and Chul-Woo Lee (2012), "overseas Koreans" have not only received limited avenues to naturalize as South Korean citizens, they have also been allotted differing legal statuses and social positions according to their country or region of origin. For example, while most co-ethnics from wealthy Western nations such as the U.S., Canada, and Australia have immigrated as teachers and professionals using the F-4 visa designation that grants them economic rights akin to those of South Korean citizens, "returnees" from most Asian states have until recent years only been allowed entry through the H-2 low-wage work visa that excluded them from many of the legal and employment benefits afforded to F-4 visa holders (Seol & Skrentny 2009). This hierarchizing has significantly impacted the social standing of "returnees" in South Korea. For example, research shows that ancestral homeland migrants from China and the CIS are more highly stigmatized and discriminated against by South Koreans than their American and Canadian counterparts because of the occupational and socioeconomic constraints placed on them by their visa statuses (Seol & Skrentny 2009; Song 2009; H. Lee 2018). Even as a country with strong ethnonational rhetoric in its political and social spheres, it is thus apparent that the notion of a Korean nationhood extends unevenly across its supposed "diaspora."

For these reasons, scholars maintain that the affective expectations of Korean "returnees" also tend to go unfulfilled. This is especially true for Korean migrants originating from other neighboring countries such as China and Russia, where the hopes associated with relocating to South Korea are met with the reality of living as low-wage laborers who frequently bear the brunt of anti-immigrant rhetoric and politics (Seol & Skrentny 2009; Song 2009; Yi & Jung 2015; H. Lee 2018). Studies about Korean "returnees" from the U.S. also illustrate how cultural alienation remains a significant barrier even to those with comparatively privileged legal and socioeconomic positions, such as 1.5/2nd-generation Korean Americans and Korean American adoptees (N. Y. Kim 2009; E. Kim 2012; H. Lee 2013; S. Suh 2017). Though the benefits provided by their visa statuses, nationality, and relatively high levels of human capital may initially act as buffers to discrimination, these studies illustrate how many eventually encounter significant roadblocks to their societal incorporation not unlike those experienced by "returnees" from other Asian states. Thus, regardless of their countries of origin, feelings of alienation appear to remain a constant among the narratives of all Korean return migrants, indicating the glaring disjuncture between rhetoric and reality that exists for "returnees" at both the personal and state-policy levels.

## METHODS AND SAMPLE

Data for this chapter were collected between 2010 and 2018 through in-depth semi-structured qualitative interviews and ethnographic observation. Fifty-six people were interviewed in total, fifty-four of whom were interviewed in-person during four fieldwork trips to South Korea. Two people were interviewed remotely using video conferencing software. Initial research participants were either prior contacts or identified through mutual networks. Subsequent interviews were respondent driven, with interviewees connecting me to potential people of interest who resided in South Korea. Discussions focused on interviewees' formative lives in the United States, reasons for departing the United States, their experiences as migrants in South Korea, and the manner in which certain factors (such as their citizenship status, cultural/linguistic fluency, gender, and race/ethnicity) impacted their ability to adapt to South Korean society. In-person interviews occurred at a mutually agreed-upon location. To differentiate migrants from those who were temporarily visiting the country without the need for an extended stay visa, I included only Korean American adults who had resided in South Korea for more than half a year with the intention to stay for a year or longer. The median length of residence in South Korea among participants was five years, although this figure ranged from as few as ten months to as many as twenty-five years. Interviewees were between the ages of twenty-four and fifty-two, with a median age of thirty-two years. All but five interviewees held a B.A. degree or higher. Twelve were either married or engaged to be married at the time of our interview. Four of the participants were parents of at least one child. Participants held the following residency statuses in South Korea: F-4 "overseas Korean" visa (42), A-series "U.S. diplomat" visa (10), Republic of Korea citizen or dual R.O.K. and U.S. citizen (3), and F-5 "permanent resident" visa (1).

Only U.S.-raised Korean Americans were interviewed for this project, meaning that one or more of their biological parents were of South Korean origin, and that they were born in the U.S. or moved to the U.S. prior to adolescence and raised in the country into adulthood. I focus on U.S.-raised Koreans Americans for a few reasons. Above all, this serves to incorporate all individuals of Korean ancestry who are raised in the U.S. into one measurable analytic group, whether they are the children of one or more Korean immigrant parent, or international adoptees. This is done not to diminish the undoubtedly different biographies and identities of the interviewees in this study, but rather to draw attention to their analogous connections to the U.S., especially concerning their racialization as Asian Americans, as well as their comparably weak connections to South Korea relative to first-generation Korean Americans (aka Korean emigrants/immigrants).

## FINDINGS

### Koreans Only by Blood

Of the fifty-six Korean American "returnees" interviewed for this study, few held illusions about being embraced as "Korean" upon moving to South Korea, cognizant that they were relocating to their ancestral homeland as both foreign nationals and cultural strangers. Still, many arrived in South Korea confident that their Korean ancestry would grant them higher levels of societal acceptance relative to the country's other immigrant populations. Interviewees were partially justified in their optimism. After all, most had relocated to South Korea under the F-4 "overseas Korean" visa designation, the existence of which itself seemed to indicate that the South Korean state supported their "return" and that there was an intrinsic value to having Korean ancestry in South Korea regardless of one's citizenship status. To that end, many interviewees were aware of the sociocultural weight that Koreans placed on ethnicity and its conceptual variants (such as "blood" or race), and were thus hopeful, if not expectant, that they would be socially accepted upon "returning."

This optimism would be tested early and frequently. For many, the move to South Korea marked the very first time in their lives that they were non-citizen residents of a nation-state, meaning that they were not only socially but legally differentiated from the South Korean nationals who they crossed paths with daily. This legal differentiation was immediately observable even through their visa designations. That the legal residents who held the F-4 visa were designated as "overseas Koreans" even as they lived and worked in South Korea was telling. Though as "overseas Koreans" these individuals were, sans voting, technically privy to most of the same rights and privileges as South Korean citizens, it became quickly apparent to most that there were many caveats to this rule.

Interviewees revealed a plethora of ways through which they, as "overseas Koreans," or *kyop'o*,[4] came to understand the superficiality of their connections to a South Korean nation and populace. Many of these were presented as formal or legal barriers to their societal integration—as limitations to their receipt of or access to basic rights and resources that stemmed from their positions as non-citizens. One oft-referenced issue concerned the thirteen-digit resident registration numbers (RRN) provided to them by the South Korean government. The RRN is a national identification number provided by the South Korean state to all its citizens and most of its legal residents (Korea Legislation Research Institute 2016). It is an integral part of South Korean life, as it is required to sign up for basic services and resources throughout the country. An individual's RRN is also typically required for many non-essential but useful services, such as purchasing goods from on-line merchants, registering for store rewards programs, or even accessing web-based apps. It was perhaps because of its seeming ubiquity that the South Korean resident registration number posed so many issues for "returnees." The problem with the RRN and the services that required it was two-fold. First, not all "returnees" possessed an RRN. Though many "returnees" resided in South Korea with a domestic visa that provided them with a RRN, there were some with A-type "foreign diplomat" visas or U.S. military clearances who were not issued one. While these individuals were technically legal residents in South Korea, they were not legal residents *of* South Korea, meaning that they remained under the jurisdiction of the United States even as they lived abroad. These individuals often possessed very limited access to services and utilities in South Korea or were required to work through affiliate programs provided by the U.S. embassy or their employers to receive such access. Taking these alternative routes usually enabled these "returnees" access to special bare-bones "foreigner" accounts at banking and telecom institutions, but little else.

Second, while it was undoubtedly preferable to possess a resident registration number while living in South Korea, access to social services was not demonstrably better for "returnees" who possessed one. In fact, several interviewees maligned that the RRN assigned to resident aliens appeared to serve more as a legal formality than a meaningful societal benefit, citing their ineligibility to register for many South Korean web-based apps and other web-based services because the "system" would not recognize them. Even signing up for retail rewards programs, let alone anything that involved access to a line of credit, proved challenging for RRN-holding "returnees." For many, the limited functionality of their resident registration numbers was emblematic of the numerous formal restrictions to their societal incorporation and, for respondents such as Jason, served as an indication that "returnees" were "not quite Korean."[5]

As "returnees" delved deeper into South Korean society, the types of barriers that they faced because of their precarious legal statuses became progressively more noticeable, making it increasingly difficult for them to write off their bouts with exclusion as merely a nuisance. These structural barriers proved particularly troublesome for those with entrepreneurial aspirations. Rebecca, one of the fifteen business owners in the study, knew from firsthand experience the challenges that non-citizen entrepreneurs faced when attempting to navigate through the South Korean legal and tax systems. Rebecca explained that as a foreigner she was required to work through a seemingly endless number of roadblocks when endeavoring to open her two small businesses in South Korea:

> In one of our companies we have three shareholders; one Korean and two foreigners. And when we were making our corporate license, our Korean partner said, "Well, I will use my accountant because that is who I've been working with." But his accountant had no experience with foreigners. So, when the Korean partner went to the accountant and told him that he needed to make a Korean corporation with two foreign shareholders, the accountant told him that he couldn't do that—that foreigners couldn't be shareholders in Korean corporations. And we had to tell the Korean accountant that it was possible, that our other business also had foreign shareholders. It was obviously possible. Anyone can be a shareholder in the business. They may not have a working visa, or be a South Korean citizen, but they can still be shareholders. So really, I think these are indicative of the fact that once you get deep enough into the system here you hit this mentality that foreigners aren't allowed, some of which actually has a legal precedent. Basically, the deeper you go the harder it is to be a foreigner within this system.

While Rebecca focused primarily on the difficulties associated with entrepreneurship in South Korea as a non-citizen, her statements also highlight the general sentiment of exclusion that she and other "returnees" encountered as they made their way through various state and private institutions that were clearly not designed with non-citizens in mind. Rebecca stated as much, arguing that the "deeper" foreigners pushed into South Korean society, the more pushback they received from the laws and institutions that stood as the foundations of the country's civil society, forcing "returnees" to reconcile the marginality inherent in their legal statuses. Unsurprisingly, it was the interviewees who had resided in South Korea for several years, such as Rebecca and Jason, who were most cognizant of these barriers to access.

In addition to the legal or formal barriers to societal incorporation mentioned above, there were many informal or socio-cultural barriers that marginalized Korean American "returnees" in South Korea. Though these informal barriers were seldom devised to explicitly discriminate or exclude, they still reinforced interviewees' perceptions that, even as ethnic Koreans, they inhabited a lesser social status in South Korea than their native counterparts.

The informal barriers that "returnees" faced in South Korea operated much in the same manner as the microaggressions that they had encountered while growing up as ethnic/racial minorities in the U.S. (Sue et al. 2007). This meant that the examples of social exclusion that interviewees referenced were seldom explicitly hostile or antagonistic in their nature, but rather playfully or even complimentarily called attention to their status as foreigners. Beyond questions concerning one's country of origin (such as "Where are you from?"), microaggressive comments made toward Korean American "returnees" often took the form of backhanded compliments about fluency. One interviewee named Jin Soo provided a few examples of the array of microaggressions he received on a regular basis from his interactions with South Koreans:

> As soon as they know you're *kyop'o*, they don't really treat you like a Korean. I hear this comment a lot if I do something that they didn't expect me to do. They'll say, *"han'guk saram ta toenne!"* ["You're almost Korean!"] I hear it all the time! Like, if I tell a joke that Koreans would actually tell, or when we go to Korean restaurants and I order a "Korean" dish, They'll do the whole "Can you eat that?" or "When did you start eating that?" Or they'll ask me if I miss eating hamburgers. So yeah, they absolutely do treat me differently.

For interviewees such as Jin Soo, interactions with South Koreans were often mired with comments and questions that consistently called to attention their seeming non-normativity. Though in most cases "returnees" could write off these types of statements as stale attempts at humor, they still had the residual effect of forcing interviewees to question their participation in social settings with South Korean nationals. Much like the way that interviewees' race or ethnicity had served as their tokenizing characteristic in majority white settings in the U.S., it was their nationality (and the "cultural" attributes connected to it) that appeared to stand out as their unintentionally foreignizing feature in South Korea.

Nowhere were the detrimental effects of these informal barriers more apparent than with the accounts of multiracial or mixed-race "returnees." Because many multiracial "returnees" were immediately recognized as being foreign through their physical appearances, they tended to experience levels of discrimination that far exceeded those of other "returnees." Whereas monoracial "returnees" tended to experience social marginalization because of their lack of cultural and linguistic fluency, many took solace in their ability to blend in or "pass" as South Korean phenotypically. Such was a luxury typically not afforded to the multiracial "returnees" in this study, many of whom drew unwanted attention in public spaces because of their appearances. Victor was a self-identified "Amerasian"[6] who was all too familiar with receiving unwanted attention in South Korean public spaces because of his appearance. As a "returnee" with fair complexion (Victor's father was white), Victor explained that South Koreans generally presumed that he was not of Korean descent and thus interacted with him accordingly:

> It's hard to talk about these things because they're various forms of microaggressions. So, if I say, someone yelled "Hello" at me on the street, people will be like, "big fucking deal!" But the thing is that I cannot go anywhere in Korea without having to deal with bullshit! I can't go to the *p'yŏnŭijŏm* [convenience store]. I can't walk down the street. I can't ride the bus. I can't ride the train. Any kind of daily activity; going to a restaurant, even.

While Victor recognized that the attention he received in public spaces was likely a product of his appearance being a "novelty" in a purportedly monoethnic South Korean society, the inability to complete ordinary tasks without soliciting gazes and comments from strangers was something that exasperated him deeply. As Victor explained, it was not so much the intent of the actions themselves that affected him as it was their relentless frequency and the contexts in which they occurred. In a milieu where it was generally uncommon for strangers to greet one another in public settings, Victor's constant receipt of undesired attention illuminated the harsh truth of his non-normative corporeality. The accumulating impact of these incidents was so detrimental that Victor revealed that he and his Amerasian peers would plan their daily routines in ways that minimized their potential encounters with these microaggressive acts.

Adoptees were another group of "returnees" who encountered their own unique set of microaggressions. Adopted "returnees" explained that the microaggressions they faced were oftentimes voiced as pity or as expressions of guilt for the presumed ordeals that they had endured as orphans and adoptees. Nicholas, one of the five adopted "returnees" in the study, elaborated upon the different kinds of microaggressions that adoptees confronted in South Korea, and the impact that these incidents had:

> If you're [a non-adopted] Korean American, sometimes Koreans will give them shit because they can't fully speak Korean. For us, once they find out that we're adopted, they don't get mad at us, but they pity us. And that's a whole different kind of feeling of exclusion. We don't want to be pitied. It's not your fault that 200,000 kids got shipped out of Korea in 50 years. It's the government's fault.

For Nicholas and other adopted "returnees," being the subject of "pity" called to attention the liminality of their statuses in South Korea, as well as the non-normativity of their own American upbringings. Though adopted "returnees" recognized that these expressions of pity were meant to be empathic, they nevertheless found them to be mostly empty gestures. Moreover, given that the adopted "returnees" whom I interviewed tended to already hold complicated relationships with their Korean ancestry, incidents such as these tended only to make matters worse. It was for these reasons that most adoptees admitted to being hesitant about revealing their biographies to others in South Korea. For example, an adopted "returnee" named Dee explained that, even though she maintained strong ties to the adoptee community in South Korea, she had resigned to referring to herself as simply *kyop'o* in most social settings. Doing so, she argued, took away much of the uneasy tension that she had previously encountered when publicly identifying as an adoptee. Ultimately, while identifying as *kyop'o* in South Korea may have provided adopted "returnees" such as Dee a momentary reprieve from the stigma of non-normativity, she and numerous others recognized that there were shortcomings intrinsic to the social status of all "returnees."

## Not Completely Foreign Either

While interviewees were undeniably frustrated by their inability to shed their outsider status in South Korea, what they claimed made matters worse was their incapacity to simply adopt the role of foreigner. "Returnees" lamented that because of their Korean ethnicity, they were not afforded the same flexibility to operate outside of Korean cultural norms as other foreign residents in South Korea. "Returnees" thus appeared to occupy a nebulous, double-edged role within South Korean society where they were neither insiders nor outsiders, neither South Korean nor foreigner.

The inability of "returnees" to simply act as foreigners, or what many referred to as "playing the foreigner card," was evinced in numerous capacities. The South Korean workplace, for example, was an area of contention for many "returnees" because of the uneven treatment or expectations they received from their co-workers and bosses. This was especially the case for individuals who worked in spaces with few other foreign employees. Though nearly all "returnees" were largely ignorant of South Korean workplace customs and practices, many realized the hard way that they were not excused from adhering to these unwritten rules as were other foreign employees. Dorothy, one of the few interviewees with some success navigating this cultural maze, detailed the difficulties that "returnees" experienced in trying to transition to the South Korean work environment:

> For Korean Americans who are in majority Korean work environments, like public schools for example, they are in many cases given the same expectations that are given to other Koreans. For example, they need to speak Korean, or are asked to do tasks x, y, and z that non-Korean foreigners wouldn't be expected to do. I think the reason why I've been able to assimilate so well in Korea is that all of that is natural for me. But Korean Americans who don't have that kind of background, they're constantly asked, "Why don't you do this? Why aren't you like this?" Non-Korean foreigners can often just use what we call the "foreigner card." Where they get excused from doing things or knowing things because they're a foreigner. Korean Americans don't really get to use that card.

According to Dorothy and numerous others, "returnees" were typically not awarded the same amount of leeway as non-Korean foreigners for matters concerning Korean language and cultural proficiency. Whereas foreigners not of Korean ancestry could be excused from specific workplace expectations by playing the "foreigner card," this was generally not viewed as an option for Korean Americans. As another "returnee" named Amelie put it, "If you're Korean American . . . [locals] feel that you should be able to just figure things out."

Granted, even "returnees" with high enough levels of linguistic and cultural proficiency to obtain jobs in South Korean companies still struggled with the expectations placed on them. Many of these grievances lay in the ambiguity of their positions within workplace environments that were predominately comprised of South Koreans. Jin Soo, for instance, was hired as his company's sole foreign legal counsel, meaning that he was tasked with nearly all paperwork written in English and/or dealing with international trade law. He also happened to be the only non-South Korean citizen employed within any of the company's ranks. Because of the uniqueness of his position and his limited Korean proficiency, Jin Soo quipped the following: "I've felt so isolated in the company during the entire five years I've been there! [Laughs.] I feel like they don't know what I'm doing and they just kind of leave me alone to do my own thing. It's been pretty difficult because I still have a hard time figuring out what they expect from me." Though he had been with his company for over five years, Jin Soo felt that there was still a level of ambiguity surrounding his position, as well as the types of workplace and social expectations that his co-workers expected of him. Though during business hours he tended to work alone, Jin Soo still felt the immense pressure to learn and abide by South Korean office norms, even if they came at the detriment of his personal wellbeing. Participating in office teamwork and morale boosting exercises, such as *hoesik* (or after work social gatherings) and *yagŭn* (or non-paid overtime work), were things that Jin Soo learned to incorporate into his work schedule early on so that he could appear as more of a team player to his colleagues and seniors. While he had traditionally not been one to consume alcohol during workdays, he quickly discovered that after work drinking with co-workers was a staple of South Korean work culture to which he needed to adapt. Despite disliking this aspect of his job, Jin Soo acknowledged that he had felt the need participate in these "team-building exercises" regularly in order to win over the favor of his co-workers. Roughly two years into his job, however, Jin Soo explained that he started to abstain from participating in *hoesik* because it was adversely affecting his health and workplace productivity. His non-participation gradually led to his exclusion from future team social events, further isolating him in his own workplace.

More disheartening for interviewees was how their inability to "play the foreigner card" directly impacted their employability on the job market. Nearly all interviewees with experience applying to or working in the private English-language sector suspected that South Korean employers hired Korean American "returnees" only as an alternative to fielding qualified white candidates. Though some "returnees" downplayed these discriminatory hiring practices by claiming that they were no longer practiced as widely, other interviewees such as Dee asserted that these practices were instead implemented more covertly:

> They used to discriminate really blatantly in their ads. Now they do it more subtly by visa status. They used to say "no Koreans," or "white applicants only." But now they say "no F-4 or E-2 visa holders." Or they'll require a picture on your application. In the past, if they wanted a Korean American they usually wanted them to be fluent in Korean, too. So, they would give you language tests over the phone. Or they would offer you positions without any benefits even if you had more qualifications than other people.

According to Dee, while it was now less common for companies to explicitly state their racial, ethnic, national, or gender preferences in the job advertisements, application requirements such as visa status and professional headshots still allowed them to actively discriminate against a wide pool of foreign candidates.

Through the examples provided by interviewees, it was clear that South Korean employers placed preference on candidates who (1) supposedly embodied the nationality or race of a native English speaker (white) or (2) were not foreign at all. Using these metrics, to be a competitive foreign applicant in the South Korean job market meant that one had to either appear the part or exhibit native levels of Korean language and cultural proficiency. Ultimately, and ironically, these hiring practices appeared to Orientalize and tokenize U.S.-raised Korean "returnee" candidates even in their ancestral homeland.

## Becoming the "Good Ambassador" in South Korea

A consequence of this in-between status was that it encouraged interviewees to police their own actions. Much of this revolved around a "politics of respectability,"[7] with interviewees endeavoring to present themselves in ways that highlighted their status as upstanding foreigners. Teresa, while reflecting on her behavior in public settings in South Korea, even likened her self-policing tendencies to that of Asian Americans internalizing and adopting the role of the "model minority" in the U.S. Much in the way that some interviewees admitted embracing the "model minority" discourse while growing up in a discriminatory American society, "returnees" like Teresa revealed embracing a similar typology in South Korea so as not to be perceived as an "ugly kyop":[8]

> I guess on a broader level, there's sort of this constant thinking of how my actions will be perceived. And this may be something that I put upon myself, but I feel like I need to be a great ambassador for Korean Americans. If I try to be full Korean, or "KoKo" as I like to say, people can tell. As soon as I open my mouth and I don't sound quite native, people know I wasn't raised here or educated here. So, I'm constantly thinking about being a good ambassador for Korean Americans or North Americans or expats. Or whatever else kind of group I'm assumed to represent. I think about that a lot. Basically, I don't want to be the ugly "kyop." . . . Funny enough I never felt the pressure of being the model minority in the States. But here I feel like I should be.

According to Teresa, her impetus to self-police in South Korea was buttressed by her desire to be a "good ambassador" for the larger "returnee" and expat communities. In effect, Teresa felt the need to bear the burden of an entire group of migrants so as not to reinforce their stereotyping as "ugly" Americans or "kyop'os." The problem with this reasoning, as Teresa herself later mentioned, was that the image of the "good ambassador" necessitated the social proliferation of an "ugly kyop"-type figure—an individual who was socially derided for his/her inability to display high levels of Korean cultural competency. In effect, the pressure to self-police relied on a politics of respectability that lauded and privileged those "returnees" who were both willing and able to abide by certain social norms while subordinating those who could not. Akin to the paradoxical allure of the "model minority" discourse in the U.S., then, the pressure for "returnees" to align their actions and behaviors to that of the "good ambassador" had the effect of minimizing the systemic barriers that worked to disadvantage not only Korean Americans but all "returnees" in South Korea.

## DISCUSSION AND CONCLUSION

This chapter demonstrates how Korean American "returnees" are not explicitly excluded from South Korean society, but rather differentially included. That is, they are explicitly included in the formulation of a South Korean populace and in the conceptual embodiment of the Korean diaspora, insofar as they are willing to occupy a subordinate or transient position within the country. Though at times certainly profiting from the human capital bestowed upon them by their upbringings in and connections to the U.S., this chapter illustrates how "returnees'" statuses as foreign nationals ultimately serve to complicate their positioning within South Korean society the longer they reside, eventually situating them in a liminal social status that straddles the line between co-ethnic insider and non-citizen foreigner. In particular, I drew attention to the seeming "double-edged" nature of interviewees' experiences in South Korea—where, on the one hand, as "overseas Koreans" they come to face many of the same socio-legal hurdles to societal incorporation encountered by other ethnic Korean and non-citizen migrants in the country, while on the other hand, their co-ethnic status also disqualifies them from unabashedly embracing the opportunities and identities afforded to other American migrants. These Korean American "returnees" thus find themselves in a puzzling predicament in South Korea where they are at once foreign yet not quite foreign enough. Much like in the U.S., where the differential inclusion of Asian American populations can be said to contribute to their embrace of "model minority" characteristics and discourses, the differential inclusion of Korean American "returnees" appears to promote similar practices of "model minority" and "respectability" politics that work to minimize the encounters with discrimination and stigmatization faced by migrants in South Korea.

These experiences are important when taking into consideration that the Overseas Korean Act is oftentimes couched as legislation that recognizes the far reach of Korean "ethnizenship," or extends the embodiment of Koreanness beyond the nation's borders and into the "blood" of former citizens and their offspring who live abroad. This rationale has served as the basis for the preferential immigration of hundreds of thousands of ancestral Koreans from the U.S. and elsewhere since 1999. While much is made about South Korea's efforts to include members of Korean ancestry in its conceptions of ethnonationality, little is stated about the ways in which Korean American "returnees," even as a privileged immigrant population in South Korea, continue to experience marginalization as they live and work within the country. As argued throughout this chapter, this process ultimately reifies a political framework where ancestral homeland migrants are both formally and informally deemed as existing outside of the purview of the South Korean state, and by extension, Korean-ness, even as it is this very quality that helped to initiate their "return."

## NOTES

1. In her examination of Japanese Americans living in Japan, Jane Yamashiro (2017) uses the term *ancestral homeland migration* instead of *ethnic return migration* or *diasporic return* to "argue that the relationship of Japanese Americans to Japan is not that of a 'diaspora' and a 'homeland'" but of different branches of what she refers to as a global ancestral group (5). The utility of the concept of a global ancestry group lies in its ability to recognize the ancestral ties shared by far-reaching, diverse populations while not making assumptions about "how people of shared ancestry identify with each other or with the ancestral homeland" (Yamashiro 2017, 5). While I share Yamashiro's critique of "diaspora" as a catch-all designation for those of shared ancestry, I nevertheless continue to implement the terminology of "return" alongside her conceptualizations. I do this because all participants in my study are 1.5- or 2nd-generation Korean Americans, meaning that for most a sense of "Korean-ness" or Korean identity, however abstracted, played an important if not central role in their decisions to migrate to South Korea. In this sense, it was not only a shared ancestry that linked my participants to one another and to South Korea, but an actual sense of co-ethnicity.

2. I use the term *"returnee"* (with quotations) generally to denote individuals who migrate to an ancestral homeland. The term *returnee* (without quotations) refers to individuals who migrate to a natal homeland or country of origin.

3. South Korea removed regional restrictions for F-4 visa eligibility in 2008, greatly increasing the number of F-4 visa holders from Asia and the CIS. In a report filed by the Korea Immigration Service in 2017, for instance, the number of F-4 visa holders from China, 275,342, vastly outnumbered those from the U.S., 45,784, and Canada, 15,846 (Korea Immigration Service 2017).

4. Interviewees frequently used the word *kyop'o* to refer to those with Korean ancestry who were born and/or raised abroad. The term is somewhat of a misnomer, given that *kyop'o* most directly translates to "expatriate" or "émigré."

5. All interview subjects in this study have been provided pseudonyms.

6. *Amerasian* is a term used to designate the status of children who are born to an Asian mother and a non-Asian, American G.I. father (Le 2018).

7. Fredrick C. Harris (2014) describes respectability politics as a neoliberal ideology where "virtues such as self-care and self-correction are framed as strategies to lift the black poor out of their condition by preparing them for the market economy" (32) and "where uplift entails transforming individuals rather than transforming communities" (33). While Harris's focus lies on the entrenchment of neoliberal ideology among elite and aspirational black Americans, similar logics can be applied to Asian Americans' pursuits of "model minority" characteristics.

8. Teresa's term, "ugly kyop," was a play on the popular stereotype of the "ugly American." In this case, "kyop" is used as a stylized and condensed version of the Korean word "kyop'o."

# REFERENCES

Espiritu, Yen Le. 2003. *Home Bound: Filipino American Lives across Cultures, Communities, and Countries*. Berkeley: University of California Press.

Harris. Frederick C. 2014. "The Rise of Respectability Politics." *Dissent* 61(1): 33–37.

Kim, Elaine H. 2012. "Human Capital: Transnational Korean Adoptees and the Neoliberal Logic of Return." *Journal of Korean Studies* 17(2): 299–327.

Kim, Nadia Y. 2008. *Imperial Citizens: Koreans and Race from Seoul to LA*. Palo Alto, CA: Stanford University Press.

Kim, Nora Hui-Jung. 2008. "Korean Immigration Policy Changes and the Political Liberals' Dilemma." *International Migration Review* 42(3): 576–596.

Korea Immigration Service. 2017. "Annual Report 2016." Accessed December 26, 2017. http://www.immigration.go.kr/HP/COM/bbs_003/ListShowData.do?strNbodCd=noti0095&strWrtNo=59&strAnsNo=A&strOrgGbnCd=104000&strRtnURL=IMM_6040&strAllOrgYn=N&strThisPage=1&strFilePath=imm/.

Korea Legislation Research Institute. 2016. "Resident Registration Act." *Statutes of the Republic of Korea*. Accessed December 10, 2018. https://elaw.klri.re.kr/eng_service/lawView.do?hseq=40157&lang=ENG.

Le, C.N. 2018. "Multiracial/Hapa Asian Americans." *Asian-Nation: The Landscape of Asian America*. Accessed December 4, 2018. http://www.asian-nation.org/multiracial.shtml.

Lee, Chulwoo. 2012. "How Can You Say You're Korean? Law, Governmentality, and National Membership in South Korea." *Citizenship Studies* 16(1): 85–102.

Lee, Helene K. 2013. "'I'm My Mother's Daughter, I'm My Husband's Wife, I'm My Child's Mother, I'm Nothing Else': Resisting Traditional Korean Roles as Korean American Working Women in Seoul, South Korea." *Women's Studies International Forum* 36(1): 37–43.

———. 2018. *Between Foreign and Family: Return Migration and Identity Formation among Korean Americans and Korean Chinese*. New Brunswick, NJ: Rutgers University Press.

Seol, Dong-Hoon, and John D. Skrentny. 2009. "Ethnic Return Migration and Hierarchical Nationhood: Korean Chinese Foreign Workers in South Korea." *Ethnicities* 9(2): 147–174.

Skrentny, John, Stephanie Chan, Jon E. Fox, and Denis Kim. 2009. "Defining Nations in Asia and Europe: A Comparative Analysis of Ethnic Return Migration Policy." In *Diasporic Homecomings: Ethnic Return Migration in Comparative Perspective*, edited by Takeyuki Tsuda, 44–72. Palo Alto, CA: Stanford University Press.

Song, Changzoo. 2009. "Brothers Only in Name: The Alienation and Identity Transformation of Korean Chinese Return Migrants in South Korea." In *Diasporic Homecomings: Ethnic Return Migration in Comparative Perspective*, edited by T. Tsuda, 281–304. Palo Alto, CA: Stanford University Press.

Sue, Derald Wing, Jennifer Bucceri, Annie I. Lin, Kevin L. Nadal, and Gina C. Torino. 2007. "Racial Microaggressions and the Asian American Experience." *Cultural Diversity and Ethnic Minority Psychology* 13(1): 88–101.

Suh, Stephen Cho. 2017. "Negotiating Masculinity across Borders a Transnational Examination of Korean American Masculinities." *Men and Masculinities* 20(3): 317–44.

Yamashiro, Jane H. 2012. "Ethnic Return Migration Policies and Asian American Labor in Japan and Korea." *AAPI Nexus* 10: 21–39.

———. 2017. *Redefining Japaneseness: Japanese Americans in the Ancestral Homeland*. New Brunswick, NJ: Rutgers University Press.

Yi, Joseph, and Gowoon Jung. 2015. "Debating Multicultural Korea: Media Discourse on Migrants and Minorities in South Korea." *Journal of Ethnic and Migration Studies* 41(6): 985–1013.

*Chapter Seven*

# (Dis-)connectedness and Identity Negotiation

*Lived Experiences of Korean Chinese Students in South Korea*

Ruixin Wei

## ETHNIC KOREANS IN CHINA: FROM CHAOXIANREN TO CHAOXIANZU

Among the 56 official ethnicities in the People's Republic of China (hereafter China), ethnic Koreans are the fourteenth largest ethnic minority, with a population of 1,830,929 (The Sixth National Population Census of the People's Republic of China, 2010). Their home in China, the Yanbian Ethnic Korean Autonomous Prefecture (hereafter Yanbian), where the borders of China, the Democratic People's Republic of Korea (hereafter North Korea), and Russia meet, is an ethnic minority autonomous prefecture that was established in 1952. Large numbers of Korean migrants or *Chaoxianren* (*Chosŏnin* in Korean, referring to people from Chaoxian) moved from the Korean Peninsula to Manchuria and settled in what is currently Northeast China during the mid-19th century, and approximately 2 million *Chaoxianren* remained in the Northeast region to the end of the Second World War (Cui 2014, 86). Having experienced a civil war in modern China and have witnessed the establishment of the People's Republic of China in 1949, ethnic Koreans in China have been recognized as an official ethnic minority with Chinese citizenship and have been referred to as *Chaoxianzu* (*Chosŏnjok* in Korean) since. The English term *Korean Chinese* is used in this work.

# KOREAN CHINESE IN SOUTH KOREA:
## KYOP'O, TONGP'O, OR CHOSŎNJOK?

Before China and the Republic of Korea (hereafter South Korea) established diplomatic relations in 1992, it was North Korea that mainly acted as the ancestral homeland for Koreans in China. With economic reforms made in China and the end of the Cold War, frequent exchange emerged between China and South Korea from the 1990s. A continuous outflow of Korean Chinese migrating transnationally to South Korea occurred.

Varying and inconsistent terminologies have been used to describe Korean Chinese in South Korea. For example, *Chosun Ilbo* published a news article on September 13, 1986, about a Chinese national shooter who is ethnically Korean and happily visited his parents' homeland (South Korea). Though the national athlete referred to himself as *Chosŏnjok*, the newspaper article described him as a *Kyop'o* living in Communist China (overseas Korean from Communist China). Similarly, on September 20, 1988, *Donga Ilbo* published a news article on *Chungguk Kyop'o* (overseas Koreans from China) reuniting with their relatives in South Korea during the 1988 Olympic Games. This is described as a joyful reunion occurring after more than 40 years of separation between families who share the same bloodline. Sometimes, the terms *Tongp'o* and *Kyop'o* are used in the same context. For example, on July 8, 1991, Donga Ilbo published an article titled "Let's build our trust in *Kyop'o* from China," while the author refers to Korean Chinese as *Tongp'o* in the article. This inconsistent use of terminologies reflects the complexity of the identity of Korean Chinese and South Koreans' confusion towards it. According to the National Institute of Korean Language, the term *Tongp'o* (compatriots) refers to those who belong to the same nation or ethnicity, while the term *Kyop'o* refers to *Tongp'o* who settle in another country and become citizens of the receiving country (National Institute of Korean Language 2019). The term *Chosŏnjok*, as noted above, refers to ethnic Koreans with Chinese citizenship. The use of a different terminology could reflect its specific emphasis on certain dimension of the identity of Korean Chinese. Since the late 1990s, it seems that the terms *Kyop'o* and *Tongp'o* are gradually being overtaken by the term *Chosŏnjok* in newspapers when referring to Korean Chinese.

When the first wave of Korean Chinese migrant returnees appeared in South Korea in the late 1980s, they were welcomed with nostalgia and sympathy as long-lost brothers. However, this touching scene did not last long. Some Korean Chinese made fortunes by selling Chinese herbal medicine in South Korea, and this was followed with accusations of them selling fake herbs in some cases, which affected views of South Korean society towards Korean Chinese. Furthermore, their perceived advantages in terms of their Korean language proficiency and cultural proximity to South Korea did not provide them access to expected occupations. On the contrary, their financial needs and fluency in Korean catered to the unskilled labor market in South Korea, and they were in turn mainly recruited for work in 3D labor (dirty, dangerous, and demanding). In spite of this, the wage difference between China and South Korea in the 1990s still drove many Korean Chinese to quit their stable jobs in China and to take advantage of opportunities in South Korea. It has been reported that the three-month income of those working in a factory can cover a year and a half of living expenses in China (Donga Ilbo, February 29, 1992). High levels of mobility between China and South Korea and the follow-up effects of transnational remittances created "anomie" in Yanbian (Kwon 1997, 17; Choi 2001, 139). The desire to leave for South Korea formed a "Korean wind" (Kwon 2015, 477) that swept Yanbian, and more Korean Chinese came to South Korea to realize the "Korean dream." Many of them moved as illegal migrants or remained undocumented for years. Several criminal acts committed by Korean Chinese intensified society's antipathy towards Korean Chinese. Socially, news reports depicting Korean Chinese as undocumented migrants, unreliable medicine retailers, and Sinicized opportunists emerged, and negative impressions gradually grew more entrenched (Song 2009, 291–292; Fang 2013, 100–101). Legally, Korean Chinese were excluded under the Overseas Koreans Act passed in 1998, which was intended to encourage overseas Koreans to move to South Korea (Lee and Lee 2016, 283). As ethnic Korean returnees, Korean Chinese are viewed as less than Korean citizens and overseas Koreans from the West. South Korea in turn became a country of "hierarchical nationhood" (Seol and Skrentny 2009) that drew distinctions among ethnic returnees. Though the Korean government later expanded Overseas Koreans Visa (F-4) coverage to include Korean Chinese, the stigmatized *Chosŏnjok* image was not easily overcome. On April 16, 2018, to prevent semantic discrimination while promoting linguistic standardization, a list of potentially misused terms was modified by the Seoul Metropolitan Government, according to which the term *Chungguk Tongp'o* (Korean compatriots in China) officially took the place of the term *Chosŏnjok* (Seoul Metropolitan Government 2018). While this call for a change in terminology did not immediately resolve confusion and misunderstanding surrounding *Chosŏnjok*, it reminds us that issues related to Korean Chinese must be taken seriously.

## THE KOREAN CHINESE IDENTITY
## AND THE YOUNGER GENERATION

As of March 2018, there were 850,007 registered foreign national Koreans in South Korea, and Korean Chinese accounted for 80.87 percent of them (Korea Immigration Office, 2018 March). Previous studies on Korean Chinese identity are based on different time periods and areas. As the two largest sub-groups of Korean Chinese in South Korea, Korean Chinese marriage migrants and Korean Chinese laborers have attracted the most academic attention (Piao 2011, 222). When it comes to Korean Chinese, the question of who the Korean Chinese are has never faded out of the discussions. Discussions surrounding their identity has been approached from several different angles and have mainly focused on its hybridity, dual nature, and changeability.

Regarding the hybridity of Korean Chinese identity, two representative metaphors have been used. Some scholars (Kim 1994, 303; Chong 1997, as cited in Xu 2012, 456) describe Korean Chinese as a daughter who has married into a new family and who grieves her own parents' (North and South Korea) divorce. Korean Chinese scholar Kim Hyok compares Korean Chinese to the Yanbian delicacy the apple pear, a local grafted fruit. "The Chosŏnjok crossed the border and settled down in a new land 150 years ago; they dedicated themselves to this hinterland, went through innumerable hardships and eventually cultivated the apple pear, which contains Chosŏnjok's joys and sorrows. Just like how we migrated and settled down in China, Chosŏnjok's identity can be sensed from the apple pear" (Kim 2011, 144). Many other works have been conducted based on the dual identity framework, further investigating to what extent the dual identity is contested, contradictory, and conflicted. For example, Kang (2008) investigates the dual identity of Korean Chinese from a political perspective since the Japanese colonial period and notes that Korean Chinese are caught between racial and diplomatic conflicts through which their national identity has been re-created from a culturally centered identity to a nationality centered identity. Along the same line of reasoning, similar perspectives are given by Lee (2005, 118) who examines Koreans' perspectives of overseas Koreans and especially in relation to Korean Chinese who have a dual identity as both "Joseon (Korean)-Chinese" and "Chinese Joseon (Korean)." However, not all scholars agree on the conclusions of the dual identity argument. Huang (Huang 2011, as cited in Xu, 2012) argues that it is not reasonable to conclude that Korean Chinese have a dual identity as a result of identifying with both a Chinese national identity and Korean ethnic identity. The two are considered total different conceptions and should not be confused with one another. Huang further states that the dual identity argument may prevent Korean Chinese and especially the younger generation from integrating into mainstream Chinese society (Huang 2011, as cited in Xu 2012, 475).

As identity is not static but instead fluid and changeable (Choi 2014, 97), in recent years, some researchers (Choi 2014, 2016, 2019; Shin 2016) have called for a rethinking of Korean Chinese from a local perspective to a global one and from ethno-nationalism to cosmopolitanism. After decades of development, as one of the first migrant groups to follow trends of transnational migration, Korean Chinese have entered a "post-Joseonjok stage" (Choi

2016, 247) in which networks, exchanges, and mobility can occur in a global space. The third generation plays a leading role in this global space and the "post-Joseonjok stage." On one hand, they develop competencies in shifting between cultures and navigating their sense of belonging. On the other hand, they preserve the identity inherited from previous generations while further developing their own understanding of what it means to be Korean Chinese. As noted by Kim (2010, 111), generational differences exist in the Korean Chinese community. The potential dissolution of the Korean Chinese community concerns the older generation, the dilemma of being positioned between the "fatherland" and "motherland" makes the middle generation anxious, and the rapid change and challenge inspire the younger generation with more possibility. However, less attention has been specifically given to the third generation of Korean Chinese. While there are studies on the third generation (Li 2014; Piao 2009, 2011), few detailed individual narratives are presented. Jo (2002) investigates how Korean Chinese students understand their mother country and ethnicity and uncovers the difficulties encountered in their daily lives by analyzing their narratives. Due to changes in policy and economic conditions occurring over the past decade, findings from previous studies may not be applicable to current conditions. A survey of how South Koreans view different ethnic groups in South Korean society conducted in 2010 shows that 60% of participants regard Korean Chinese as the same or almost the same as South Koreans (Yoon 2011, 184). However, this percentage decreased to 45.6% in 2015 (Yi and Yoon 2016, 287). Therefore, it is necessary to conduct qualitative research to develop an updated and in-depth understanding of Korean Chinese from their narratives based on their daily experiences.

This work focuses on the third-generation Korean Chinese students and investigates their (dis-)connectedness and identity negotiation in transnational space. Connectedness refers to a sense of belonging or affinity with the Korean Chinese community; accordingly, disconnectedness denotes a sense of lacking contact with the Korean Chinese community or of feeling disconnected from it when faced with certain situations. The experiences of this particular group could offer a useful dimension to our understanding of the younger generation. Their (dis-)connectedness and identity negotiation in transnational space are presented in their agency (the power to negotiate) in the given situation.

## Korean Chinese Students in Transnational Space

Faist (2017, 3–4) defines transnational space as "relatively stable, lasting and dense sets of ties reaching beyond and across the borders of sovereign states. They consist of combinations of ties and their contents, positions in networks and organizations, and networks of organizations that cut across the borders of at least two nation-states." Four types of transnational spaces are described according to their degrees of formalization or institutionalization and longevity. The first type of transnational space involves the exchange of goods, capital, information, practices, etc. The second type is generated from small groups based on kinship. A typical example is transnational family. The third type issues networks. And the fourth type exists in transnational communities and organizations (Faist 2017, 8–10). In light of implications of the definition of transnational space, the transnational space in which Korean Chinese students are positioned in this study is divided into two dimensions: the public sphere and the private sphere. The public sphere of transnational space mainly refers to the space in which ideas and information regarding both China and South Korea are exchanged on or off campus and within or outside of Korean Chinese community. The private sphere here refers mainly to the family and home.

Transnational migration between China and South Korea has altered the experiences of the children of many Korean Chinese families. The younger generations have been embedded in cross-border connections between and beyond China and South Korea. The experiences of younger Korean Chinese generations may be a reflection of whether or not there are real long-term structural problems with the integration process into South Korean society. At the same time, the difficulties that they face may also offer a more accurate account of constraints and challenges faced than modes of discrimination experienced by their parents and grandparents. Different from previous generations, third-generation Korean Chinese studied in this work are characterized by unique features. Many Korean Chinese parents are devoted to their children's education (Kwon 1997, 10). The third generation has access to better education and living conditions. Findings from previous studies show that language can be a source of conflict for some Korean Chinese women in South Korea (Schubert, Lee, and Lee 2015, 242) and especially in regard to communicating in English, as a result of which they will feel isolated. For many Korean Chinese students, language is not an impediment to adaptation. In addition, with China's economic development, students not only achieve their Korean dream but also their Chinese dream. Their aspirations for the future can be distinguished from those of previous generations.

As part of a research project that involves interviews with Korean Chinese students of higher education, a total of 21 female and 17 male Korean Chinese students participated in the research project by snowball sampling. In this study, 12 of the 38 interviewees' narratives are selected for analysis. All interviewees studied for this work are Korean Chinese born in China and only moved to South Korea in their late teens or early 20s. They are free to choose the interview language that they feel comfortable with. Almost all the interviewees chose Mandarin Chinese to communicate, but Korean vocabularies were used from time to time during interview. In-depth semi-structured interviews were conducted, and each interview lasted 30 to 60 minutes. All participants were interviewed anonymously, and the interviews were recorded with consent to use for a narrative analysis only.

## FINDINGS

### Public Sphere: Fitting in But Not Necessarily Belonging To

In transnational space there is a difference between ways of being and belonging. According to Levitt and Schiller (2004, 1010), ways of being refer to "the actual social relations and practices that individual engage in," and this is not necessarily associated with one's self identification; ways of belonging refer to "practices that signal or enact an identity which demonstrates a conscious connection to a particular group." Korean Chinese students may communicate with local Korean students every day, but building friendship is never easy. While many Korean Chinese students have Koreanized their fashion choices, their sense of belonging is not necessarily the same. Kyeongnam was a university student who used to take an active part in club activities on campus. He recalled his first attempt to make local friends:

> I knew no one from my department in the first semester, and I was so eager to make some new friends. There was one time that some of my classmates were talking about Gag Concert [개그콘서트], and I thought they were talking something about a dog (the first Korean character in "Gag Concert" is pronounced the same as the word for dog in Korean), so I joined their conversation and started talking about dogs, which turned out to be very embarrassing. Because the Gag Concert [개그콘서트] they were talking about is a comedy show. (Kyeongnam, 2016 July)

Kyeongnam has graduated from his master program and is now working in Seoul. He seems to have made many local friends during his last few years of studying in Seoul. However, he indicated that even though he fits in, this does not necessarily mean that he has developed a sense of belonging with the local community. He explained,

> I believe that whether one can make many friends depends on one's personality, but it is hard to make friends at least in the beginning in a foreign country. Even the foreign country is South Korea, a country we [Korean Chinese] are supposed to be familiar with, it never makes it easier. In school, most of my close friends are still Korean Chinese. Korean Chinese students and South Korean students grow up in different backgrounds. The cartoons we liked, the TV dramas we watched, the fashion styles that used to be popular, etc. are different. We have different collective memories from childhood. (Kyeongnam, 2016 July)

Similar narratives can be found in Piao and Kim's (2012, 326) study, which is an oral history study regarding the lived experience of 22 Korean Chinese in South Korea. Interviewee S, who first came to South Korea as a marriage migrant and changed her nationality, noted that changing one's nationality to South Korean does not mean that one is no longer Chinese. "It is not that I expect to be taken as South Korean, but I have made great efforts to get well along with all of the people around me here." Being able to adapt to the given society has very much to do with personal efforts. The ethnic link between Korean Chinese students and their local peers is not always necessarily helpful in building peer friendships. There are even hierarchies among international students of Korean higher education. According to Jon's (2012) research on power dynamics among international students, the economic status of an international student's original country and the language that one speaks largely determine whether he or she is preferred as a friend of local Korean students (Jon 2012, 446–447). Although students from China compose the largest proportion of international students in South Korea, they are not Korean students' preferred friends (Jon 2012, 447). This doesn't mean Korean Chinese students are totally being ignored. Their identity sometimes gets special attention as well. Many interviewees remarked that their reflections on Korean Chinese identity started after they came to South Korea. Hyanglim, a graduate student, described the first time when a South Korean asked about her identity,

> I didn't know my identity is such a hot issue until I came to South Korea. I was teaching Chinese at a language institute, one of my students, who is an old Korean businessman, came to me and asked if I am Korean. I said that I am Chinese, but Korean Chinese. He obviously wasn't satisfied with my answer and asked if my grandfather is a Korean, and I said "Yes, my grandfather is originally from Korean Peninsula." He then told me bluntly, "If your grandfather is a Korean, you are a Korean," and left. (Hyanglim, 2016 July)

The positioning of Korean Chinese between China and South Korea has become a long-standing question to many Korean Chinese students when they are in South Korea. One interviewee, Hamhyang, added another similar experience:

> One of the questions that many of us [Korean Chinese] hate the most is that "If there is a football match between China and South Korea, which team will you support?" And I know that it doesn't matter which team I choose, because the person who asks this question will always take my identity into account to interpret my answer. I'm not even a fan of football, and if I have to make a choice between the two, shouldn't I choose the one that plays better? (Hamhyang, 2016 July)

Although special attention to their identity is sometimes unwanted, when the interviewees are asked about their feelings regarding their Korean Chinese identity, all of them exhibited relatively positive attitudes. "It is a bit annoying of getting questions about our identity all the time, but I am proud of being a Korean Chinese because it adds more dimensions to who I am" (Hamhyang, 2016 July). When this pride is sometimes challenged, not all Korean Chinese students can laugh it off. Some of them decide to argue back. Most Korean Chinese from Yanbian are originally from the Hamkyeong area of the Korean Peninsula, which now belongs to North Korea. Thus, many Korean Chinese share a similar accent to North Koreans (Fang 2013, 106). Yonghwa, an exchange student from Yanbian University said,

> There was one time at a hair salon when a Korean hairdresser asked me if she could use a curling iron to style my hair after recognizing that I am Korean Chinese probably from my accent. She picked up the curling iron and said, "See, this is a curling iron, shall I use it on your hair for styling?" She probably didn't have bad intentions, but it was ridiculous to me. What kind of life does she think Korean Chinese have in China? Had I never seen or used a curling iron before? I told her that whatever they have here in South Korea you can find in China. (Yonghwa, 2016 February)

Similar experiences can be found in many other interviewees' narratives. Experiences like above are subtle discrimination that unnecessarily emphasizes their ethnic distinctiveness. And this eventually serves to re-affirm their Korean Chinese identity. In the meantime, in response to the given situation, some interviewees had even developed strategies in pursuit of their goals. Linyang, a university student who has been living in Seoul for many years, said, "These days if I go to Myeongdong for shopping, I'd rather pretend that I cannot speak Korean. They will always have someone in the store who speaks Mandarin Chinese. I get better service when I speak Chinese because Chinese people always buy a lot" (Linyang, 2016 July).

The strategies adopted by the students in certain situations have nothing to do with transforming their identities. They were more likely to exploit their agency of being a Korean Chinese in a given situation. Individual negotiations and strategies (re-)draw ethnic boundaries out of ongoing social encounters. However, even the students who identify with both Korean and Chinese cultures don't identify with both equally. Basically, they have a stronger sense of belonging towards Korean culture, and this tendency largely stems from their growth experiences and family background.

## Private Sphere: Inheritance and Innovation

For many interviewees, the seeds for ethnic Korean identification were sown as far back as childhood. Their growth environment has ingrained a sense of

Koreanness into their daily lives and subconscious since they were very young. Korean language as the family language in addition to the traditional culture formed their ethnic consciousness that was distinct from the majority Han Chinese identity. A sense of ethnic pride among Korean Chinese students can be seen in the following narratives from an interviewee named Juntae: "I was raised in a traditional Korean Chinese family. My grandparents are very typical Korean Chinese, and many values and rituals that have been lost in South Korea are still maintained by our family, which makes us special. I would say that my Korean Chinese peers are doing better with respect to courtesy than my Han Chinese peers" (Juntae, 2016 July).

The results show a strong sense of ethnic maintenance among younger generations of Korean Chinese, and they actively take part in ethnic cultural activities while appearing to fit well into the mainstream South Korean society, as there is no fundamental culture shock for them. Most respondents acknowledged their Korean heritage is a vital reflection of who they are in a cultural dimension. But in relation to the maintenance of the Korean heritage, generational divergent understanding emerged when it comes to seeking a spouse as a Korean Chinese. For example, the interviewee Yonghwa mentioned,

> For many younger Korean Chinese, ethnic background is not that important when it comes to looking for a boyfriend/girlfriend or husband/wife, but it will be a very important issue if you ask your parents and grandparents. My mom even gave me a ranking of preferences. The most preferred Sawitkam [son-in-law material] would be a Korean Chinese who had gone to a Han Chinese school, the second preferred would be a Han Chinese who had attended a Han Chinese school or a Korean Chinese school, the least preferred is a Korean Chinese who had attended a Korean Chinese school. (Yonghwa, 2016 February)

As the number of Korean Chinese ethnic schools has been decreasing dramatically, the quality of formal ethnic education has subsequently become worrying in the past few decades. More Korean Chinese parents are sending their children to Han Chinese schools for education (Piao 2014, 163–164). The mother's wish reflects, one the one hand, the general high expectations of Korean Chinese integrating into Han Chinese society, and on the other hand, the older Korean Chinese generations maintain a conservative mindset and keep the Korean Chinese identity in a relatively exclusive way. In other words, many of them still believe that being Korean Chinese means sharing the same bloodline in the first place. Different from the older generations, the Korean Chinese students make concerted efforts to adapt to society in a more open attitude. And many of them believe that staying exclusively within one's own community will not change the stigmatized images of Korean Chinese and their neighborhood promulgated by the public media. On August 29, 2017, a group of Korean Chinese activists gathered at Daerim Station in Seoul to protest negative portrayals of Korean Chinese and of their neighborhood in the action comedy film *Midnight Runners*. This high-profile film has led to a new upsurge in attention to the images of Korean Chinese and their neighborhoods. Daerim-dong is located in southwestern Seoul where there are many Chinese restaurants and shops. Meilin is a university student majoring in piano at a prestigious women's university in Seoul. Her parents had worked in Seoul throughout her childhood. She decided to apply for universities in Seoul after graduating from high school in Yanji city, Yanbian. Though the family members now all live in the same city, they still live separately. Meilin says,

> My parents live in Daerim-dong, but I moved out and live close to campus. Daerim is not an ideal neighborhood for students. It is like Korean Chinese are living in one city with South Koreans but in two parallel societies. Daerim-dong looks too different from the other neighborhoods. It is good that we [Korean Chinese] show our solidarity, but if we only stay in our community exclusively, we will never let other people know who we really are. (Meilin, 2016 July)

Third-generation Korean Chinese are just like social image brokers. They are eager to improve the image of Korean Chinese in South Korean society. Their understanding of how to prove themselves to the given society is different. Meilin further explained,

> My grandparents and parents are very much proud of having preserved what they believe to be the most authentic sense of Koreanness, and this is the most important thing when they demand equal rights with other ethnic Koreans. But I think if we [the younger generation] want to destigmatize and improve our image in South Korea. More efforts should be made in educational achievement and career planning. (Meilin, 2016 July)

Third-generation Korean Chinese are experiencing the "globalization of Joseonjok" (Choi 2016, 246). Their horizon is neither limited within China nor South Korea. Many will not stop navigating by settling in Korea. The way in which many first- and second-generation Korean Chinese have chosen to return to and stay in South Korea regardless of the prejudices or discrimination is not applicable to the younger generation. In a globalized world, Korean Chinese are closely interacting with and connecting to both overseas Korean communities and overseas Chinese communities (Choi 2019, 42). Appadurai (2004) argues that aspirations are cultural capacities that oriented toward future and plans. As for the Korean Chinese students, on the base of the capital accumulation made by the previous generations, their aspiration of being global elites in the future is their cultural capabilities which motivate them to break through the limits of ethno-nationalism.

## CONCLUDING NOTES

The demographic composition of South Korea has changed dramatically since the late 1980s, when thousands of ethnic returnees migrated back to South Korea. The growth of the Korean Chinese community in South Korea is well documented in previous research. Much of the related research has mainly focused on Korean Chinese marriage migrants and unskilled laborers in South Korea. However, few works have been conducted on how younger Korean Chinese generations negotiate their identity. The stereotyped or stigmatized image of Korean Chinese in South Korean society has been a long-standing social issue since the 1990s. As there are no physically visible or distinctive cultural traits that differentiate Korean Chinese from South Koreans, their ethnic identity negotiation is mainly reflected in subtle lived experiences.

The findings of this study can be summarized into three main conclusions. First, though many Korean Chinese students exhibit a strong capacity to adapt to campus life, this does not necessarily mean that they feel a sense of belonging to South Korean society. Expressions of ethnic identity are situational and dynamic, and this is a result of a dialectical process involving insiders (Korean Chinese) and outsiders (non-Korean Chinese and especially South Koreans). Identity is not as much related to a common origin as it is a result of the interaction between personal agency and given situations in both the public and private spheres.

Second, the interviewees' ethnic pride in being Korean Chinese had barely been disrupted regardless of the interminable questioning. Some of them underwent a process of re-confirming their identity as something that they should be proud of. What the students do in specific situations does little to reshape or transform their identity into a different one. It is simply done to exploit their identity to cope with situations. Identity negotiation involves not only drawing and redrawing boundaries but also assigning meanings. For example, some students stated that being Korean Chinese enables them to enjoy a higher level of geographical mobility and a sense of cosmopolitanism. Some of them defend Yanbian while speaking to Korean nationals and defend Korean Chinese while speaking to non-Korean Chinese, and this becomes a regular part of their lives. They defend both cultures vigorously while trying to point out the favorable features of both. In this way, students can create a niche from which they can freely express who they are.

Third, it is important to pay attention to issues of globalization and the necessity to be globalized for third-generation Korean Chinese. Demographically, overseas Korean Chinese now live in more than 20 countries around the world. It is estimated that roughly 53,000 Korean Chinese reside in Japan, that over 30,000 Korean Chinese live in the U.S., that more than 3,000 reside in Russia, and that approximately 20,000 reside in other countries (Piao 2014, 161). On the one hand, the younger Korean Chinese generation is clearly aspiring for a global identity (Lee 2017, 100). On the other hand, Korean Chinese society has witnessed a decline in population and a surge in urbanization, and it is undeniable that high levels of geographical mobility and rapid urbanization are disintegrating traditional Korean Chinese communities (Kim 2010, 96). It is foreseeable that the success of ethnic Korean entrepreneurship will not last forever. Many previous studies have described Korean Chinese as "ideal intermediaries" (Lankov 2007, 6) in communications between China and South Korea or in the potential unification of the Korean Peninsula in the future. However, in recent years, Korean Chinese as mediators are no longer as essential as before, since more and more Han Chinese have joined the cohort of Chinese–South Korean exchange through various activities (Shin 2017). Fundamentally, it is also inevitable for the third-generation Korean Chinese to be involved in globalization.

## REFERENCES

Appadurai, A. 2004. "The Capacity to Aspire: Culture and the Terms of Recognition." In *Culture and Public Action*, edited by V. Rao and M. Walton, 58–84. Stanford, CA: Stanford University Press.

Bae, Jungsul. 1991. "Chunggukkyop'oe shilloegam shimŏjuja [Let's build our trust in Kyop'o from China]." *Donga Ilbo*, July 8.

Chosun Ilbo. 1986 "Pumonimnarae wa kippŭda [I'm so happy to visit my parents' homeland]." Chosun Ilbo, September 13, 1986.

Choi, Sumak. 1992. "Junggugin chwigeum bulman dongjokttatteutanpoyong aswiwo geonseolhyeonjang eumsikjeom dabang mangucheonyeomyeong [Promote social inclusion of the ethnic Koreans: 19,000 Koreans got employed on site]." *Donga Ilbo*, February 29.

Choi, Woo-Gil. 2001. "The Korean Minority in China: The Change of Its Identity." *Development and Society* 30(1): 119–141.

———. 2014. "Chosŏnjok chŏngch'esŏng tashi ikki: se ch'awŏnŭi ŭishige kwanhan shiron [Rereading the identity of Korean Chinese: three dimensions of their existence]." *Studies of Koreans Abroad* 34: 95–131.

———. 2016. "The transformation of the Korean Chinese community: the case of the age of migration in China." *Journal of Contemporary Korean Studies* 3(1–2): 245–264.

———. 2019. "Chosŏnjok yŏn'gu 30nyŏn hoego, kwaje kŭrigo chŏnmang [The 30 years' studies on Joseonjok: retrospection, tasks, and prospect]." *Studies of Koreans Abroad* 47, 29–54.

Cui, Fengchun. 2014. "Chaoxianzude mingchengyoulai jiqi jibentezheng [The origin of Chaoxianzu as a terminology and its characteristics]." In *Chaoxianzu yanjiu 2013*, edited by Zhongguo chaoxianminzu shixuehui [China Korean Minority History Association], 86–89. Beijing: Minzu chubanshe.

Donga Ilbo. 1988. "Chunggukkyop'o mogukpangmun churiŏ [Overseas Koreans from China waiting in line to visit home country]." *Donga Ilbo*, September 20.

Fang, Meihua. 2013. *Idonggwa chŏngch'agŭi kyŏnggyeesŏ chaehan chosŏnjogŭi shilch'ŏjŏllyakkwa chŏngch'esŏng* [Mobility and settlement on the borderland: the practical strategy and identity of Korean Chinese in South Korea]. Paju: Idam Books.

Faist, T. 2017. "The Border-Crossing Expansion of Social Space: Concepts, Questions and Topics." In *Transnational Social Spaces: Agents, Networks and Institutions*, edited by T. Faist and E. Özveren, 1–36. Abingdon, Oxon: Routledge.

Jo, Hye-Young. 2002. "Haeoedongp'o moguksuhaksaenge taehan yŏn'gu—chungguktongp'o haksaengdŭrŭi moguk kwan min minjokkwanŭl chungshimŭro [A study on Korean-Chinese students studying in Korea: focusing on their meaning of mother country and ethnicity]." *Studies of Koreans Abroad* 12(1): 65–114.

Jon, Jae-Eun. 2012. "Power Dynamics with International Students: From the Perspective of Domestic Students in Korean Higher Education." *High Education* 64(4): 441–454.

Kang, Jin Woong. 2008. "The Dual National Identity of the Korean Minority in China: The Politics of Nation and Race and the Imagination of Ethnicity." *Studies in Ethnicity and Nationalism* 8(1): 101–119.

Kim, Hyok. 2011."Chunggung chusŏnjogŭi aehwan tamgin myŏngmul 'sagwabaeo' [The Korean Chinese specialty: Apple pear and the embedded joys and sorrows]." *Minjog* 21, 126, 144–149.

Kim, Sung Ho. 1994. "Chunggung chosŏnjokkwa han'gukkwan'gye-sanghoraewangesŏ nat'anan ilbuŭi munjerŭl chungshimŭro [Relation between Chosŏnjok and South Korea: Centered on the problems emerged in the process of interactions]." *Hwanghae Review* 4, 301–311.

Kim, Wang-Bae. 2010. "Nostalgia, Anxiety and Hope: Migration and Ethnic Identity of Chosŏnjok in China." *Pacific Affairs* 83(1): 95–114.

Korea Immigration Office. 2018. "Ch'uripkuk oeguginjŏngch'aek t'onggyewŏlbo [Korea Immigration and Foreign Policy Monthly Report, 2018 March]." Accessed February 18, 2019. http://www.korea.kr/archive/expDocView.do?docId=37969.

Kwon, Jun Hee. 2015. "The Work of Waiting: Love and Money in Korean Chinese Transnational Migration." *Cultural Anthropology* 30(3): 477–500.

Kwon, Tai-Hwan. 1997. "International Migration of Koreans and the Korean Community in China." *Korean Journal of Population and Development* 26(1): 1–18.

Lankov, Andrei. 2007. "China's Korean Autonomous Prefecture and China-Korea Border Politics." *The Asia-Pacific Journal* 5(8): 1–8.

Lee, Jung Tae. 2017. "Chunggugŭi sosuminjokchŏngch'aekkwa chosŏnjong tiasŭp'oraŭi chŏngch'esŏng [China's minority policy and the identity of the Korean diaspora]." *Korean Journal of Political Science* 25(2): 81–106.

Lee, Junsik. 2005. "The Changing Nature of the Korean People's Perspective on National Issues, and Fellow Korean Living Abroad." *The Review of Korean Studies* 8(2): 111–140.

Lee, Seokwoo, and Hee Eun Lee. 2016. *The Making of International Law in Korea: From Colony to Asian Power.* Leiden & Boston: Brill.

Levitt, Peggy., and N. G. Schiller. 2004. "Conceptualizing Simultaneity: A Transnational Social Field Perspective on Society." *International Migration Review* 38(3): 1002–1039.

Li, Dongzhe. 2014. "Chaehan chosŏnjong 3serŭl wihan chiptansangdam p'ŭrogŭraem: tamunhwa kajŏng adongt'pch'ŏngsonyŏnŭl wihan nori chiptansangdam p'ŭrogŭraem [Group counseling for the third-generation Chinese-Koreans living in Korea: Group counseling for children youths in multicultural homes]." *Yonsei Journal of Counseling and Coaching* 2, 51–70.

National Institute of Korean Language. 2019. "Definitions of Kyop'o and Tongbo." Accessed February 19, 2019. http://stdweb2.korean.go.kr/search/View.jsp?idx=393901 and http://stdweb2.korean.go.kr/search/View.jsp.

Piao, Tingji. 2014. "Chaoxianzu shehui chongzu yu minzujiaoyufazhan duice [The reconstruction of Korean Chinese society and ethnic education development strategy]." In *Chaoxianzu yanjiu 2013*, edited by Zhongguo chaoxianminzu shixuehui [China Korean Minority History Association], 159–168. Beijing: Minzu chubanshe.

Piao, You. 2009. "Chaehan chunggung yuhaksaengŭi ijuhyŏnhwanggwa t'ŭksŏnge kwanhan yŏn'gur hanjok, chosŏnjong yuhaksaeng pigyorŭl chungshimŭro [A study on migration and characteristics of Chinese foreign students in China: Focusing on the comparison between Han and Korean Chinese students]." *Studies of Koreans Abroad* 19: 155–181.

———. 2011. "Han'gugŭi t'echaehanjosŏnjokt'e yŏn'gu hyŏnhwang [Trends of studies of "Korean Chinese in Korea" in Korean Academic]." *Studies of Koreans Abroad* 25: 207–228.

Piao, You, and Yong-Seon Kim. 2012. *"Uriga mannan han'guk: chaehan chosŏnjogŭi kusul-saengaesa* [The South Korea we met: the oral history of Korean Chinese in South Korea]." Seongnam: Book Korea.

Schubert, Amelia L., Youngmin Lee, and Hyun-Uk Lee. 2015. "Reproducing Hybridity in Korea: Conflicting Interpretations of Korean Culture by South Koreans and Ethnic Korean Chinese Marriage Migrants." *Asian Journal of Women's Studies* 21(3): 232–251.

Seol, D. H., and J. D. Skrentny. 2009. "Ethnic Return Migration and Hierarchical Nationhood." *Ethnicities* 9(2): 147–174.

Seoul Metropolitan Government. 2018. "Haengjŏng sunhwaŏ tŭng parŭn konggongŏnŏ sayong allim [Notice on administrative standard use of terminology]." Accessed November 23, 2018. https://opengov.seoul.go.kr/sanction/15035011?fileIdx=0#pdfview.

Shin, H. R. 2016. "Urinŭn modu chosŏnjogida: nyumoltŭnesŏ ch'ingdaokkaji, onŭlto ttŏnanŭn saramdŭl [We are all Chosŏnjok: from New Malden to Qingdao, and those who are also leaving today]." Seoul: Imagine.

———. 2017. "Joseonjok and Their Evolving Roles as Mediators in Transnational Enterprises in Qingdao, China." *Asian and Pacific Migration Journal* 26(1): 108–127.

The Sixth National Population Census of the People's Republic of China. 2010. Accessed February 18, 2019. http://www.stats.gov.cn/tjsj/pcsj/rkpc/6rp/indexch.htm.

Song, C. Z. 2009. "Brothers Only in Name: The Alienation and Identity Transformation of Korean Chinese Return Migration in South Korea." In *Diasporic Homecomings: Ethnic Return Migration in Comparative Perspective*, edited by T. Tsude, 281–304. Stanford, CA: Stanford University Press.

Xu, Mingzhe. 2012. "Chosŏnjong chŏngch'esŏng tamnon [Studies on Korean-Chinese identity]." *Journal of Chung-Ang Historical Studies* 36: 451–470.

Yi, Naeyong, and Injin Yoon. 2016. *Han'guginŭi chŏngch'esŏng: pyŏnhwawa yŏnsok, 2005–2015* [South Korean identity: changes and continuity, 2005–2015]. Seoul: The East Asian Institute.

Yoon, Injin. 2011. "From Ethnicity to Citizenship: The Change of Perspective on Overseas Koreans, North Koreans, and Foreign Immigrants." In *Han'gugin, urinŭn nuguin'ga? yŏronjosarŭl t'onghae pon han'guginŭi chŏngc"esŏng* [Understanding Korean identity through the lens of opinion survey], edited by Wontaek Kang and Naeyong Yi, 165–187. Seoul: The East Asian Institute.

*Chapter Eight*

# "Uh . . . Well, We're . . . Russians"

*Identity and Resistance to Ethnic Hierarchy Among*
Koryŏ Saram *Diasporic Returnees in South Korea*

## Changzoo Song

Ethnic return migrants are those who return-migrate to their ethnic home-lands after having lived for more than one or more generations overseas (Sheffer 2003; Tsuda 2003).[1] While descendants of migrants tend to live in their host countries, in the late 1980s and early 1990s, there emerged a substantial number of "ethnic return migrants" (or "diasporic return migrants") in many parts of the world. In Europe this happened in the late 1980s when the Cold War eased, which was followed by the collapse of the Soviet Union. Thousands of the German *Aussiedler* returned to Germany from the former communist countries of Eastern Europe. Ethnic Russians from the newly independent republics of Central Asia and Eastern Europe returned to Russia, and Jewish people from the former Soviet Union returned to Israel (cf. Münz & Ohliger 2003; Remnnik 1998). The economic downturns of Latin America in the 1980s also pushed many ethnic Spaniards, Italians, and Portuguese to return to their ancestral homelands in Europe.

Around the same time, similar ethnic return migrations took place in East Asia as well. Between the late 1980s and late 2000s, nearly 300,000 *Nikkeijin* Japanese migrated from Brazil and Peru to their ethnic homeland of Japan (Tsuda 2003; 2009). Almost at the same time, tens of thousands of ethnic Koreans from China (*Chosŏnjok*) migrated to South Korea. Though much smaller in scale, ethnic Koreans of the former Soviet Union (*Koryŏ saram* or former "Soviet Koreans") also migrated to South Korea from the late 1990s. These ethnic Koreans from China and the former Soviet Union (mostly from the post-Soviet Uzbekistan, Kazakhstan, and Russia) came to South Korea mainly as migrant workers.

Regarding the phenomenon of these ethnic return migrations, academic research has focused on the causes and processes of ethnic return migration, policies of receiving countries, and post-migration ethno-national identity changes (cf. Gal, Leoussi & Smith 2010; Tsuda 2010). Though some of the ethnic return migrations—e.g. the German, Russian, and Jewish cases—were caused by political reasons, most recent ethnic return migrations have been due to economic reasons (Tsuda 2009). The common push and pull factors behind most ethnic return migrations were due to the differences in employment opportunities and wage differentials between their host countries and ethnic homelands. The *Nikkeinjin*, *Chosŏnjok*, and *Koryŏ saram* ethnic return migrations are all attributable to the differences in employment opportunities and wages between the sending and receiving countries.

Those ethnic return migrants who migrate from less developed host countries in the Global South to more developed ethnic homeland countries of the Global North mostly tend to work as low-paid, unskilled, and manual laborers. In so doing, they tend to have negative experiences such as discrimination, alienation, and marginalization in their ethnic homelands. In addition, co-ethnic return migrants from different countries tend to form hierarchical relationships among themselves in their ethnic homelands. Those who are from wealthier countries normally take up higher paying and more prestigious jobs while those who are from poorer countries tend to be engaged in low-paid menial jobs. Such unequal and hierarchical relationships between individuals from wealthier countries and others from poor countries, and also between them and their co-ethnics in the host countries, tend to give those from poorer countries disappointment and a sense of ambiguity toward their ethnic homelands (cf. Tsuda 2009). Such negative experiences in their ancestral homelands also make the ethnic return migrants reflect on their ethnonational identities. In such circumstances, they often reject or weaken their given ethnic identities and, as a result, they may opt for new identities tied to their natal homelands rather than their ethnic homelands. This intriguing phenomenon of the newly emerged hierarchical relationship among co-ethnics and post-ethnic return migration identity changes call for more academic attention.

In this very context, this chapter examines their post-ethnic return migration ethno-national identity changes. In particular, it explores the former Soviet Korean (*Koryŏ saram*) ethnic return migrants in South Korea, with a focus on the hierarchical relationship between them and their co-ethnics in South Korea and those from other countries such as China.

## *KORYŎ SARAM*: A HISTORY

The Korean migration of the mid-nineteenth and early twentieth century to the Russian Far East (more accurately the Maritime Province of Russia) was similar to that of Korean migration to Manchuria of the time. Just like those Koreans who migrated to Manchuria, the Koreans who migrated to the Maritime Province of Russia before the twentieth century were mainly from North Hamgyeong Province in the northeastern tip of the Korean Peninsula. Russia gained the large territories of the "Maritime Province" from Qing China after the Treaty of Beijing in 1860. The first presence of Korean migrants in the Russian Far East was reported in the early 1860s, and by 1883, there were over 30,000 Korean settlers in the region. Impoverished Korean peasants were pushed by the economic and political turmoil of Joseon Korea, and the land across the Tumen River allured them. Sometimes the Russian authority tolerated Korean migrants and even encouraged them to settle in the region. Some other times, however, they dealt with Koreans with suspicion and hostility. By 1910, there were over 50,000 Koreans in the Russian Far East, and most of them were residing around the city of Vladivostok (Gelb 1995). As Japan formally colonized Korea in 1910, more Koreans fled to the Russian Far East and to Manchuria. The Russian Revolution (1917) and the establishment of the Soviet Union in 1922 attracted more Korean peasants to the region with the expectation that the new communist regime in Russia would be generous to them. By the end of the 1920s, there were nearly 200,000 Koreans in the Russian Far East, and their numbers grew continuously. Vladivostok and vicinities were a centre of Korean community, where Koreans had their own newspapers, schools, theatres, and a teachers' college.

However, in late 1937 these Koreans were suddenly forced to relocate to Kazakhstan and Uzbekistan by the Stalinist government. This was not to let the Koreans provoke Japan with their anti-Japanese activities, which might give Japan an excuse to invade the Soviet Union at the time when the Soviet Union was expecting a war with Germany in Europe (cf. Huttenbach 1993). There also was a strong need to develop Central Asia's agriculture in preparation for the imminent war with Hitler's Germany, and the forced relocation of the Korean farmers to Central Asia was potentially beneficial for such a need. In the process of the forced migration, however, the Soviet Koreans were branded as an "enemy nation" (who helped Imperial Japan) and were stripped of their rights as citizens of the Soviet Union. Such harsh treatment of Koreans in the Soviet Union distinguishes them from other Korean migrants in China, Japan, and the U.S. (Min 1992).

After the forced relocation, *Koryŏ saram* had to rebuild their lives anew in the wild fields and semi-deserts of southern Kazakhstan and Uzbekistan. Not having freedom to move or travel to other areas or cities, they had to concentrate only on agricultural activities. They proved their agricultural acumen quickly, and Korean collective farms in Central Asia became rather successful and wealthy. This made *Koryŏ saram* a "model minority" within the Soviet Union, and they regained their rights as citizens of the Soviet Union after Stalin's death in 1953. Since then, many Soviet Koreans moved to big cities throughout the Soviet Union, while others stayed in local collective farms in Central Asia. Those who migrated to urban areas mostly became professionals, while many of those who stayed in the agricultural sector launched entrepreneurial agricultural practices of market gardening. The latter would move around southern Russia and Ukraine in search of a suitable climate and fertile lands for their commercial agricultural business (Kim & Kim 2016; Baek 2001; Brooks 1988). They would grow cash crops such as onions and watermelons in southern Russia, Ukraine, and Uzbekistan and sell them in the markets of large cities such as Moscow and Leningrad. Many of them made wealth through such agricultural business, and in the 1970s an increasing number of *Koryŏ saram* were engaged in such activities.[2]

Then, new serious challenges came when the Soviet Union collapsed at the end of 1991. As the new republics gained independence, there rose local ethnic nationalisms, which made the life of non-locals such as *Koryŏ saram* extremely difficult (Kim 2003). Particularly in Uzbekistan, those who did not speak the vernacular language were not allowed to keep their professional positions, which resulted in the loss of jobs for many *Koryŏ saram* in the new republic. Many of them moved to the private business sector including market gardening. As Russians in Central Asia returned to Russia, many *Koryŏ saram* also chose to "return" to their old homeland in the Russian Far East in the hope that they would rebuild their new life near to their ancestral homeland of Korea.

## DIASPORIC RETURN OF *KORYŎ SARAM*

During the Cold War, the Soviet Union and the People's Republic of China did not recognize South Korea as a legitimate country, and there were no contacts between *Koryŏ saram* in the former Soviet Union and South Koreans. There was no contact between *Koryŏ saram* in the Soviet Union and *Chosŏnjok* in the People's Republic of China before the 1990s. For this reason *Koryŏ saram* did not have much information and knowledge of Korea even though they originated in the northeastern part of the Korean peninsula which is North Korea today. It was only after the late 1980s that *Koryŏ saram* came to have more realistic information on South Korea. In particular, the 1988 Summer Olympic Games held in Seoul provided momentum, with both *Chosŏnjok* and *Koryŏ saram* reviving a strong sense of connection to South Korea as their ethnic homeland. As they learned more about South

Korea from the media during the 1988 Olympic Games, both the ethnic Koreans in China and the former Soviet Union developed strong ethnic affinities toward South Korea and their co-ethnics there. In particular, due to their precarious status in Central Asia where ethnic nationalisms rose after the collapse of the Soviet Union in 1991, *Koryŏ saram* quickly nurtured a more favorable opinion towards South Korea and came to consider South Korea as a part of their ethnic homeland (Myong & Nurzhanov 2012). While *Chosŏnjok* started to arrive in South Korea from the late 1980s, and their number grew rapidly after the establishment of diplomatic relationship between PRC and South Korea in 1992, *Koryŏ saram* ethnic return migration happened at the end of the 1990s. Through the 2000s the number of *Koryŏ saram* migrants in South Korea grew steadily, and today there are over 40,000 of them living in South Korea.

The rising sense of ethnic affinities to ethnic homeland was not only among the *Chosŏnjok* and *Koryŏ saram* in the late 1980s and early 1990s. In fact, a similar sense of ethnic sentiment rose among South Koreans toward their long-lost co-ethnics from China and the former Soviet Union, and both *Chosŏnjok* and *Koryŏ saram* were generally welcomed by South Koreans in the early 1990s. The South Korean government, however, did not recognize any special status of Korean diasporic returnees until 1999 when it legislated the Act on the Immigration and Legal Status of Overseas Koreans (or commonly called the Overseas Koreans Act) (cf. Seol & Skrentny 2009; Park & Chang 2005). This law bestows special status to ethnic Koreans to visit, stay, work, and conduct business in their ethnic homeland. Nevertheless, *Chosŏnjok* and *Koryŏ saram* were excluded from the special treatments offered by this law. This was due to both international and domestic reasons. First of all, there were protests from China and the former Soviet Union republics, which worried that South Korea might incorporate their citizens into its influence. The South Korean Ministry of Labor also supported this exclusion due to possible disruptions in the country's labor market if too many of them migrated to the country. Only after 2004, when the law was revised, did *Chosŏnjok* and *Koryŏ saram* come to be included in the law. Since then the number of ethnic return migrants from these groups rapidly increased. In 2007, with the new "Visitor Employment Scheme" policy, entry visas and employment for *Chosŏnjok* and *Koryŏ saram* in South Korea became much easier.

These policy changes in South Korea, together with the grim situation in post-Soviet Central Asia and Russia, exhorted *Koryŏ saram* to seek for opportunities in South Korea. However, the process of migrating to South Korea did not happen quickly. As stated above, in the early 1990s Soviet Koreans in Central Asia became anxious as they witnessed the rise of local nationalisms and the exoduses of Russians, Germans, and Poles, who were returning to their ethnic homelands. This made *Koryŏ saram* wish to leave if they had a country to "return" to, but they did not have one, and migration to South Korea did not happen until the late 1990s. First of all, the distance between Central Asian republics and South Korea is considerable and until later the South Korean government did not have any plan to allow them to migrate to the country except in some exceptional cases (cf. Seol & Skrentny 2009). In the early 1990s, therefore, many *Koryŏ saram* left Central Asia and migrated to large cities in Russia and to the Russian Far East. In fact, the latter was considered their "homeland" as their ancestors used to live there before the forced relocation to Central Asia in 1937. There were expectations that the Russian Far East could promise them a better future once countries like Japan and South Korea started to invest in the region. In fact, the South Korean government launched a few plans to develop agriculture and fisheries industries in the region for the food security of the country. These further encouraged *Koryŏ saram* to migrate to the Russian Far East in the 1990s even though most of these plans were abandoned later.

By the late 1990s, a small number of *Koryŏ saram* from Central Asia and the Russian Far East entered South Korea. They initially arrived in South Korea as tourists, trainees, or students, and many of them stayed there as undocumented migrant workers. Once they secured legal visa status, they would bring their family and relatives to join them. There were also a substantial number of *Koryŏ saram* women who came as spouses of South Korean men, and in 2016 there were about 2,000 Uzbek Korean brides living in South Korea. There were also ethnic Koreans from Sakhalin as well.[3]

The life of ethnic return migrants from the poorer Global South to their ethnic homeland in the Global North was not easy anywhere (Tsuda 2009). They might have belonged to a higher socio-economic status in their natal homelands, but as migrant workers they normally tend to do menial work in their ethnic homelands. *Koryŏ saram* from the former Soviet Union were not an exception in this regard, and they worked mostly in the construction sector or took other manual jobs. In addition, as most *Koryŏ saram* returnees do not speak Korean well, unlike most of their co-ethnics from China, their employment status was even lower. They normally would take temporary *arŭbait'ŭ* work (miscellaneous unskilled work of handy men) as migrant workers in South Korea. They are often discriminated by their co-ethnics in their ethnic homeland, and they also experience hierarchical relationships between themselves and their co-ethnics from other countries.

## HIERARCHY AMONG CO-ETHNICS IN ETHNIC HOMELAND

*Koryŏ saram* migrant workers are less known to the general public of South Korea and the latter tend to be surprised when they hear that they are "Koreans" from Russia or Uzbekistan. As most young *Koryŏ saram* do not speak

Korean, and are not well versed in Korean customs, they tend to face more problems in daily life in South Korea and go through harsher lives than those of other diasporic returnees. *Koryŏ saram* are also not known much to *Chosŏnjok* from China even though many of their ancestors had come from the same region of North Hamgyeong Province in Korea in the late nineteenth century. As stated above, these two groups of ethnic Koreans of the former Soviet Union and China did not have contact between themselves until they encountered each other in South Korea after their ethnic return migration. Due to their lower Korean language capacities, *Koryŏ saram* workers are normally employed for lower-paid manual work in their ethnic homeland. Among all foreign workers in South Korea, *Chosŏnjok* workers tend to have jobs that require communication and thus get higher wages. In addition, the number of *Chosŏnjok* returnees is much larger in size (over 500,000) than *Koryŏ saram* (whose number is only about 40,000), and the former are better organized than the latter. This gives more political power to *Chosŏnjok* in South Korea in comparison with their co-ethnics from the former Soviet Union.

Thus, there emerges a hierarchical relationship among the three Korean co-ethnic groups: South Koreans at the top, then *Chosŏnjok* in the middle, and *Koryŏ saram* at the bottom. For *Koryŏ saram*, such a hierarchical relationship among co-ethnics is a source of frustration and resentment. In particular, *Koryŏ saram* returnees react sensitively against any discriminatory treatment and remarks towards them. My *Koryŏ saram* informants frequently expressed their discontentment and anger toward their South Korean bosses, who disregard *Koryŏ saram* as if they were inferiors or "unqualified Koreans." In particular, *Koryŏ saram* detest the way that South Koreans look down up on them by using non-honorific language to them. They are also very upset whenever their South Korean co-ethnics "insensibly" question why *Koryŏ saram*, as "Koreans," do not speak Korean. Slova, who is in his late thirties and from Tashkent, has been working as an unskilled handyman in various industrial sites near Seoul for the last seven years, testifies:

> Sometimes [South] Koreans ask me why I don't speak Korean even though I'm a "Korean." Such a question always makes me extremely frustrated. I simply don't know what to reply to such questions. I just tell them that I'm different from them [South Koreans]. At work, South Koreans generally use *banmal* (non-honorific language) to me when they order me to do something. That's outrageous and I'm very angry at that. Therefore, I sometimes pretend as if I don't understand them.[4]

Through such incidents *Koryŏ saram* returnees realize that there is a hierarchical relationship among co-ethnics in South Korea and they are below both South Koreans and *Chosŏnjok*. They feel that is totally unfair and they are frustrated. In particular, *Koryŏ saram* workers tend to disapprove of the

behavior of their co-ethnics from China. Volyodza, a handyman in his forties, is from Khabarovsk of the Russian Far East and he depicts *Chosŏnjok*
workers whom he met at construction sites:

> Chosŏnjok? They only pursue money. In the work place those guys don't work
> hard. They make us do all the hard work while they themselves only pretend to
> work. But, it is they who get paid more than us!

In the face of such unjust realities, *Koryŏ saram* tend to culturally distinguish
themselves from their co-ethnics of South Korea and China. Most of them
say that South Koreans are generally "rude" and they not only frequently use
non-honorific language to *Koryŏ saram* regardless of the latter's age, but
they also frequently use swear words at work. Another *Koryŏ saram* male
worker from Uzbekistan (in his late forties) testifies how South Korean
supervisors and bosses habitually use swear words to their workers:

> South Korean supervisors at construction sites use non-honorific language to
> us regardless of our age or background. This bothers me very much. . . . They
> also frequently say *ssibal* [fucking], and that's really unthinkable in Russian
> culture. Such swearing words are extremely humiliating and offensive to us.

Facing such disrespect and discrimination from their co-ethnics, *Koryŏ saram* tend to reaffirm their judgement that South Koreans are "not as civilized
as Russians." Inga, a female *Koryŏ saram* in her early thirties and from
Tashkent, states:

> [South] Koreans speak loudly in public places, and they're generally rude.
> They don't respect women as Russians do, and this is an indicator of the level
> of South Korean culture. [5]

In such a manner, *Koryŏ saram* returnees tend to view both South Koreans
and *Chosŏnjok* as "uncivilized," and they do not accept the imposed hierarchical relationship among the Korean co-ethnics of South Koreans,
*Chosŏnjok* and *Koryŏ saram*. Instead of accepting or internalizing such hierarchical relationships, *Koryŏ saram* returnees tend to question their identity
as "Koreans."

## POST-ETHNIC RETURN MIGRATION IDENTITY ISSUES
## OF *KORYŎ SARAM*

As the number of *Chosŏnjok* ethnic return migrants grew, the initially welcoming attitude among South Koreans toward their co-ethnics from China
dissipated and there rose more critical opinions about them. At the same
time, *Chosŏnjok* returnees also got disillusioned by the harsh realities of

working as manual laborers in South Korea as well as by the discriminatory treatment from their South Korean co-ethnics. Mostly as workers in the so-called 3D sector, *Chosŏnjok* are underprivileged, marginalized, and discriminated against in their ancestral homeland (Song 2009). The situation is even worse for *Koryŏ saram* returnees, who do not speak Korean. Like other ethnic return migrants from the Global South elsewhere, after having experienced the harsh realities of life as menial workers in their ethnic homeland, both *Chosŏnjok* and *Koryŏ saram* migrant workers tend to reflect their being "Koreans." This is particularly true for the *Koryŏ saram* diasporic returnees who face double discrimination both from their co-ethnics of South Korea as well as those of China.

As stated above, ethnic return migrations raise many intriguing questions and issues, and one of the most prominent issues is the post-ethnic return migration identity changes. What determines the identity transformation experiences of *Koryŏ saram* (and also *Chosŏnjok*) diasporic returnees are four-fold: (1) their involvement in the low-paid and undesirable jobs that South Koreans normally shun; (2) the discriminatory treatment and alienation they face in their ethnic homeland; (3) the hierarchical relationship among diasporic returnees regardless of their sharing the same ethnicity; and (4) finally, the status of their natal homeland in global political economic community (cf. Tsuda 2009).

While engaged in manual labor in South Korea, *Koryŏ saram* find themselves underprivileged and their living conditions grim. This makes them feel that their life in their ethnic homeland was relatively degraded in comparison to their pre-migration life. This, in turn, makes them nostalgic about the easier life back in their natal homelands. The more difficult challenges for these returnees in South Korea, however, are the prejudice and discrimination they experience from their South Korean co-ethnics. They feel particularly frustrated when South Koreans treat them differently from other overseas Koreans who are from wealthy countries such as the U.S., Western Europe, and Japan (Tsuda 2009; Song 2009; Strother 2012) and even China (Song 2019).

As mentioned earlier, South Korean public opinion on *Chosŏnjok* changed in the early 2000s when their number grew. South Korean employers frequently complained that *Chosŏnjok* workers had "weak work ethic" and are "not trustworthy" (Song 2009). *Chosŏnjok* were also criticized for being overly "Sinicized" not only in their attitude but also in their national orientation. *Chosŏnjok*, however, strongly disagree with such comments and they claim that it is South Koreans that are too "westernized" especially in their daily language use, which includes too many English words. In fact, many *Chosŏnjok* returnees state that for them one of the most difficult things in South Korea is the numerous foreign words that South Koreans use in daily life but they do not comprehend (Song 2009). The experiences of alienation and discrimination in their ethnic homeland, however, not only make *Chosŏnjok* returnees critical about South Korea and its people, but also drive them to reflect on their being "Koreans." This and other cases reveal how the ethnic return migration experiences of *Chosŏnjok* in South Korea actually reinforce their "Chinese" identity while weakening their emotional ties with South Koreans in their ethnic homeland (Song 2009). This is similar for *Koryŏ saram* ethnic return migrants even though they have a somewhat different experience from their co-ethnics from China.

Though they always thought of themselves as "Koreans" (and Russians call them *Koreitsyi*, which means Koreans) in the former Soviet Union, *Koryŏ saram* were very much "Sovietized" (or "Russified"). This is visible in their language and food culture. Their daily language is Russian, and even though they live in Central Asia they normally do not speak the local languages such as Uzbek or Kazakh.[6] Meanwhile, their culinary culture is a mixture of Korean, Russian, and Central Asian (Song 2016). Even in the cases when they eat "Korean" cuisines, they are not really "Korean" from the perspective of South Koreans. One example is "Korean carrot" salad (*Koreisky markov*, as it is called in Russian, which means "Korean carrot"). Such a food (figure 8.1) is not known to South Koreans, but it is widely spread throughout the former Soviet Union. Another example is seaweed salad, which is called *morskaya kapusta salat* in Russian, literally meaning "marine cabbage salad" (figure 8.2). This kelp salad is consumed as a salad in the former Soviet Union, but such a food is not known among South Koreans or *Chosŏnjok*. These culinary examples show how the two Korean diasporic groups of *Chosŏnjok* and *Koryŏ saram*, whose ancestors originally came from the same region of the northeastern province of the Korean Peninsula, have gone through remarkable transformations in their cultural practices. Such cultural distinctions gave *Koryŏ saram* returnees an identity that is distinguished from those of *Chosŏnjok* and South Koreans.

While criticizing South Koreans and their culture as "less civilized" than that of Russians, *Koryŏ saram* tend to identify themselves with the culturally superior "Russians." When asked about their identity, many of them reply that they are more like "Russians" in their heart and culture. Vitalyi (in his early seventies) from Tashkent states:

> We are heavily Russified. If one thinks in a certain language, this means that the person belongs to the ethnic/national group of that language. I do think and dream in Russian, and this means that I'm more of a Russian than a Korean. . . . Though I have the idea that I'm a Korean and Korea is my homeland, that's only in my head, and my heart and feelings are very much Russian.

Most of my respondents share exactly the same feelings as Vitalyi. Regardless of their being "Korean" and being born in Uzbekistan (and not in Rus-

**Figure 8.1.** *Koreisky markov* ("Korean carrot").

**Figure 8.2.** *Morskaya kapusta salat* (kelp salad).

sia), most *Koryŏ saram* returnees tend to feel they are Russians. Vitalyi explains again:

Do I feel I'm an Uzbek? Not really. Though I was born there in 1941 and lived there throughout my life, Uzbekistan is not my fatherland (*rodina*).[7] . . . These days, anyway, in Uzbekistan my children cannot be successful there as they aren't Uzbeks. However, things are different in Russia. Russia is a big country and for that reason there are less discrimination and more opportunities.

The description "Russia is a big country" was shared by many of my *Koryŏ saram* interviewees. They all seem to share the belief that Russia, as a multi-cultural country with abundant natural resources, and also as a country of "European" civilization that is "higher" than that of Korea (or China), is a good country for them to live. This is clear from what Slova from Tashkent (in his thirties) states:

My face is Korean, but my heart is Russian. I don't feel any commonality with Koreans in South Korea at all. They're total foreigners to me and I'm here only to work. My plan is to settle in Yekaterinburg in Russia once I save some money here. . . . . I'll be successful in Russia. Russia has abundant natural resources. But, Russians do not work hard. We *Koryŏ saram*, however, work hard. That's why we can be successful there.

While *Chosŏnjok* ethnic return migrants, after the hard realities of migration experience in South Korea, tend to feel they are more "Chinese" than "Korean," *Koryŏ saram* from Uzbekistan (or elsewhere in Central Asia) tend to feel that they are "Russians."

## CONCLUSION

As seen above, *Koryŏ saram* ethnic or diasporic return migrants arrived in South Korea after the late 1990s in search of work opportunity in their ethnic homeland. Nevertheless, these "homecomings" of diasporic groups were not a simple or smooth process. Though the *Koryŏ saram* returnees from the former Soviet Union expected a warm ethnic welcome in their ancestral homeland (just as their *Chosŏnjok* co-ethnics did), the realities of their ethnic return migrations betrayed their expectation. They were engaged only in low-paying manual work that local South Koreans tend to avoid, which resulted in their economic marginalization particularly because they went from less developed natal homeland countries to a more developed ethnic homeland. They also have been culturally discriminated and socially alienated by their South Korean co-ethnics. In addition, the people and government of South Korea treat them differently from their co-ethnics who are from wealthy and developed countries, which creates a hierarchy among co-ethnics depending on their geographical origin. Interestingly, however, there also rose a hier-archical relationship between *Chosŏnjok* and *Koryŏ saram* as well. This is due to the fact that *Chosŏnjok* can speak Korean while *Koryŏ saram* mostly do not speak the language, which resulted in different level of employment opportunities and wages between them.

Such negative experiences in their ethnic homeland, South Korea, make *Koryŏ saram* returnees reflect upon the meanings of their being members of the ethnic and national community of Korea. This reshapes their ethnic and national identity. As many *Chosŏnjok* returnees came to strengthen their being "Chinese" after they return migrated to South Korea (Song 2009), *Koryŏ saram* returnees from the former Soviet Union also go through the post-ethnic return migration identity change. First of all, as Koryŏ *saram* ethnic return migrants lost their language and tradition, from the beginning they do not feel they are as strongly "Koreans" as did their co-ethnics from China. Facing the discrimination from their South Korean co-ethnics and also an unfair ethnic hierarchy among the Korean co-ethnics in South Korea, *Koryŏ saram* feel bitter toward both their Chinese co-ethnics and South Koreans. They see South Koreans and their society as culturally "uncivilized" and inferior to Russia, with which they tend to identify themselves. Therefore, they say they are "Russians" even though they were not born in Russia or have never been there. This is because their natal homeland, Uzbekistan, does not give an empowering feeling to them as Russia does. In any case, their mother tongue is Russian and their culinary culture is also heavily "Russian." Russia is also a big country with "liberal" and multicultural values and also with abundant natural resources. As such, the post-ethnic return migration identity changes of *Koryŏ saram* diasporic return migrants in South Korea presents a very important and interesting case in the study of migration and identity.[8]

## NOTES

1. A part of the Chosŏnjok identity in this chapter was quoted and rephrased from from my own research included in Takeyuki Gaku Tsuda & Changzoo Song (eds.), 2018, *Diasporic Returns to the Ethnic Homeland: The Korean Diaspora in Comparative Perspective*, with permission of the publisher, Palgrave Macmillan.
2. Truck farming (or market gardening) is large-scale commercial farming, which was a uniquely Soviet Korean business during the Soviet era. They would organize agricultural work groups among themselves and grow cash crops such as onion, rice, or watermelon on the land which they rented out from collective farms. They would sell those products in big cities such as Moscow and Leningrad. This "capitalist" agribusiness was not legal in the Soviet Union, but many Soviet Koreans were involved in this.
3. Ethnic Koreans from Sakhalin are different from *Koryŏ saram* in terms of their migration history, geographical origin, and also legal status. They were given the right to return due to historical reasons.
4. All names of interviewees in this chapter are pseudonyms.
5. Such a comment was interesting as most Korean Chinese normally state that South Koreans are more "knowledgeable and smart" and "streets are cleaner here than in China," but "their hearts are cold" (a female *Chosŏnjok* restaurant-helper in her fifties).
6. This is the reason why they could not keep their professional positions in the nationalizing new republics in Central Asia, and many of them chose to migrate to Russia.

7. *Rodina* means "homeland" or "motherland" in Russian.

8. This work was supported by the Core University Program for Korean Studies through the Ministry of Education of the Republic of the Korea and Korean Studies Promotion Service of the Academy of Korean Studies (AKS-2017-OLU-2250001).

## REFERENCES

Back, Thae Hyeon. 2001. "Kobondzhil' koreitsev Srednei Azii i Kazakhstana" [*Gobonjil* of Koreans in Central Asia and Kazakhstan] PhD dissertation, Bishkek University.

Brooks, Karen. 1988. "Soviet Union: The Anomaly of Private-cum-Socialist Agriculture: Discussion." *American Journal of Agricultural Economics* 70(2): 437–438.

Gal, Allon, Athena S. Leoussi, and Anthony D. Smith, eds. 2010. *The Call of the Homeland: Diaspora Nationalisms, Past and Present*. Boston: Brill.

Gelb, Michael. 1995. "An Early Soviet Ethnic Deportation: The Far Eastern Koreans." *The Russian Review* 54(3): 389–412.

Huttenbach, Henry R. 1993. "The Soviet Koreans: Products of Russo-Japanese Imperial Rivalry" *Central Asian Survey* 12(1): 59–69. DOI: 10.1080/02634939308400800.

Kim, German. 2003. "*Koryo Saram*, or Koreans of the Former Soviet Union: In the Past and Present" *Amerasia Journal* 29(3): 23–29.

Kim, German & Young Jin Kim. 2016. "Gobonji as a Phenomenon of Ethnic Entrepreneurship among the Koryo Saram in the Soviet Economy." *Korea Journal* 56(4): 92–119.

Min, Pyong Gap. 1992. "A Comparison of the Korean Minorities in China and Japan." *International Migration Review* 26(1): 4–21.

Münz, R. & Ohliger, R. eds. 2003. *Diasporas and Ethnic Migrants: Germany, Israel, and Post-Soviet Successor States in Comparative Perspective*. London: Frank Cass.

Myong, Soon-ok, and B.G. Nurzhanov. 2012. "Identity Politics of Former Soviet Korean: One of the Most Prominent Heritages of the 1988 Seoul Olympics." *International Scholarly and Scientific Research & Innovation* 6(6): 1369–1376.

Park, Jung-Sun, and Paul Y. Chang. 2005. "Contention in the Construction of a Global Korean Community: The Case of the Overseas Korean Act." *Journal of Korean Studies* 10: 1–27.

Remnnick, L.I. 1998. "Identity Quest among Russian Jews of the 1990s: Before and After Emigration." In *Jewish Survival: The Identity Problems at the Close of the Twentieth Century*, edited by Krausz, E. and G. Tulea, 241–258. New Brunswick, NJ: Transaction Publishers.

Seol, Dong-Hoon, and John Skrentny. 2009. "Ethnic Return Migration and Hierarchical Nationhood." *Ethnicities* 9(2) : 147–174.

Sheffer, Gabriel. 2003. "From Diasporas to Migrants, from Migrants to Diasporas." In *Diasporas and Ethnic Migrants: Germany, Israel, and Post-Soviet Successor States in Comparative Perspective*, edited by Rainer Münz and Rainer Ohliger, 21–55. London: Frank Cass.

Song, Changzoo. 2009. "Brothers Only in Name: the Alienation of Korean Chinese Return Migrants in South Korea." In *Diasporic Homecomings: Ethnic Return Migration in Comparative Perspective*, edited by Takeyuki Tsuda, 281–304. Stanford, CA: Stanford University Press.

———. 2014. "Engaging the Diaspora in an Era of Transnationalism." *IZA World of Labor*. doi:10.15185/izawol.64.

———. 2016. "Kimchi, Seaweed and Seasoned Carrot in the Soviet Culinary Culture: The Spread of Korean Food in the Soviet Union and Korean Diaspora." *Journal of Ethnic Foods* 3(1): 78-84. DOI: 10.1016/j.jef.2016.01.007.

———. 2019. "Chosŏnjok and Koryŏ Saram Ethnic Return Migrants in South Korea: Hierarchy Among Co-ethnics and Ethnonational Identity." In *The Korean Diaspora in Comparative Perspective*, edited by Takeyuki Tsuda and Changzoo Song, 57–77. London: Palgrave Macmillan.

Strother, Jason. 2012. "Ethnic Koreans from China Hit by Seoul Visa Policy." *Voice of America News*. https://www.voanews.com/a/ethnic-koreans-china-seoul-visa-policy/940039.html. Date accessed May 23, 2016.

Tsuda, T. Gaku. 2003. *Strangers in the Ethnic Homeland: Japanese Brazilian Return Migration in Transnational Perspective*. New York: Columbia University Press.

———. 2009. *Diasporic Homecomings: Ethnic Return Migration in Comparative Perspective*. Stanford, CA: Stanford University Press.

———. 2010. "Ethnic Return Migration and the Nation-State: Encouraging the Diaspora to Return 'Home.'" *Nations and Nationalism* 16(4): 616–636.

*Part IV*

# Transnational Mobility from a Historical Perspective

*Chapter Nine*

# Korean Immigration to the United States, 1903–1905

*A New Look at Japanese Imperialism*

## Wayne Patterson

Scholarly studies on the causes of the Japanese takeover of Korea have generated considerable academic debate during the past half century.[1] In particular, three books stand out. The first was Hilary Conroy's book *The Japanese Seizure of Korea, 1868–1910: A Study of Realism and Idealism in International Relations*, published in 1960 by the University of Pennsylvania Press. Using primarily Japanese sources, that study argued that Japan did not have a long-term plan to take over Korea. This book was followed seven years later by C. I. Eugene Kim and Han-Kyo Kim's book *Korea and the Politics of Imperialism, 1876–1910*, published by the University of California Press in 1967. That study argued that Korea's lack of self-reliance allowed it to become a pawn of the major powers surrounding the peninsula. Finally, in 1995 came Peter Duus' book *The Abacus and the Sword: The Japanese Penetration of Korea, 1895–1910*, also published by the University of California Press. Duus argued that annexation occurred because Japan had been unsuccessful in finding suitable collaborators among the Korean elite to assist in its modernization project for Korea. Although all three books used different sources and focused on different aspects of the takeover process, all three had in common the thesis that security concerns were at the center of the decision of the Japanese government to take over Korea, first as a protectorate in 1905 and finally as a colony through annexation in 1910. This chapter will not argue against the central motif of security in explaining the takeover. Rather, it will argue that an additional and heretofore unexplored issue arose late in the process and, while not displacing security as the primary motivation, provides not only an additional explanation for why the takeover occurred (ends) but also an additional explanation for how Japan was able to take over Korea so easily (means). That issue was the overseas emigration of Koreans at the end of the Chosŏn dynasty.[2]

The sugar planters in Hawaii started bringing in Koreans in 1903 as strikebreakers against the majority Japanese because the planters could no longer use Chinese now that Hawaii had become a U.S. territory and had to abide by the 1882 Chinese Exclusion Act. The American minister in Seoul, Horace Allen, in his version of dollar diplomacy, helped the planters obtain Koreans in the hope that increased American business interests might spill over to increased American political interest, which might help keep Korea out of the clutches of Japan. And the Korean emperor Kojong approved of Koreans going to the United States because it served as yet another link with a seemingly benevolent country. Accordingly, Kojong issued an imperial edict in 1902 creating a department of emigration (Yuminwŏn) charged with issuing passports and adopting rules and regulations to protect emigrants (Harrington 1944, 133; Hwangsŏng sinmun 1902; Allen 1902, section, titled "Enclosure with Allen," to Secretary of State John Hay).

Although it turned out that the Koreans who were arriving in Hawaii, being largely city folk, were not good agricultural laborers, they were good enough to serve as strikebreakers against the Japanese. Consequently, wages remained low for the sugar plantation workers at about 75 cents per day, since all the strikes by Japanese were broken by the Koreans. But now that Hawaii was part of the United States, Japanese could freely move from Hawaii to California, where the wages were nearly twice as high at $1.50 a day. Soon, an average of one thousand Japanese a month were crossing over to San Francisco from Hawaii. As more and more Japanese appeared in California, the same racist attitudes that had manifested themselves twenty years earlier against the Chinese now began anew against the Japanese. Editorials in newspapers published by William Randoph Hearst, speeches by San Francisco mayor James Phelan, broadsides from labor organizations, and the formation of the Asiatic Exclusion League were all indicators of growing anti-Japanese sentiment, triggered by this massive influx from Hawaii. The Japanese government, particularly Consul-General Saitō Miki in Honolulu, tried to stem the tide by having the Japanese government issue passports with the words "To Hawaii Only," by printing circulars "forbidding" Japanese to go to the west coast, and by asking the planters to raise the wages—all to no avail. Japanese continued their exodus from Hawaii to California, and anti-Japanese agitation in California continued to increase. Meanwhile, Korean immigration to Hawaii produced no shortage of opponents, both Japanese and Korean (Daniels 1962, 22 and 27; Gaimushō 1973, 119; see also Ibid., 317f, section titled Saitō Miki to Chinda Sutemi, April 22, 1905).

Japanese imingaisha agents who recruited Japanese for work in Hawaii resented the fact that the arrival of Koreans meant that fewer Japanese were needed, cutting into their profits. Three of them wrote a letter to Foreign Minister Komura Jutarō complaining that Korean strikebreakers were depressing the wages of Japanese in Hawaii, propelling them to the west coast and the higher wages there. But Japan was in the middle of the war against Russia, and Komura made no reply. However, the foreign minister, a Harvard Law graduate, was now aware, as a result of this letter, of the economic forces propelling the Japanese to move from Hawaii to California (Gaimushō 1905a, section titled Morioka Makoto, Hyūga Terutake, and Tomiochi Chūtarō to Komura Jutarō, February 5, 1905).

A second opponent was the head of the Korean Imperial Household Department (Kungnaebu), Yi Yong-ik, who asserted that Koreans in Hawaii were treated like slaves. Yi persuaded the malleable Kojong to cancel his imperial edict of the previous year while Horace Allen was on home leave, effectively legislating out of existence the Department of Emigration (Yuminwŏn) and its rules and regulations. Although Koreans still continued to leave for Hawaii, now with passports issued by the Korean Foreign Office (Oebu), there were no longer any rules and regulations to protect them. Moreover, there was no Korean diplomat in Hawaii to tend to the needs of the growing number of Koreans there, the nearest one being in Washington, DC, despite the fact that Horace Allen had urged the Korean government to appoint a consul to Hawaii to refute Yi's claims of slave-like treatment (*Cheguk sinmun* 1903; Allen 1902, section "Allen to J. Sloat Fassett," May 17, 1903).

A third opponent of Korean immigration to Hawaii was the Japanese minister to Korea, Hayashi Gonsuke, who, like Horace Allen, saw franchises or concessions as a means to strengthen political interest. Hayashi was on the lookout for a way to terminate this American-sponsored project to make it easier in the long run for Japan to take over Korea. Despite these formidable opponents, Koreans continued to go to Hawaii, Japanese continued to go to California from Hawaii, and the resentment of Californians toward Japanese continued to increase (*Hwangsŏng sinmun* 1903; Cooke 1903, section Bishop to Cooke, March 19).

Then, in the spring of 1905, events in California took an ominous turn for Japan when the Japanese consul in San Francisco cabled Foreign Minister Komura that the California Assembly had just passed a resolution calling on Washington to enact a Japanese exclusion act. By this time, Japan had prevailed over Russia, and Foreign Minister Komura could now focus on this new crisis. Komura could not abide the prospect of a Japanese exclusion act, passage of which would demote Japan to the lowly rank occupied by China, that "sick man of Asia," and serve to negate all the attributes of great power status that Japan had secured: defeating two major powers (China and Russia) in war, amassing the third largest navy in the world, cementing an alliance with Britain, and enacting Asia's only constitution. With the nation's prestige at stake on a global scale, Komura, thanks to the letter from the imingaisha recruiters revealing that it was Koreans who were driving the Japanese from Hawaii to California and thus driving anti-Japanese sentiment there, determined that Korean immigration had to be stopped. If Koreans were prevented from leaving Korea, a salutory series of events would ensue: Japanese in Hawaii would win their strikes; their wages would go up; the wage disparity between Hawaii and California would shrink; fewer Japanese would move to California; anti-Japanese sentiment in California would subside; and, in the end, a Japanese exclusion act would no longer be needed, and Japan could retain its status as a major power, its prestige intact. Ironically, Japan had determined to exclude Koreans from the United States so its own nationals would not be excluded (Gaimushō 1905a, section "Komura to Saitō," March 9; Gaimushō 1905b, section "Ueno to Komura," March 3).

But stopping Koreans from going to Hawaii was easier said than done, since Korea was still a sovereign nation that could send its people anywhere they would be accepted. Of course, Japan possessed enough power in Korea that it could have simply stopped Koreans by fiat from departing. There were, after all, thousands of Japanese troops on the peninsula at the end of the war against Russia, and during that war the Japanese government had forced the Korean government to accept Japanese-nominated advisers into several key ministries. But Japan had embarked on a campaign to assure the United States that it had only humanitarian concern for the Korean people and that it would act benevolently in the event that Japan took over Korea. If Japan was unilaterally to prevent Koreans from going abroad without any justification, that might invite embarrassing questions from the United States about the claim that Japan had only the best interests of the Koreans at heart.[3]

As Komura searched for a way to stop Koreans from going abroad without dismantling Japan's humanitarian façade and appearing like a bully to the United States, his subordinate in Seoul, Hayashi Gonsuke, acting on his own, used a fatal misstep by the Korean government to effect a temporary prohibition on emigration. In April 1905, the Korean government apparently did not notice that one thousand Koreans had just departed for Mexico. Hayashi immediately sprang into action, going to Korean foreign minister Yi Ha-yŏng's office to point out that: (1) the Koreans who had just departed had no passports to Mexico; (2) Mexico's working conditions were so abysmal that no civilized nation (including Japan) would allow its subjects to work there; (3) Korea did not even have diplomatic relations with Mexico; (4) hence, there was no Korean ambassador or consul there to assist these hapless victims; (5) the emigration was illegal, since Kojong had permitted emigration only to Hawaii; and (6) there were no rules or regulations to protect emigrants since they had been legislated out of existence when the

Yuminwŏn was dissolved. Foreign Minister Yi agreed that emigration to Mexico had to be temporarily prohibited, but Hayashi insisted successfully that all emigration stop, including emigration to Hawaii, where there was still no Korean consul in place, until the Korean government could demonstrate that it could control emigration in an organized and responsible manner. Hayashi knew full well that there was little chance of that given the disorganized nature of the Korean government (U.S. Department of State 19–, sections titled "David Deshler to Huntington Wilson, Charge d'affaires, United States Legation, Tokyo, January, 1906" [undated] and "Enclosure with Wilson to Elihu Root, Secretary of State, January 27, 1906." See also Gaimushō 1905a, section "Wilson to Katō Takaaki [Foreign Minister]," January 19).[4]

Komura was in Tokyo when he learned that the Korean foreign minister had temporarily suspended emigration and immediately cabled Hayashi in Seoul instructing him to make the temporary prohibition on emigration a permanent one. In that way, Japan would not have to bully Korea to stop its subjects from going abroad, and Japan could maintain the pretense with the United States that it had only the best interests of the Koreans at heart. In fact, the Mexico fiasco played right into Japanese hands, as the Japanese government had been putting pressure on the Korean government to withdraw all its diplomats stationed abroad and replace them with Japanese diplomats to represent Korean interests. Now, Hayashi pointed out to Korean foreign minister Yi that since Japan did enjoy diplomatic relations with Mexico, the Koreans who had been sold into virtual slavery on the henequen haciendas in the Yucatan peninsula could be represented by the Japanese minister to Mexico. In addition, the Japanese government successfully pressured the Korean government to appoint Saitō Miki as Korean consul in Honolulu to look after the interests of Koreans in Hawaii (Gaimushō 1905a, sections "Komura to Hayashi, April 6, 1905," "Komura to Takahira Kogorō, April 12, 1905," and "Komura to Saitō, April 12; 1905, 1970, 540-541, no. 8632." For Saitō in Hawaii, see Hansŏng sinbo 1905 and Hwangsŏng sinmun 1905a).

But the Korean government was determined not to go down without a fight. Foreign Minister Yi assigned his deputy, Vice-Minister Yun Ch'i-ho, to visit Hawaii and Mexico to investigate the conditions of Koreans there and then return to draw up new rules and regulations that would allow the temporary prohibition on emigration to be lifted, and lay the groundwork for the stationing of Korean diplomats in Hawaii and Mexico. If Yun's mission was successful and Korea stationed its own diplomatic representatives in Hawaii and Mexico and emigration resumed, it would not only increase the probability of a Japanese exclusion act but it would also make Japan's takeover of Korea's diplomatic functions that much more difficult. Japan had to make sure that Yun's mission did not succeed. Otherwise, Japan would have to bully Korea to stop Koreans from going abroad, revealing Japan's real motives in Korea—motives that were hardly benevolent, as they were all about Japan's prestige as a leading nation on the world stage and not about concern for the welfare of the Korean people. All this came just at the time in the summer of 1905 when the United States and Japan were preparing to sign the Taft-Katsura Memorandum giving Japan the green light to take over Korea in return for American freedom of action in the Philippines (Yun 1973, entry no. 6:139, dated June 20, 1905).

Yun's first stop was Hawaii, where he spent most of September visiting all the sugar plantations that had Korean workers. At the end of his visit, he pronounced that the Koreans were well-treated by the sugar planters and that he would recommend a resumption of emigration to Hawaii when he returned to Seoul. His next stop was Mexico, where the reputed problems lay. However, Yun had been so scrupulously honest in an attempt to avoid bias that he had refused to allow the planters to pay for his transportation, lodging, or meals, so as not to be placed in their debt. In doing so, he had expended his entire travel allotment of 1000 yen (about $500). When the Foreign Office sent him an additional 490 yen ($242) for the remainder of his trip, the planters informed Yun that it was insufficient to get to Mexico and back to Seoul. Consequently, Yun wired back to Seoul requesting an additional $300, and the Korean Foreign Office requested the Finance Ministry to forward the money to Yun in Honolulu. Luckily for Japan, however, it had fortuitously placed an "adviser," Megata Tanetarō, in the Finance Ministry. Megata naturally vetoed the expenditure, forcing a disappointed Yun to return to Korea without going to Mexico, and thus dooming his mission. The Korean government now could neither enact new rules and regulations nor could it send diplomats to Hawaii or Mexico. So the prohibition on Korean emigration remained in place, as Komura had wanted. Japan had been able to avoid acting like a bully, and the United States, having agreed to the Taft-Katsura memorandum, remained convinced that Japan had Korea's best interests at heart and remained unaware that Japan had manipulated the Korean government behind the scenes to prevent Koreans from going to Hawaii. When the protectorate was established in November of 1905, without any objection from the United States, Japan was now legally in charge of Korean emigration and could prohibit it permanently to reduce the chances that a Japanese exclusion act would be enacted by the United States (Hwangsŏng sinmun 1905b; *Korea Review* 1905, 393; 395).

We now return to the original question of the linkage between Korean immigration and the Japanese takeover of Korea. First, it is important to state once again that a realist consideration of security on the peninsula, in place since 1868, remains the most salient factor in the takeover. Within that framework, however, we find that the issue of Korean emigration is related to the Japanese takeover with respect to both ends and means. As far as ends are concerned, Korean emigration to Hawaii made a Japanese takeover of

Korea even more desirable over and above the benefits of ensuring Japan's security, as that would allow Japan legally to prevent Koreans from leaving for Hawaii and prevent the loss of national prestige that a Japanese Exclusion Act would entail.

Second, regarding means, the incompetence of the Korean government over emigration made it easier for Japan to assume control of Korea's diplomatic functions, and thus more easily pave the way for a protectorate, by allowing Japan to point to the Korean government's failure to station representatives in Hawaii and Mexico (and Vladivostok) where Koreans had migrated. In such a situation, Japan could quite logically argue that Korea should permit Japanese diplomats stationed in those places specifically and more generally abroad to handle Korea's diplomatic affairs.

Third, again related to means, the emigration blunders by the Korean government also allowed Japan to conceal its real motive for wanting to prohibit Koreans from going abroad and to maintain the façade that it would treat Koreans benevolently. Japan did not care about the plight of the victimized Korean emigrants, as it claimed. Rather, Japan was concerned solely with its prestige as one of the leading nations of the world. The missteps of the Korean government allowed Japan to operate skillfully behind the scenes so it would not have to bully the Korean government openly into stopping emigration. The United States never learned the real reason behind Japan's stopping of Korean emigration, continued to believe that Japan's motives in Korea were benevolent rather than mean-spirited, and did not object to the Japanese takeover of Korea.

## NOTES

1. An earlier version of this chapter first appeared in *Acta Koreana*, 14:1 (June 2011). The author is grateful to editor, Michael Finch, for permission to reprint it.

2. The details surrounding this additional issue are spelled out in my book, *The Korean Frontier in America: Immigration to Hawaii, 1896–1910* (Honolulu: University of Hawai'i Press, 1988; revised edition, 1994), which uses documentary sources in Japanese, Korean, and English that are different from those used in the three aforementioned books.

3. The advisers were Durham White Stevens in the Korean Foreign Office and Megata Tanetarō in the Korean Finance Office. See the account by the apologist for Japan, George Trumbull Ladd, *In Korea with Marquis Ito* (London: Longmans, Green, and Co., 1908), 252, 365.

4. One might argue that Hayashi's words carried considerable persuasive weight considering the presence of nearly 6,000 Japanese troops in the Korean capital. Moreover, Yi was fairly new at the job of foreign minister, having been appointed to that position only the year before, in 1904. He would be replaced the following year by Pak Che-sun.

## REFERENCES

Allen, Horace. 1902. Enclosure with Allen to Secretary of State John Hay, December 10, 1902. *Horace Allen Papers*. Microfilm. New York Public Library.

*Cheguk sinmun.* 1903. May 12, 1903.

Cooke, Charles. 1903. *Charles M. Cooke Papers.* Honolulu: Hawaiian Mission Children's Society Library.

Daniels, Roger. 1962. *The Politics of Prejudice: The Anti-Japanese Movement in California and the Struggle for Japanese Exclusion.* Berkeley: University of California Press.

Gaimushō. 1905a. *Kankoku seifu Hawai oyobi Mokushika yuki Kankoku imin kinshi ikken— tsuki hogo itaku kankoku no ken* [The prohibition of Korean emigration to Hawaii and Mexico by the Korean Government—Recommendation and protection]. Tokyo: Gaimushō.

———. 1905b. *Zai Bei ryōji rai* [Incoming from the United States]. Tokyo: Gaimushō.

———. 1973. *Nihon gaikō bunsho: Tai Bei imin mondai keika gaiyō fuzokushō* [Documents on Japanese foreign policy: Annexes to summary of the course of negotiations between Japan and the United States concerning the problem of Japanese immigration to the United States]. Tokyo: Gaimushō.

Harrington, Fred Harvey. 1944. *God, Mammon, and the Japanese: Dr. Horace N. Allen and Korean-American Relations, 1884–1905.* Madison: University of Wisconsin Press.

*Hansŏng sinbo.* 1905. May 5, 1905.

*Hwangsŏng sinmun.* 1902. November 21, 1902.

———. 1903. February 9, 1903.

———. 1905a. May 6, 1905.

———. 1905b. October 2, 1905.

*Korea Review.* 1905. Seoul: Methodist Publishing House.

*Kwanbo* [Official Gazette]. 1902. November 20, 1902.

Ladd, George Trumbull. 1908. *In Korea with Marquis Ito.* London: Longmans, Green, and Co.

Patterson, Wayne. 1994. *The Korean Frontier in America: Immigration to Hawaii, 1896–1910.* Honolulu: University of Hawai'i Press, 1988; Revised Edition 1994.

Unknown. 1970. "KuHan'guk oegyo munsŏ. Ilan [Documents relating to the foreign relations of Old Korea. Japan]." *Asea munje yŏn'guso* 7: 540–541.

U.S. Department of State. 19–. *Dispatches from U.S. Ministers to Japan, 1855–1906.* Washington: National Archives.

Yun, Ch'i-ho. *Yun Ch'i-ho's Diary.* 1973. Seoul: National History Compilation Committee.

*Chapter Ten*

# Korean Activists in Tōkyō, *The Asia Kunglun,* and Asian Solidarity in the early 1920s

## Dolf-Alexander Neuhaus

During the early 1920s, Tōkyō, as the capital of an expanding empire, attracted many independence activists, students, and intellectuals from Korea and adjacent countries in Asia. The city can thus be seen as a contact zone in which the transgressive lives of peoples with different backgrounds, but similar objectives and ideas converged (Pratt 1992, 6; Goebel 2015, 6). This chapter explores the pan-Asian journal *The Asia Kunglun* (Jap.: Ajia kōron; Kor.: Asia Kongnon) which was published in Tōkyō by the Korean independence activist Yu T'aekyŏng between May 1922 and January 1923, bringing together a wide array of authors from Korea, Taiwan, India, and China and Japanese proponents of Taishō liberalism. Unfulfilled hopes of national liberation in the wake of the March First Movement in Korea and the Paris Peace Conference 1919 had prompted reconfigurations within the Korean independence movement, including the adoption of new ideologies such as Marxism or pan-Asianism without relinquishing the ultimate goal of independence. Against this backdrop, the question of how Korean authors drafted new visions of a united "Asia" and utilized them as expedient devices to denounce Japanese colonial rule in Korea and other parts of Asia in their contributions to *The Asia Kunglun* warrants closer inspection. While they found common ground with Japanese pan-Asianists in rejecting the outcome of the peace conference, at the same time they refused to accept Japanese hegemony in Asia under the given conditions. The transnational mobility of Korean activists, students, and intellectuals facilitated the interaction with anti-colonial activists from China and Taiwan residing in Tōkyō. The transnational intellectual space that resulted from the encounter in the contact zone prevented Korean contributors of *The Asia Kunglun* from becoming ensnared in Japanese narratives of assimilation policy based on common ancestry (Jap.: *Nis-Sen dōsōron*) in Korea. Efforts by diasporic Korean activists to create an egalitarian version of Asian solidarity have nevertheless attracted only insufficient scholarly attention (Tikhonov 2002, 198–199), despite the fact that the movement for regional solidarity in Asia occurred within the broader context of globally emerging alternative conceptions of civilization, which was no longer simply regarded as a signifier of Euro-American superiority (Duara 2001, 101–102).

This chapter draws on recent historiography, which has shown that the responses of Asian audiences to the perceived promise of national self-determination as well as the disillusionment with it were complex and not simply confined to the reductive pattern of nationalist anticolonialism. Such interpretation exaggerates the influence of the United States of America and Europe while downplaying the agency of non-Westerners (Zachmann 2017, 3; Garon 2017, 67; Manela 2007). Moreover, research still largely fixates on state-based approaches to pan-Asianism in Japan and China, resulting in a conspicuous dearth in terms of scholarship on visions of Asia of the interwar period that originated outside Japan and China (Hotta 2007; Saaler and Szpilman 2011a, 2011b). Exploring the role that Tōkyō-based Korean students and activists during the 1920s took on in putting forward alternative deliberations of Asian solidarity, this article is divided into three sections. To contextualize the publication of *The Asia Kunglun*, the first section briefly delineates the historical trajectory of pan-Asianism in Korea in relation to Japan and China. The chapter will then discuss the motivations that led to the publication of the journal before the last part investigates the alternative concepts of Asia's role within the international order by analyzing selected articles of *The Asia Kunglun* and how they were utilized as anti-imperial critiques of Japan.

## KOREA IN ASIA, 1880–1924

Generally speaking, pan-Asianism was a broadly defined and by no means monolithic ideology, encompassing diverse strands of thought and ideas that viewed Asia as a cohesive body determined by geographic, linguistic, and racial or cultural communalities as the smallest common denominator (Saaler 2007, Saaler and Szpilman 2011a; Hotta 2007; Huebner 2016, 5). Increasing contact among Asian elites in the early twentieth century resulted in the emergence of pan-Asianist ideas, which hinged on an understanding of a common destiny in an Asian struggle against Western imperialism. Consequently, culturist or racialist concepts of Asian unity often encompassed a strong anti-Western component, particularly in Japan (Weber 2008; Duus

1971). Eventually, the Japanese state sought to harness anti-Western and pan-Asian rhetoric in order to ideologically legitimize its imperial expansion in Asia and the Greater East Asia Co-Prosperity Sphere during the 1930s and 1940s. During the second half of the nineteenth century, the seemingly inexorable advance of Euro-American powers into Asia accelerated the collapse of the Sinocentric world order and traditional modes of diplomatic and economic interaction between the countries of East Asia. Following the Meiji Restoration in 1868, Japan enthusiastically adopted modern technology as well as political, economic, and social institutions from Western powers in order to "self-strengthen." After it was forced to sign the unequal Treaty of Kanghwa in 1876, the crisis-stricken Chosŏn dynasty finally succumbed to Japan's overwhelming efforts to colonize it in 1910.

Whereas the "rule of colonial difference" was a key concept in many Euro-American colonies (Chatterjee 1993, 16; Burbank and Cooper 2010, 11–22), Japanese colonial authorities in Korea asserted racial and linguistic similarities (*dōbun dōshu*) and common ancestry to construct unity between colonizer and colonized as the ideological groundwork for assimilation policy (Oguma 2002, 64–80). In Japanese colonial ideology, the main dividing line was thus not drawn between Japanese and Koreans, but rather between Japan and Korea on the one side and the Euro-American nations on the other (Lee 2017, 61). The official colonial narrative notwithstanding, Japanese imperialism was still firmly based on the assumption of Korean inferiority. In retrospect, it therefore seems hard to understand how independence activists like An Chungkŭn, who in autumn 1909 assassinated the Japanese resident-general in Korea, Itō Hirobumi, were able to reconcile their ardent Korean nationalism with the idea of East Asian regional unity. At the turn of the century, however, the landscape for Asian nationalists was defined by the threat of a resurgent Russia as well as the United States which, after the Spanish American War of 1898, had started to establish military outposts and garrisons on islands reaching all the way to the Philippines. In Japan, leading civil rights activist Sugita Teiichi and Tarui Tōkichi had put forward ideas of Asian commonalities as early as the 1880s (Weber 2018, 67–68). Although initially marginalized in political discourse, these ideas inspired later pan-Asianists from World War I onwards (Weber 2018, 67). In his treatise *Daitō Gappōron*, published in 1893, Tarui promoted a close alliance between the countries of the East (*tōkoku*)—unified Japan and Korea would form a union with China. Yet, neither Sugita's nor Tarui's proposal made any attempt to empathize with the Korean perspective, who by then were already subjected to the unequal Treaty of Kanghwa (Kim KH 2011, 76). Eventually, Japan's pivot away from solidarity to domination unveiled the contradictions in the conceptions of Sugita, Tarui, and other Japanese pan-Asianists like Okakura Tenshin.

Support for pan-Asian ideas grew consistently among Japanese, Chinese, and Indian ideologues in the first decade of the twentieth century, but similar ideas also enjoyed some popularity in Korea. Prior to 1905, the notion of Asian solidarity had been embraced by a part of the Korean elite, especially by progressive reformers and newspapers including the *Hwangsŏng Sinmun* (Imperial Capital News). The praise of Japan as the new guide of Asia was based on the traditional worldview in which the more "civilized" country aided the "less civilized" (Lee 2011, 206). However, Koreans soon became increasingly wary of the menace to their sovereignty which the proposition of Japanese (or Chinese) leadership in Asia entailed. Important Korean intellectuals entertained reasonable doubts about Japan's sincerity to serve as the altruistic leader of Asia (Schmid 2002, 92–100). Eventually, the impending annexation of Korea prompted nationalist historian Sin Ch'aeho to write a passionate repudiation of "Easternism" (*tongyangjuŭi*), which he denounced as a mere tool of Japanese expansion in the guise of Asian solidarity against Euro-America (Kim B 2011, 191–193). His critique aimed at pro-Japanese sympathizers (Kor.: *ch'inilp'a*) such as the leadership of the *Ilchinhoe* (Advance in Unity Society). Stigmatized as unadulterated pro-Japanese collaborators, the *Ilchinhoe* maintained excellent relations with the Japanese pan-Asianist society *Kokuryūkai* (Amur River Society) that actively lobbied for a merger of Korea and Japan, which was simply a euphemism for annexation (Hatsuse 1980, 99–110, Saaler 2014). However, being an anti-Japanese nationalist and a pan-Asianist were not always mutually exclusive: charged with the assassination of Itō Hirobumi, the Japanese resident-general in Korea, in autumn 1909, An Chungkŭn drafted the introduction and the first chapter of the unfinished *Tongyang p'yŏnghwaron* (A discourse on peace in East Asia) while awaiting trial in prison. An condemned Japan for jeopardizing the security of Korea and the region by creating tension among Japan, Korea, and China. In his view, Japan had thereby betrayed its position as the defender of the East in the wake of the Russo-Japanese War (Shin 2006, 31–35). In the treatise, An furthermore detailed a plan for close cooperation between Korea, Japan, and China that comprised the organization of an oriental peace conference, the issuance of a common currency, and the establishment of a common military force (Lee 2011, 208).

Such auspicious visions might seem utopian in light of the looming annexation of Korea, which ultimately revealed Tōkyō's will to define regional stability as empire in East Asia. Yet, visions of a supranational region rooted in cultural communalities continued to unite significant numbers of anti-colonial and anti-imperialist activists, who nonetheless argued for the nation as the main reference for belonging during the interwar period (Huebner and Weber 2013, 12–13). This persistent sense of historical connectedness of East Asian peoples and anti-Westernism led thinkers like Li Dazhao, the co-founder of the Chinese Communist Party, to envision an Asian federation of nations liberated from Japanese domination. Between 1915 and 1920 Li devised the concept of "New Asianism" in order to oppose Japanese "Greater Asianism," which he unmasked as an excuse for Japanese expansion on the Asian continent. Korean activists and students abroad remained integrated in such regional networks even after political resistance inside Korea was stymied in a crackdown on the leading patriotic society *Sinminhoe* (New People's Association) and by the ensuing suppression of free speech immediately following the annexation. While "Asia" in the Japanese perception became increasingly synonymous with empire, intellectual challenges to Japanese colonialism emerged from the interaction between various groups of Asian students and activists who resided in the colonial capital of Tōkyō. The formation of the Asian Solidarity Society in 1907 is a conspicuous example for such an attempt in which Chinese, Japanese, Vietnamese, and Koreans participated. Although the society was ephemeral and spawned few activities, its legacy lay in the emergence of alternative approaches to creating cultural and regional unity that stood in contrast to state-sponsored nationalist concepts of Asian regionalism (Karl 1998, 1097, 1110–1117; Shiraishi 1982). In a similar fashion, the New Asia Alliance (Jap.: *Shin'a Dōmeitō*) was another clandestine effort to institutionalize anti-imperialist cooperation among East Asian activists in Tōkyō, including two Taiwanese students between 1915 and 1917 (Ogio 2004, 55). Kim Ch'ŏlsu, a founding member, recalled that the group strove "to defeat Japanese imperialism and to build a new Asia" in order to achieve Korean independence. However, the aims of the alliance were not limited to the Korean problem; it fought for the liberation of all Japanese colonies, including Chōsen (Korea), Taiwan, and semicolonial China (Ono 2013, 117). Progressive non-state approaches to Asian solidarity lingered at the pan-Asiatic conferences in Nagasaki in 1926 and Shanghai in 1927, where Chinese and Korean delegates demanded that Japan abrogate its imperialist aspirations on the continent (Aydin 2007, 156–157).

## YU T'AEKYŎNG AND *THE ASIA KUNGLUN*, 1922–1923

Following the annexation, suppression of alternative ideologies that were deemed subversive to Japanese rule intensified, causing the center of resistance to shift outside the Korean peninsula. Epicenters of Korean anti-colonial activity formed in Manchuria, Shanghai, the United States, and Japan, where a very active student movement emerged around the outbreak of World War I (Neuhaus 2017, 618–622). In 1919, Korean discontent with Japanese military rule peaked during the March First Independence Movement, which the Japanese were only able to quell by force of arms. Yet, this movement in Korea was not detached from other movements including the proclamation of independence by Korean exchange students at the Korean

Young Men's Christian Association in Tōkyō on 8 February 1919 (Neuhaus 2017, 618–619).

During the Taishō period (1912–1926), the Japanese capital of Tōkyō hosted a vibrant community of students and activists from various Asian countries. The overall political and intellectual climate in Japan during the Taishō period was considerably more liberal when compared to the stifling conditions in Korea, where Governor-General Terauchi Masatake had established a repressive system of military rule between 1910 and 1919. However, underneath its liberal rhetoric, the Japanese state maintained tight control over opposition even in mainland Japan, as exemplified by the government's reaction to the escalating Rice Riots of 1918 (Choi 2015, 37).

Following the failure of the independence movements across large parts of Asia, disillusioned Korean intellectuals realized that Korean independence could hardly be accomplished without support from Japanese sympathizers. The mounting frustration over the double standards of Western democracies typified by the discriminatory immigration policy toward Asians in the United States was reflected in the emphasis on Asian solidarity as an ideological alternative to Wilsonian idealism or dogmatic socialism. The lingering skepticism toward Western civilization reverberated intellectually through the interwar period in the thinking and writing of pan-Asianist activists who challenged the conception of international society as an arrangement of sovereign nation-states vying for power by proposing culturally defined regions as important building blocks of a new world order.

In an extraordinary effort to harness these potential synergies and create an intellectual forum for young authors from different parts of the Japanese Empire, as well as sympathetic Japanese, Korean independence activist Yu T'aekyŏng edited the trilingual journal *The Asia Kunglun* between May 1922 and January 1923. Prior to his involvement with the journal, Yu had spent some time as an exchange student at Waseda University around 1907 before participating in the resistance movement against Japanese annexation. In 1912, he enrolled at Qingdao University, then, after the Japanese assault on the former German colony, he relocated to Beijing (Bae 2013, 93). In the wake of the March First Movement, he was incarcerated for conspiring against the Japanese colonial authorities in Manchuria. After his release he moved to Tōkyō, where he made provisions for the publication of *The Asia Kunglun* (Bae 2013, 97; Gōtō 2009, 149).

*The Asia Kunglun* produced nine issues until January 1923, defying regular interference and censorship by the authorities and the Home Ministry. Its successor, *The Orient Review* (*Daitō Kōron*), published by Yu's acquaintance Park Ch'iho, was discontinued after the release of the first issue in July 1923 (Gōtō 2009, 151–152). Official records attributed this to the Great Kantō earthquake on September 1, 1923, although an unsuccessful attempt to resuscitate the journal seems to have been undertaken in February 1924 with the distribution of 1,200 copies. Publication was suspended for good from March 1924 (Chōsen Sōtokufu 1975, 144). After the discontinuation of *The Asia Kunglun,* Yu immigrated to the United States to study at Susquehanna University before returning to Korea in 1930. Residing in Shanghai during the Second Sino-Japanese War, he moved to Chongqing with the Provisional Government to evade advancing Japanese troops in 1940. Yu returned to liberated Korea in 1946 but vanished during the Korean War after he was abducted by a North Korean special operations unit (Kwon 2014, 100).

Many liberal intellectuals and international students who contributed to *The Asia Kunglun* were affiliated with Waseda University (Chi 2012, 319). In 1922, when the journal was first published, authorities recorded a total of 3,222 Korean students in Japan. All but 54 of them, who received a government scholarship, were self-sponsored. The following year saw a sudden decline to merely 936 privately financed students due to the lynching of Koreans in the aftermath of the Great Kantō earthquake in September 1923 (Weiner 1989, 142). From 1924 onwards numbers began to slowly recuperate to the effect that in 1925 1,318 students, including 150 women, were registered at schools in Tōkyō alone (Naimushō 1975, 309). According to official data, only a small fraction of the students were enrolled at universities, while the bulk attended technical colleges (Jap.: *senmon gakkō*), language schools, girls' schools, or high and middle schools. Waseda University and its adjacent high schools and technical colleges hosted a total of 177 students (Naimushō 1975, 310–312).

When the millenarian belief in a new and improved world order arising from the devastation of World War I in Europe went unfulfilled due to the denial of national self-determination and the perpetuation of colonialism in Asia after the Paris Peace Conference, independence activists in Asia began to contemplate modifications to materialistic liberalism and nationalism to guide them in their struggle against imperialism. While the ideological direction of Korean independence activists began to bifurcate into leftists and moderate nationalists, the major figures of exile organizations in Japan, China, Manchuria, Siberia, and the United States were brought together in the Shanghai-based Provisional Government of the Republic of Korea (Kor.: *Taehan Min'guk Imsi Chŏngbu*). During the war, Korean writers like Yi Kwangsu had already expressed the expectation that the existing order would disintegrate once the war in Europe ended. Hence, he argued for a "new culture" *(sin munhwa)* based on the "Oriental civilization" *(tongyang munmyŏng)* (Yi 1917, 4; Choi 2015; Shin 2000, 254–255). Yi, who had studied at Waseda University before establishing himself as a pioneer of modern Korean literature with the serialized novel *Mujŏng* (The Heartless) in 1917, also drafted the February 8 Declaration of Independence in Tōkyō (Shin 2000, 249). In his article "Our Ideals" (Kor.: *Uri ŭi isang*) Yi insinuated that Asian civilization was superior to European culture in that "Westerners only entirely understand Western civilization [*sŏyang munmyŏng*], they must acknowledge the respectable values of Oriental civilization, which has its roots in India and China. Ever since Schopenhauer and Bergson, the tendency to include Eastern thinking [*tongyang sasang*] into Western civilization had become obvious" (Yi 1917, 5; Neuhaus 2017, 621). The gradual shift in emphasis from "civilization" and enlightenment towards "culture" was at the time also observable in China (Fung 2010, 72–76).

*The Asia Kunglun* carried this regional legacy, and by embracing the diversity of Asia it linked the imaginations of Korean, Taiwanese, Chinese, and Japanese activists and intellectuals who envisioned a new world order based on Asia's awakening. Generally, *The Asia Kunglun* sought to enhance a new Asian civilization based on humanism (*jinrui shugi*) and righteous humanitarianism (*seigi jindō*) by implementing universal love of mankind (*jinruiai*), freedom (*jiyū*), and equality (*byōdo*) (Bae 2013, 93; Gōtō 2009, 151). The regionalist vision of world order did not outright oppose Wilsonian idealism, but rather argued to replace it with its own Asian (read: better and more equitable) version (Zachmann 2017, 5). Antagonized by the omission of the racial equality clause which the Japanese delegation proposed for incorporation in the Covenant of the League of Nations, the irritation about continuing discriminatory immigration policies in the United States and Australia is palpable in the writings of *The Asia Kunglun*. This skeptical stance towards the West concurred with the assertions of Japanese pan-Asianists like Konoe Fumimaro, who in his treatise *A Call to Reject the Anglo-American Centered Peace* reviled the Paris settlements as dictated by the desire of Great Britain and the United States in order to maintain their dominant position within the international system (Hotta 2011, 312). Konoe's polemic denunciation addressed a domestic audience arguing for a Japan-centered way of thinking in order to secure Japan's "legitimate right to survival" (Hotta 2011, 315), but nonetheless encapsulated the main arguments of non-Western opponents of the Versailles order (Zachmann 2017, 6).

Anti-imperialist critiques voiced by Koreans, Taiwanese, and Chinese generally concurred with Japanese pan-Asianism in reproaching Euro-American colonial powers, which many of them had hailed as guarantors of long-desired liberation from colonial rule prior to 1919. The English-language newspaper *Japan Times* neatly captured this sentiment in February 1919 in a report about "a meeting of Japanese, Chinese and Korean students . . . held at the YMCA Hall yesterday afternoon." According to the article, the participants were discussing anti-racial discrimination and speakers "complained that the white race is trying to dominate the world." A "professor of Keiō University" was quoted as saying that "anti-racialism must be removed in Japan and discrimination against Koreans, Formosans and Chinese stopped" (*Japan Times* 1919). After its founding in 1906, the Korean YMCA emerged as a hotbed of the student movement of the 1910s and, for a time after 1919, it retained its leading role as an important space to mediate the interactions between Koreans, Chinese, and Japanese (Neuhaus 2016, 624–625). Yet the assertions of anti-racialist codes and practices voiced by Japanese intellectuals like Yoshino Sakuzō must not be misunderstood as fundamental and essential critiques of empire. In fact, such criticism was almost exclusively directed toward the repressive style of military rule in the Japanese colonies of Korea and Taiwan (Han 2012, 105–111). The subsequent transition of Japanese rule in Korea and Taiwan from "military" to "cultural" policy merely substituted outright repression with subtler forms of assimilation by granting certain liberties to the colonial subjects. In retrospect, this strategy of assimilation proved more effective than the preceding "military rule," thus paving the way for the co-optation of colonial elites. (Robinson 2007, 49).

In reality, the dividing line between imperialist oppressor and the oppressed did not run neatly along the East-West divide (Weber 2017, 78–79). While Konoe revealed the hypocrisy and egoism behind the "Anglo-American version of democratic humanitarianism," his social Darwinist interpretation of international relations left no room for Koreans and other colonized peoples. Despite a universal moralistic argument of "justice and humanity," Konoe did not call for an Asian alliance to counter Western racism (Shimazu 1998, 64). Nevertheless, *The Asia Kunglun* declared as its motto the strife for justice and humanitarianism, which superficially overlapped with the demands made by Konoe in 1918. Although the majority of articles was written in Japanese as a *lingua franca*, the journal also included pieces in Chinese and Korean, particularly in the first issue. The periodical featured a ream of articles penned by renowned proponents of Taishō liberalism, such as Ōyama Ikuo, Yoshino Sakuzō, and postwar prime minister Ishibashi Tanzan, as well as early writings by the Korean writer Hwang Sŏku (Kwon 2014). The resulting multiplicity of ideological beliefs and approaches to East Asia underscore *The Asia Kunglun*'s significance for Taishō liberalism, despite its lifespan of less than a year (Bae 2013, 93).

## *THE ASIA KUNGLUN*, THE "KOREA QUESTION," AND EAST ASIA

Accentuating the Confucian principle of justice and humanitarianism, *The Asia Kunglun* articulated criticism of Japanese suppression in Asian countries. In doing so, the editor of the journal pursued clearly defined political and anti-imperialist objectives. Although the contributors never openly called for Korean independence and did not unanimously agree on the question of how this new concept of Asia should take shape, the journal's historical significance derives from its Korean and Taiwanese authors' unequivocal disapproval of Japan's policy toward Asia and its collusion with imperialist Euro-American powers. Notwithstanding its critical stance toward Japanese dominance in Asia, the publication of the first issue of *The Asia Kunglun* caused a stir that was covered by the *Tōkyō Asahi Shinbun* (Gōtō 2009, 150). Remarkably, the journal's editors received congratulatory notes from Japanese members of Parliament, as well as from such enigmatic figures as Tōyama Mitsuru, the notorious right-wing power broker and godfather of Japanese ultra-nationalism, despite the explicit criticism of Japan's oppressive policy toward adjacent countries in Asia (Gōtō 2009, 152).

The disillusionment, caused by the self-destruction of Europe during World War I coupled with the disenchantment with Wilsonian idealism, invigorated intellectual efforts to forge regional solidarity in order to supplant the Eurocentric international order with a more egalitarian one. Many Japanese right-wing proponents of anti-Westernism and pan-Asianism like Tōyama Mitsuru and Ōkawa Shūmei conceived of such positions as tools for stabilizing Japanese supremacy in Asia by adopting a vision of Asia that was entrenched in the belief in irreconcilable antagonism between East and West. However, the contributors of *The Asia Kunglun* did not unanimously share this perception and proposed a more egalitarian alternative to the existing international order of the Washington-Versailles system, one that would originate from Eastern culture. In fact, the journal tried to clearly dissociate itself from what it considered "militarism." Responding to an apparent critique of the emphasis on Asia in the journal's designation as "militarist" (*gunkokushugisha*)—i.e., promoting Japanese imperialism—a section of the inaugural issue featured a prize contest in search of a more fitting label while clarifying the objectives of the publication: "The Asia Kunglun is not such a narrow-minded [*kechikusai*] idea as a union [*danketsu*] or the unification [*tōitsu*] of the Asian peoples. . . . [T]he happiness of mankind is the happiness of all peoples." In order to achieve world peace, the text continued, it was therefore imperative for Asia to compare favorably in terms of character with Euro-Americans [*ōbeijin*]. "As a first step Asia must awake [*kakusei*]!" (*The Asia Kunglun* 1922b).

The journal furthermore strongly disavowed any relationship with another Japanese pan-Asian group, the *Dōkōkai* (The Same Light Society). Uchida Ryōhei, one of the leaders of the *Kokuryūkai* (Amur River Society) who had lobbied for annexation during the protectorate period after the Russo-Japanese War, founded the *Dōkōkai* in 1921 with the professed objective to "improve and reform" the administration of the Korean Peninsula in order to create real equality between Koreans and Japanese as a response to the March First Independence Movement (Saaler 2011, 63–66). Aside from Uchida's participation, the *Dōkōkai* assembled the who's who of the Japanese pan-Asianist community including Tōyama Mitsuru and the parliamentarians Ogawa Heikichi and Sugita Teiichi. Despite harsh criticism concerning official policies in Korea, the independence of Korea had never been a viable option for the group (Saaler 2011, 65). Without hesitation, *The Asia Kunglun* pilloried the *Dōkōkai* for such inconsistencies. An anonymous reader contribution to *The Asia Kunglun* published in the section "Under the microscope" entitled "What does the Dōkōkai do?" [Dōkōkai ha nani wo suru?] issued a fiercely critical analysis of the *Dōkōkai* (*The Asia Kunglun* 1922a, 70). In unambiguous language the text attempted to expose the hypocrisy and sinister motives of the association's central figure, the *"rōnin"* Uchida Ryōhei. The label *"rōnin"* originally alluded to medieval masterless samurai roaming the countryside, but a reader in the 1920s would also have associated the term with the so-called *tairiku rōnin* (continental ruffians). Around the turn of the century Uchida had been a member of such a band called *Ten'yūkyō* (Chivalrous Knights of Heavenly Assistance) which did not confine itself to campaigning for Japanese territorial aggrandizement on the continent but conducted covert operations for the Japanese Imperial Army in Manchuria and was involved in illicit drug smuggling (Jennings 1997, 52; Saaler 2014, 131–132).

Warning Koreans and Japanese against Uchida's scheming machinations by reminding them of Uchida's lobbying activities in Korea during the protectorate, the author wrote: "It is impossible for Koreans to forget Uchida's role as advisor to the *Ilchinhoe* prior to annexation." According to the anonymous author, the *Dōkōkai* would only pretend to attack the Governor-General for his misguided policy in Korea but secretly agree with it. Uchida would regard Koreans as cattle and be only interested in the "filthy lucre" (*The Asia Kunglun* 1922a, 70). In contrast, *The Asia Kunglun* would aim to "root out the different kinds of negative effects that come from the notion of racist discrimination in many countries of Asia and to encourage a consciousness of universal love of mankind [*sekaiteki jinruiai*] toward the people of all countries" (Bae 2013, 96). While the editorial entitled "The Purpose of the Release of this Journal" acknowledged the existence of many journals and magazines that were addressing the "Oriental Problem" or the "Asian Problem," it asked,

> How many are there that impartially speak about how in reality a certain country continues to oppress Asia, and how many are published on the basis of human justice and humanitarianism? It is safe to say that except for this publication there is no other that focuses particularly on the Korea problem, an issue of critical importance to Japan and Korea, and formulates impartial critique. (Bae 2013, 96)

"Dawn of East Asia" (Tōa no Akebono), an article by Korean author Ch'oe Ungpong that appeared in *The Asia Kunglun*, epitomized the idea of the awakening of Asia (Ch'oe 1922). Ch'oe declared that the "whites" (*hakujin*) advocated the equality of men and universal brotherhood (*shikai dōhō*) but pointed to the obvious discrepancy between words and deeds (*genkō fuitchi*). Ch'oe highlighted Western hypocrisy by reminding his audience that Asians were banned from migrating to the United States and that even the white people of Ireland were suppressed. However, Japan had abandoned her fellow yellow race and colluded with the white race by forging an alliance with England (Ch'oe 1922, 50). Debunking the Japanese rhetoric of uniting the peoples of Asia to oppose Euro-American world domination, Yu T'aekyŏng in a similar fashion alleged that "some unrestrained [*rōnin*] scholars and politicians who were intoxicated by militarism" simply wanted to usurp hegemonic leadership (*meishu*) in Asia (Yu 1922, 109). The familiar topos of Japanese betrayal in pursuit of her own imperial gain to the detriment of neighboring Asian countries harked back to An Chungkŭn. Coupled with the accusation of collaboration with Euro-American powers, Japan's treachery was attributable to the acceptance and adoption of an international system created and imposed by Euro-America in order to consolidate global dominance.

As an alternative to the existing international system and Euro-American hegemony, Ch'oe invoked the concepts of justice and humanitarianism (*seigi jindō*) that "sustained freedom and equality." On the basis of the Confucian and Buddhist principles of kindheartedness (*jijin*) and benevolence (*jihi*), people should create peace and guarantee the independence of the nation and freedom of humanity (Ch'oe 1922, 50–51). Ch'oe's opinion was representative of the main thrust of the journal: after European civilization had brought disaster upon itself, it fell to the Asians to form a new world civilization. According to the article's author, this would ensure stability and peace throughout the world. The treatise "Dawn of the East" constitutes a salient example of *The Asia Kunglun*'s intellectual challenge to Euro-American and Japanese imperialism. Yet Ch'oe and other contributors never clearly articulated how the alternative world order could materialize under the given conditions.

The relevance of *The Asia Kunglun* for pan-Asian thought is further emphasized by the fact that it assembled contributors from different parts of the Japanese Empire. Taiwanese intellectual and political activist Cai Peihuo concurred with the critiques of the Korean authors Yu and Ch'oe. Cai was the publisher of the first Taiwanese journal in Tōkyō, *The Tâi Oân Chheng Liân* (Taiwan youth), and he had devised a Romanized written Taiwanese vernacular (Yokoji 2014, 166). In his article "How to Reach Peace in the Far East?" [Kyokutō no heiwa hatashite ikan?], Cai attached great importance to the awakening of the peoples of the Far East in order to combine forces and establish basic peace (Cai 1922, 24). Yet Cai's assertion that the "Far East is for the Far Eastern people" did not imply the same elements of xenophobia that the Japan-centered version of an Asian Monroe Doctrine contained (Chi 2012, 261; Pierson [1980] 2014, 368–389). In fact, criticizing the outcome of the 1921 Washington Naval Conference, Cai must have been aware of the idea of the Japanese Monroe Doctrine for Asia, a recurring theme in Japanese writing, as he explicitly distanced himself from its main proponent, Tokutomi Sōhō (Cai 1922, 24; Hotta 2007, 95–97). Using excoriating language, Cai decried Japanese rule in Taiwan and Korea as "an act of absolutely tyrannical and egoistic government policy under which colonial subjects are barred from education and free development. While obedience is demanded from them, they do not possess the smallest amount of legal freedom." He continued:

> As a first step toward peace building in the Far East, the peoples of the Far East have to first sort out the bad sentiments toward one another. Here, I propose that Japan establishes a China policy of good faith and in particular fundamentally reforms her policy toward Korea and Taiwan to demonstrate true great spirit of coexistence and commonness. (Cai 1922, 27)

Confined by political subjugation to Japan and influenced by the cultural dominance of China, Cai in his later work *Son of East Asia* sought to construct East Asia as a space that transcended colonial Japaneseness and national communities alike (Chi 2012, 262). In his lengthy contribution to *The Asia Kunglun*, Cai already envisioned East Asian unity and cooperation as an instrument not only to guarantee peace and stability, but also to overcome the unjust rule of Japan in Taiwan and Korea.

While a common theme of the journal was stressing the Asian capability for replacing the Western-dominated system, not all authors unequivocally rejected Japanese imperial policy. For instance, Indian revolutionary Rash Behari Bose, who had fled to Japan in 1915 after the Ghadar conspiracy to end the British Raj had failed, contributed to the journal. In the *Orient Review* he postulated that Asia represented the cradle of civilization: "In the past Asia had given true civilization and religion to Europe under much sacrifice. Even Europeans today have to acknowledge the fact, that Asia was the mother of world civilization" (Bose 1923, 53). Like others, Bose argued that the war in Europe had destroyed European civilization and culture, which it was now unable to reconstruct: "As a result of Europe's self-inflicted politics many young people have died in the war and that's why Europe is no longer able to rebuild civilization. As in the past, the onus was on Asia to generate a new civilization and true religion to help Europe" (Bose 1923, 53–54). Given his anti-British background, Bose's contributions to the journal reiterated his hypothesis about the spiritual superiority of India and her strong ties with Japan by referring to a glorified past. Influenced by Okakura's works, this sentiment was generally shared by Japanese rightwing agitators like Ōkawa Shūmei or Kita Ikki, who took an antagonizing stance toward the existing Western-centered international order (Hotta 2006,

120–121). While Ch'oe, Cai, and Yu combined their critiques of the international system with an attack on Japanese colonial rule in East Asia, Bose was extremely reticent about Japan's failure to live up to the rhetoric of Asian solidarity.

Although the contributors to *The Asia Kunglun* criticized the prevailing international order dominated by Euro-American powers, their critiques did not lure them into assuming a leading role for Japan in their conception of Asia. Instead, the overall vision of Asia advocated by *The Asia Kunglun* was grounded in the belief in equality, humanitarianism, and justice, values based on centuries-old, but vague, Asian values. Early Japanese pan-Asianists like Okakura or Tarui also proposed a union of Asian countries but under the leadership of Japan. They thus laid the groundwork for a state-based Japanese pan-Asianism that legitimized imperial dominance in Asia. The main thrust of *The Asia Kunglun*'s idea of "Asia" was directed against exactly this "Greater Asianism." This approach was rather informed by Li Dazhao's "New Asianism," An Chungkŭn's visions of an Asian union, or Rabindranath Tagore's Asia as a spiritual counter-narrative to Europe. Bose's standpoint, on the other hand, while certainly not unaware of Tagore, was fiercely anti-British, a stance that eventually ensnared him in the alluring anti-Western narrative of Japanese fascism fighting British and American imperialism in Asia during the 1940s.

## CONCLUSION

Yu's biography exemplifies the transnational life stories of many Korean independence activists during the colonial period. During the early 1920s, the Japanese capital constituted a contract zone where significant numbers of East Asian students and independence activists crossed paths. The actors' transnational mobility and interaction facilitated the formation of an intellectual space within which anti-colonial and anti-imperialist movements could thrive. Within the liberal atmosphere of the Taishō period, pan-Asian ideas clearly influenced the ideological orientation of *The Asia Kunglun*. It furthermore enabled Yu and likeminded Asian campaigners to create an intellectual platform that explored alternative paths to national liberation by transcending national and imperial boundaries. While Yu and others advocated a utopian construct of Asia that hinged on an international reality that faced the problem of imperialist encroachment, the example of Rash Behari Bose illustrates that the backgrounds of the contributors to *The Asia Kunglun* were as diverse as their perspectives.

Faced with the double constraint of Western and Japanese imperialism, the Korean activists of *The Asia Kunglun* viewed national liberation as inextricably tied to the creation of a new international order within which Asia would assume cultural leadership. While emphasis clearly lay on culture, this does not necessarily mean the activism was apolitical (Shin 2005, 620). The profound distrust in the Western-dominated international order developed after the pivotal year 1919, fueled by the disillusionment with Wilson's United States, which failed to grant independence to Korea and guarantee Chinese sovereignty over former German possessions. For Yu and his fellow campaigners, the imagined cultural and political community of free Asian countries and peoples had the potential to replace the Eurocentric international system, which was designed to guarantee the acceptance of the "nation-state as the universally normal, legitimate form of the modern state" (Chatterjee 2012, 273).

In the end, national independence remained the main objective, even though the nation-state system as solidified by Versailles and Washington had also reified Japanese colonial rule over Korea and Taiwan. Arguing for the "awakening" of Asia, Yu and his fellow authors stressed Asian solidarity and cooperation on the grounds of an alleged cultural superiority in order to establish an alternative model to the Western-dominated world of antagonizing nation-states. This vaguely formulated cultural and spiritual superiority of "Asia" over the "West" in the post-Versailles era therefore served not only to decry the global dominance of Euro-America but also to rebuke Japan's subjugation of Asia which the activists saw as a betrayal. For the contributors to *The Asia Kunglun,* stressing cooperative solidarity among Asian peoples was therefore also a chiffre for national liberation. Even though they lacked political clout and their visions remained not much more than wishful ruminations, the historical significance of Yu's publication *The Asia Kunglun* derives from the fact that, despite its short lifespan, the journal offered East Asian intellectuals a unique forum for fecund debates on the situation in Asia which would not have been possible in other places in East Asia with the exception of Shanghai.

## NOTE

This chapter is a revised and amended version of my article "'Awakening Asia': Korean Student Activists in Japan, *The Asia Kunglun,* and Asian Solidarity, 1910–1923." *Cross-Currents: East Asian Studies History and Culture Review* e-journal 24: 105–131.

## REFERENCES

*The Asia Kunglun.* 1922a. "Dōkōkai ha nani wo suru? [What does the Dōkōkai do?]." Vol. 1 (7): 70-71.

*The Asia Kunglun.* 1922b. "'Shidai' Kenshō Boshū [Call for journal title prize contest]." Vol. 1: 28.

Aydin, Cemil. 2007. *The Politics of Anti-Westernism in Asia: Visions of World Order in Pan-Islamic and Pan-Asian Thought.* New York: Columbia University Press.

Bae Youngmi. 2013. "Zasshi 'Ajia Kōron' to Chōsen [The journal "The Asia Kunglun" and Korea]." *Koria Kenkyū* 4: 93–110.

Bose, Rash Behari. 1923. "Indo no Genkyō to Shimei [The current state of India and her mission]." *The Orient Review* 1:52–54.

Burbank, Jane and Cooper, Frederick, eds. 2010. *Empires in World History. Power and the Politics of Difference*. Princeton, NJ: Princeton University Press.

Cai Peihuo. 1922. "Kyokutō no Heiwa Hatashite Ikan? [How to reach peace in the Far East?]" *The Asia Kunglun* 1: 22–28.

Chatterjee, Partha. 1993. *The Nation and its Fragments. Colonial and Postcolonial Histories*. Princeton, NJ: Princeton University Press.

Chatterjee, Partha. 2012. *The Black Hole of Empire: History of a Global Practice of Power*. Princeton, NJ: Princeton University Press.

Chi, Hsu-Feng. 2012. *Taishōki Taiwanjin no 'Nippon Ryūgaku' Kenkyū* [Research on overseas studies by Taiwanese in Japan during the Taishō period]. Tōkyō: Ryūkei Shosha.

Ch'oe Ungpong. 1922. "Tōa no Akebono [The dawn of East Asia]." *The Asia Kunglun* 4: 48–51.

Choi, Ellie. 2015. "Yi Kwangsu and the Post–World War I Reconstruction Debate." *Journal of Korean Studies* 20(1): 33–75.

Chōsen Sōtokufu Keimukyoku Tōkyō Shutchōin, 1975. "Zai-Kyō Chōsenjin jōkyō. Taishō 13-nen [The situation of resident Koreans in Tōkyō. Taishō 13]." In *Zai-Nichi Chōsenjin Kankei Shiryō Shūsei dai 1 kan* [Collected materials concerning Koreans in Japan, vol. 1], edited by Pak Kyŏngshik, 133–150. Tōkyō: San'ichi Shobō.

Duara, Prasenjit. 2001. "The Discourse of Civilization and Pan-Asianism." *Journal of World History* 12(1): 99–130.

Duus, Peter. 1971. "Nagai Ryūtarō and the 'White Peril,' 1905–1944." *The Journal of Asian Studies* 31(1): 41–48.

Fung, Edmund S. K. 2010. *The Intellectual Foundations of Chinese Modernity: Cultural and Political Thought in the Republican Era*. Cambridge: University of Cambridge Press.

Garon, Sheldon. 2017. "Transnational History and Japan's 'Comparative Advantage.'" *The Journal of Japanese Studies* 43(1): 65–92.

Goebel, Michael. *Anti-imperial Metropolis: Interwar Paris and the Seeds of Third World Nationalism*. New York: Cambridge University Press, 2015.

Gōtō Ken'ichi. 2009. "Taishō Demokurashii to Zasshi 'Ajia Kōron': Sono Shiteki Imi to Jidai Haikei [Taishō democracy and the journal "The Asia Kunglun": Its historical meaning and background]." *Ajia Taiheiyō Tōkyū* 12: 149–166.

Han Jung-Sun N. 2012. *An Imperial Path to Modernity: Yoshino Sakuzō and a New Liberal Order in East Asia, 1905–1937*. Cambridge, MA: Harvard University Press.

Hatsuse Ryūhei. 1980. *Dentōteki Uyoku Uchida Ryōhei no Kenkyū* [A study of Uchida Ryōhei, a traditional right winger]. Fukuoka: Kyūshū Daigaku Shuppankai.

Hotta, Eri. 2006. "Rash Behari Bose and His Japanese Supporters." *Interventions* 8(1): 116–132.

Hotta, Eri. 2007. *Pan-Asianism and Japan's War 1931–1945*. New York: Palgrave Macmillan.

Hotta, Eri. 2011. "Konoe Fumimaro: 'A Call to Reject the Anglo-American Centered Peace,' 1918." In *Pan-Asianism: A Documented History*, edited by Sven Saaler and Christopher W. A. Szpilman, vol. 1, 311–317. Lanham, MD: Rowman and Littlefield.

Huebner, Stefan, and Thorsten Weber. 2013. "Introduction: National and Regional Belonging in Twentieth-Century East Asia." *Comparativ: Zeitschrift für Globalgeschichte und vergleichende Gesellschaftsforschung* 23(3): 6–16.

*Japan Times*. 1919. "Japanese, Chinese and Korean Students Meet." February 22, 4.

Jennings, John M. 1997. *The Opium Empire: Japanese Imperialism and Drug Trafficking in Asia, 1895–1945*. Westport, CT: Praeger.

Karl, Rebecca. 1998. "Creating Asia: China in the World at the Beginning of the Twentieth Century." *American Historical Review* 103(4): 1096–1118.

Kim, Bongjin. 2011. "Sin Ch'ae-ho: 'A Critique of Easternism,' 1909." In *Pan-Asianism: A Documented History*, edited by Sven Saaler and Christopher W. A. Szpilman, vol. 1, 191–194. Lanham, MD: Rowman and Littlefield.

Kim, Kyu Hyun. 2011. "Tarui Tokichi's Arguments on Behalf of the Union of the Great East, 1893." In *Pan-Asianism: A Documented History*, edited by Sven Saaler and Christopher W. A. Szpilman, vol. 1, 73–83. Lanham, MD: Rowman and Littlefield.

Kwon Junghee. 2014. "Asia Kongnon Sojae Hwang Sŏku ŭi Kŭlssŭgi [Hwang Suk-Woo's writings published in the magazine 'Asia Public Opinion']." *Han'guk munhwa Yŏn'gu* 26: 99–125.

Lee, Eun-Jeung. 2011. "An Chung-gŭn: 'A Discourse on Peace in East Asia,' 1910." In *Pan-Asianism: A Documented History*, edited by Sven Saaler and Christopher W. A. Szpilman, vol. 1, 205–209. Lanham, MD: Rowman and Littlefield.

Lee, You Jae. 2017. *Koloniale Zivilgemeinschaft. Alltag und Lebensweise der Christen in Korea (1894–1954)* [Colonial Civil Community. The Everyday Way of Life of Christians in Korea (1894–1954)]. Frankfurt am Main: Campus Verlag.

Manela, Erez. 2007. *The Wilsonian Moment: Self-Determination and the International Origins of Anticolonial Nationalism*. New York: Oxford University Press.

Naimushō Keihokyoku. 1975. "Zai-Kyō Chōsen Ryūgakusei Gaikyō. Taishō 14-nen [A general view of Korean students in Tōkyō]." In *Zai-Nichi Chōsenjin Kankei Shiryō Shūsei dai 1 kan* [Collected materials concerning Koreans in Japan, vol. 1], edited by Pak Kyŏngshik, 307–337. Tōkyō: San'ichi Shobō.

Neuhaus, Dolf-Alexander. 2016. "Assimilating Korea: Japanese Protestants, 'East Asian Christianity' and the Education of Koreans in Japan, 1905–1920." *Paedagogica Historica* 52(6): 614–628.

Neuhaus, Dolf-Alexander. 2017. "'Awakening Asia': Korean Student Activists in Japan, The Asia Kunglun, and Asian Solidarity, 1910–1923." *Cross-Currents: East Asian History and Culture Review*, 6(2): 608–638.

Ogio Fujio, ed. 2004. *Tokkō Keisatsu Kankei Shiryō Shūsei Dai 32kan: Suihei Undō, Zainichi Chōsenjin Undō, Kokka Shugi Undō* [Collection of material on the Special Higher Police, vol. 32: The Social Equality Movement, the Resident Korean Movement, and the Nationalist Movement]. Tōkyō: Fuji Shuppan.

Oguma, Eiji. 2002. *A Genealogy of "Japanese" Self-images*. Translated by David Askew. Melbourne: Trans Pacific Press.

Ono Yasuteru. 2013. *Chōsen Dokuritsu Undō to Higashi Ajia, 1910–1925* [The Korean independence movement and East Asia, 1910–1925]. Kyoto: Shibunkaku Shuppan.

Pierson, John D. (1980) 2014. *Tokutomi Sōhō, 1863–1957: A Journalist for Modern Japan*. Princeton, NJ: Princeton University Press.

Pratt, Marie Louis. 1992. *Imperial Eyes: Travel Writing and Transculturation*. London and New York: Routledge.

Robinson, Michael E. 2007. *Korea's Twentieth-Century Odyssey*. Honolulu: University of Hawai'i Press.

Saaler, Sven. 2007. "The Construction of Regionalism in Modern Japan: Kodera Kenkichi and his 'Treatise on Greater Asianism' (1916)." *Modern Asian Studies 41*(6): 1261–1294.

Saaler, Sven, and Christopher W. A. Szpilman. 2011a. *Pan-Asianism: A Documented History. Vol. 1, 1850–1920*. Lanham, MD: Rowman and Littlefield.

Saaler, Sven, and Christopher W. A. Szpilman. 2011b. *Pan-Asianism: A Documented History. Vol. 2, 1920–Present*. Lanham, MD: Rowman and Littlefield.

Saaler, Sven. 2011. "Japan, Korea, and Pan-Asianism: The Dōkōkai, 1921." In *Pan-Asianism: A Documented History*, edited by Sven Saaler and Christopher W. A. Szpilman, vol. 2, 63–67. Lanham, MD: Rowman and Littlefield.

Saaler, Sven. 2014. "The Kokuryūkai (Black Dragon Society) and the Rise of Nationalism, Pan-Asianism, and Militarism in Japan, 1901–1925." *International Journal of Asian Studies*, 11(2): 125–160.

Schmid, Andre. 2002. *Korea between Empires, 1895–1919*. New York: Columbia University Press.

Shimazu, Naoko. 1998. *Japan, Race and Equality. The Racial Equality Proposal of 1919*. London and New York: Routledge.

Shin, Gi-Wook. 2005. "Asianism in Korea's Politics of Identity." *Inter-Asia Cultural Studies*, 6(4): 616–630.

Shin, Gi-Wook. 2006. *Ethnic Nationalism in Korea: Genealogy, Politics, and Legacy*. Stanford, CA: Stanford University Press.
Shin, Michael. 2000. "Interior Landscapes: Yi Kwangsu's 'The Heartless' and the Origins of Modern Literature." In *Colonial Modernity in Korea*, edited by Shin Gi-Wook and Michael Robinson, 248–287. Cambridge, MA: Harvard University Press.
Shiraishi Masaya. 1982. "Meijiki no Zainichi Betonamujin to Ajia Shōminzoku Rentai no Kokoromi: 'Tōa Dōmeikai' naishi ha 'Ashū Washinkai' wo megutte [Cooperation between Vietnamese and Asian peoples in Japan in the late Meiji era: An Organization called the Đồng Á Đồng Minh Hội or Ashū Washinkai]." *Tōnan Ajia Kenkyū* 20(3): 335–372.
Tikhonov, Vladimir. 2002. "Korea's First Encounters with Pan-Asianism. Ideology in the Early 1880s." *Review of Korean Studies* 5 (2): 195–232.
Weber, Torsten. 2008. "Unter dem Banner des Asianismus: Transnationale Dimensionen des japanischen Asianismus-Diskurses der Taishō-Zeit (1912–1926) [Under the banner of Asianism: Transnational dimensions of Japanese discourse on Asianism during the Taishō era (1912–1926)]." *Comparativ: Zeitschrift für Globalgeschichte und vergleichende Gesellschaftsforschung* 18(6): 34–52.
Weber, Torsten. 2017. "From Versailles to Shanghai: Pan-Asianist Legacies of the Paris Peace Conference and the Failure of Asianism from Below." In *Asia after Versailles. Asian Perspectives in the Paris Peace Conference and the Interwar Order, 1919–33*, edited by Urs Matthias Zachmann, 77–97. Edinburgh: Edinburgh University Press.
Weber, Torsten. 2018. *Embracing "Asia" in China and Japan. Asianism Discourse and the Contest for Hegemony, 1912–1933*. Cham, Switzerland: Palgrave Macmillan.
Wells, Kenneth M. 1989. "The Background to the March First Movement: Koreans in Japan 1905–1919." *Korean Studies* 13: 5–21.
Yi Kwangsu. 1917. "Uri ŭi Isang [Our ideals]." *Hakchikwang* 14: 1–9.
Yu T'aekyŏng. 1922. "Iwayuru Tsuran Renmei to ha Nan zo ya? [What is this so-called Turanism?]." *The Asia Kunglun* 2: 109–122.
Yokoji Keiko. 2014. "Zasshi 'Taiwan Seinen': Jūsōteki na Nettowāku kara no naritachi [The journal "Taiwan Youth": Origins from multi-layered networks]." *Border Crossings: The Journal of Japanese-language Literature Studies* 1(1): 155–170.
Zachmann, Urs Matthias. 2007. "Blowing up a Double Portrait in Black and White: The Concept of Asia in the Writings of Fukuzawa Yukichi and Okakura Tenshin." *Positions* 15(2): 345–368.
Zachmann, Urs Matthias. 2017. "Introduction. Asia after Versailles." In *Asia after Versailles. Asian Perspectives in the Paris Peace Conference and the Interwar Order, 1919–33*, edited by Urs Matthias Zachmann, 1–19. Edinburgh: Edinburgh University Press.

*Chapter Eleven*

# Between Personal Choice and Social Exclusion

*Diaspora Identities of Korean Marriage Migrants of the Korean War Period in the Philippines*

## Minjung Kim

I would like to present some "unnoticed" histories shared by both Korea and the Philippines.[1] Korean women married to Filipinos in the Korean War period are probably the least noticed group of overseas Koreans.[2]

Marriage migration due to war during the cold war period is a crucial topic when discussing nationalism and gender issues. Yuval-Davis clearly demonstrated that constructed notions of nationhood usually involve specific notions of gender, i.e., "manhood" and "womanhood" (Yuval-Davis 1997, 1). Women have been induced to be biological reproducers of nations, and internationally married women have been a group likely to be excluded from their original nations, especially in S. Korea whose traditional state had been rooted on patrilineal kinship and Confucianism. A case in point is that a foreign husband of a Korean wife and their children were not eligible for Korean nationality and they could not be registered as a Korean family in Korea before the 1998 Nationality Law was amended to ensure equal rights for both Korean women and men in terms of the inheritance of citizenship.

Furthermore, as Moon articulates, the militarization of S. Korea under the protection of the U.S. has differentiated the term of membership in a nation, such as rights and responsibilities to the nation, between males and females (Moon 2005). Limitation or exclusion of membership in a nation within the state directly affects the recognition of membership in an overseas nation. Yeo poignantly identifies "nearly a hundred thousand" Korean Americans in the U.S. who married American military personnel during 1950 to 1989 as women who have married non-Koreans and who—regardless of their social background—are stained by presumed association with U.S. military camp towns and prostitution. Simply because they married an American soldier, they are left standing outside the bounds of both respectable Korean woman-hood and authentic Korean-ness (Yeo 2002, 3–4).

The social positioning of Korean women married to Filipinos in the Korean War period seems quite dissimilar from one of these numerous Korean marriage migrant women in the U.S. There has not been any sizable group of Korean marriage migrant women since then, and both Korea and the Philippines were categorized as developing countries until the 1970s. As a matter of fact, throughout the 20th century, both Korea and the Philippines have been under the influence of the U.S. The Philippines was a colony of the U.S. from 1898 to 1946 and has kept a close economic and political relationship with the U.S. after independence. Korea was under a U.S. military government for three years after liberalization from the Japanese colonial rule and has hosted the U.S. Army to this day since the Korean War (1950–1953) ceased.

It is this very similarity that provides the two countries with an interesting, shared historical context in which marriage migration occurred. Many Filipino males went to Korea during the Korean War as a part of the UN forces, the U.S. Navy or for U.S. companies, and Filipinos also assisted the U.S. military in various ways as civilian workers during the Vietnam War. The image of Filipinos was reminiscent of the U.S. to Koreans, though that has faded as Korea preceded the Philippines in terms of GDP ranking in the 1970s. Since Korea joined the OECD (Organization for Economic Cooperation and Development) in 1996, it has begun to take pride in becoming classified as a developed country and has a sense of superiority in becoming a destination country for other Asian immigrants, including Filipinos.

Then, how does the exclusion logic of membership in the overseas nation apply to the diaspora experiences of these Korean marriage migrants in the Philippines? And how does Korea's rapid economic growth, surpassing the Philippines economically, affect the diaspora identities of these Korean marriage migrants in the Philippines? To elucidate these questions, first, I will provide a brief history and characteristics of the relations between Korea and the Philippines. Second, I will discuss how intermarriage has been interpreted by the Korean women themselves and Korean society at large, and how these interpretations affect personal and societal perceptions of identity. Then, I will analyze how these women experience their diasporic identities as Korea has become richer and more globalized.

## "KOREANS" IN THE PHILIPPINES

Historical records show that ethnic Koreans' contact with Filipinos, before the Korean government was established, came about through Japanese trading activities in the Philippines, Catholic persecution by the Japanese shogunate and Cho-sŏn dynasty, and independent movement of Koreans under Japanese occupation. First of all, there were three occasions of a Korean's contact with Filipinos during the Cho-sŏn dynasty. The first was a man known by the name of Cho who became a captive during the second Japanese invasion of Chŏng-yu (1597). He was sent to the Philippines and Vietnam as a laborer under a Japanese merchant from 1604–1606 and finally returned home in 1607. Second, three Korean Catholics were included among 350 Japanese Catholics evacuated to Manila in November 1614, to avoid religious persecution by Tokugawa Ieyasu (Han'guktongnibundongsap'yŏnch'anwiwŏnhoe 2005, vol. 55). Finally, in 1837, three Korean theological students, including Kim Dae-gŏn who later became the first Korean Catholic saint, went to Macau to study but temporarily stayed in a monastery near Manila to escape riots in Macau (Kutsumi 2007, 61).

During the Japanese occupation period, the Korean provisional government in Shanghai appears to have communicated with pro-independence groups in the Philippines and India (*Tongailbo* April 9, 1924). Ahn Ch'angho, one of the major independence activists, traveled for two months in the Philippines to look for an alternative refuge for Koreans in Manchuria in February and March of 1929 (Kim, D. 2015, 54–58). According to the record of the colonial Japanese authorities, there were 42 Koreans in the Philippines among 2.78 million overseas Koreans in 28 countries in 1935 (Han'guktongnibundongsap'yŏnch'anwiwŏnhoe 2005, vol. 55).

Both the Philippines and Korea became independent after World War II and the two countries formed diplomatic ties in 1949, right after the establishment of the Korean government. During the Korean War, the Philippines was also an ally who dispatched around 7,000 troops to Korea. Both countries have been allied with the U.S. and have been dependent on the U.S. for their development in the newly reorganized global system. Yet until the 1960s, the Philippines was a promising developing country, while South Korea was still suffering the devastation of the Korean War. The GDP per capita of the Philippines in 1960 was USD 254.4, which was 60% higher than the GDP per capita of Korea of USD 158.2 (The World Bank n.d.). Until the 1960s the Philippines was the most westernized and therefore the most "modernized" country in Asia, except for Japan, and was considered as an exemplary country in the third world (Romulo 1974).

It is obvious that Korea showed interest in the Philippines' performance and achievement at the time. According to Korean newspaper articles on the

Philippines in the 1960s, there were great concerns regarding human exchanges between the two countries in sports, art, education, and film. This
time accords with the main period during which Korea showed a sociocultural interest towards its Southeast Asian neighbors, before entering the Yusin
period. At the beginning of the 1960s, the Philippines donated cash to help
after flood damage in Korea (*Tongailbo* June 27, 1963), Filipino journalists
saw to fund-raising for Korean bicyclists to cover their return trip expenses
from Manila after a national competition (*Kyŏnghyangsinmun* May 8, 1962),
a Korean director studied movie-making skills in the Philippines by making a
joint film (*Kyŏnghyangsinmun* December 21, 1962), and the biography of
President Magsaysay was translated into Korean (*Tongailbo* December 28,
1962). The most noticeable event during the 1960s between the two countries
was probably the summit meeting of the seven countries participating in the
Vietnam War, which was held in Manila in 1966. It was initiated by Korean
president Pak Chŏng-hŭi, who presented his resolution to strengthen the
collaborative effort of allies against the Vietnamese Communist group
(*Kyŏnghyangsinmun* October 25, 1966).

The economic ranks of the two countries, however, started to change
from 1969 onwards and were completely reversed by 1975. In 1969, Korea's
GDP per capita (USD 243.3) slightly surpassed the Philippines' (USD 241.7)
and in 1975, Korea's GDP per capita (USD 615.2) was 70% higher than the
Philippines' (USD 360.7) (The World Bank n.d.). Korean society owed its
rapid economic growth to entering the Vietnam War (1955–1975) and getting support from the U.S. It was in 1975 when the national air carrier
Korean Air (KAL) put into service a flight route between Seoul and Manila[3]
and also when the economic achievements of the two countries, equally
based on martial law, were revealed and judged. This flight route was, in
fact, targeted at increasing numbers of Japanese tourists to Manila. However,
the number of Korean travelers to the Philippines also started to grow and
their purpose diversified owing to the KAL service to Manila. The Korean
community in the Philippines started to truly emerge with World Health
Organization (WHO) and Asian Development Bank (ADB) staff members,
employees of Korean companies such as Kumho, Hanwha, and Hyundai, and
university students in the 1980s.[4] It is also said that the leadership group of
the present United Korean Community Association in the Philippines (UK-
CAP) immigrated in the 1970s and 1980s, according to Vice-President Lee
of UKCAP.[5]

In the 1980s, the long dictatorships of both nations ended and both countries had experienced major political and social changes. Korea implemented
more diverse diplomatic efforts to enhance its national image, while entering
the category of middle-income countries in the aftermath of the Cold War
(Kim and Yang 2014). President Chŏn-Duh-whan, the successor to President
Pak Chŏng-hŭi, formally visited the Philippines as head of state in 1981[6] for

the first such visit; Senator Aquino was assassinated at the Manila airport in 1983 and then People Power, the first bloodless people's revolution in Asia, happened in 1986; Korea hosted the 10th Asian games in 1986 and the 24th Olympics in 1988 in Seoul. Meanwhile, the Korean government liberalized overseas travel of Koreans in 1989 just after the Seoul Olympics. It was, however, in the 1990s when many more Koreans flowed into the Philippines, especially tourists and minors as students. The Korean president Kim Yŏng-sam started the globalization policy in 1995 by launching a special committee to pursue the globalization of Korea. English classes as an integral part of public education started, beginning in elementary school, and the names of major business groups were also changed into English, such as Kŭmsŏngsa into LG and Sŏn'gyŏng into SK (Choi 2000).

The number of Koreans in the Philippines in 1995 increased to 5,000, or almost three times the number six years previously ([Korean] Ministry of Foreign Affairs 1989; 1995). The growth in the number of Koreans in the Philippines slowed in the run-up towards the Asian financial crisis in 1997 and also because Korean society made strides in expanding its interests in other foreign countries. At the same time, Korean society's interests in the Philippines were intensified for business investment, trade, tourism, and the study of English.

During the 2000s, Korean nationals became the largest foreign visitor group in the Philippines, having overtaken U.S. nationals in 2006 with over 600,000 people. Korean visitor arrivals continue to increase, passing one million in 2011 ([Philippine] Department of Tourism 2011). This trend of increasing the number of tourists also has repercussions on the increase in the number of Korean residents in the Philippines. Especially in 2007, the number of Korean residents in the Philippines almost doubled from 46,000 to 86,800 in a single year ([Korean] Ministry of Foreign Affairs 2007). As of 2017, there are 7.4 million overseas Koreans in 194 countries and the Philippines have the 10th largest population of overseas Koreans (table 11.1).

The composition and profile of Korean residents in the Philippines is quite different from the profile of Koreans in the other top three countries. In China, the U.S., and Japan, about half or more of the overseas Koreans are local citizens, but the majority of Koreans in the Philippines occupy an intermediate status between a temporary visitor and a frequent visitor (Kim, M. 2015b). Koreans as Filipino citizens number just 22, and many of them are likely Korean women who were married to Filipinos during the 1950s.

Table 11.1.

| | Permanent resident | Overseas Koreans | | | Koreans as Foreign citizens | Total |
|---|---|---|---|---|---|---|
| | | Visitor | Student | Subtotal | | |
| **Total** | 1,049,209 | 1,354,330 | 260,323 | 2,672,202 | 4,758,486 (64%) | 7,430,688 |
| **China** | 6,602 | 275,338 | 62,056 | 349,406 | 2,198,624 (86%) | 2,548,030 |
| **U.S.** | 416,334 | 546,144 | 73,113 | 1,035,591 | 1,456,661 (58%) | 2,492,252 |
| **Japan** | 379,940 | 57,718 | 15,438 | 453,096 | 365,530 (45%) | 818,626 |
| **The Philippines** | 1,176 | 81,992 | 9,903 | 93,071 | 22 (0%) | 93,093 |

Source: Ministry of Foreign Affairs (2017). The top 10 countries are China, U.S.A., Japan, Canada, Uzbekistan, Australia, Russia, Vietnam, Kazakhstan, and the Philippines, in order.

# FAMILY DE/CONSTRUCTION DURING
# THE KOREAN WAR PERIOD

The story of Pak Yun-hwa, who became the first president of the Korean Association in the Philippines in 1967 and kept this position until 1978 when he passed away, conveys the context of international marriages among Koreans around the time of Korea's independence.

According to a series of five newspaper articles based on interviews with him (*Kyŏnghyangsinmun* February 3–28, 1977), he was born in Ŭiju in the North Korean territory in 1917 and left his hometown for the Philippines in 1935. He intended to go to the U.S. for study, but became a merchant dealing in ginseng and other herbal medicine in Manila's Chinatown. Even though Pak Y. was a civilian he was jailed twice as a prisoner of war during the Pacific War. He recollected that he was treated as a Japanese under the U.S. occupation but as a third class national under the Japanese in the Philippines. After the Korean War occurred, Pak Y. found work again with the help of a Chinese friend and decided to stay in the Philippines instead of returning home to North Korea. He married a Filipino woman in 1951, started his own company to export wood to Korea in 1958, and had five children. It is notable that it was just after the Korean War broke out that Pak Y. decided to marry a Filipino woman and settle down in the Philippines instead of returning to North Korean territory.

Regarding the size of the Korean community around the time when Pak Y. got married and decided to stay in the Philippines, there are two Korean newspaper articles that mention the number of Koreans in the Philippines during the 1950s–1960s. One mentions only nine male Korean students in the Philippines in 1959 (*Tongailbo* January 5, 1959). However, the other introduces six Korean men who married Filipino women and settled down in the Philippines under a similar situation to that of Pak Y., including one former army surgeon with Chiang Kai-shek's troops (*Kyŏnghyangsinmun* January 28, 1967). The latter newspaper article also mentioned 25 Korean women married to Filipino men and the Korean restaurant in Manila that some of these women jointly operated. However, unlike internationally married Korean men, who were referred to as "overseas Koreans" (kyop'o, 僑胞), internationally married Korean women were referred to simply as "Korean women" (han'guk yŏin, 韓國女人). If the former newspaper article didn't pay attention to internationally married Koreans who settled down in the Philippines regardless of sex, the latter considered only the six Korean men as overseas Koreans while leaving the Korean women out of the category although they were four times more numerous than the men.

In fact, there were Korean women who decided to marry Filipinos they met in Korea during the Korean War period. In the 1950s, some Filipino men came to Korea as high-ranking UN officials, officers or soldiers with the UN forces, and others as news reporters, civil technician contract workers in military camps, or employees of construction or trading corporations. Among them, Bueno, a Filipino ambassador assigned to Korea in 1962, was married to Pak Hyŏn-juk, a Korean woman (*Tongailbo* March 27, 1962). Bueno had visited Korea several times before as the Philippine representative of the UN Commission for the Unification and Rehabilitation of Korea (UNCRRK) during the 1950s and he met Pak H. at the foreigners-only Chosŏn Hotel where she worked at the front desk after graduating from Ewha girls' high school. For certain Korean girls at the time, Filipino men could be considered as promising and reliable husbands from a country better off economically.[7]

The U.S. hired Filipinos as U.S. Navy civilian workers by inserting Article 27 into the Military Bases Agreement in 1947 when the Philippines became independent. By this action, 2,000 Filipinos were hired every year by the U.S. on four- or six-year contracts around the Korean War period (Espiritu 1995, 15).[8] They belonged to the U.S. Army and were a larger group with more contact with ordinary Koreans near U.S. campsites than Philippine Army personnel in Korea who joined combat troops.

Now I would like to introduce the life stories of seven Korean women married to Filipinos in Korea in the 1950s, including two deceased women spoken for by their sons.[9] Of their husbands, six worked for the U.S. Navy as vessel electricians or navigation officers and one worked for a U.S. munitions company when they married. My interviews with them took place in the Philippines from July 2013 to May 2014. Among the seven women, five (Hayoung, Suk-hee, and Ok-ja, Diwa's mother and Yaron's mother) lived in Metro Manila, and two (Hyun-sil and Sun-young) lived in the provincial area in Luzon. Four of the women were in their eighties; one in her seventies; and the two sons of the then-deceased women were in their fifties at the time of the interviews. These two sons and their families moved to the Philippines in the mid-1960s when they were 11 and 13 years old. Therefore, they can speak Korean and also remember many things about their childhood in Korea. The women's educational backgrounds in Korea varied from none to middle school graduates. All Filipino husbands of these seven Korean women have now passed away.

Above all, mobility is a noticeable feature in their lives. They were born and raised not only in Korea but also in the North Korean territory and even in Japan, such as Daegu, Yŏngdŏk, Kimch'ŏn, Haeju, and Osaka, etc. Before they left Korea they had to move between several places and their various trajectories of movement inside Korea reflected the historical upheavals of Korean society, such as the liberation from Japanese occupation, the outbreak of the Korean War, and the post-war recovery process. However, they departed from Busan or Incheon to the Philippines after marrying to Filipinos in Korea, except for one woman who came to the Philippines through Ho Chi Minh City (Saigon).

Busan and Incheon are port cities where U.S. military camps were located at that time. Camp Hialeah was in Busan. The U.S. Forces Command was located at that camp and it had a hotel, hospital, school, officers' club, restaurant, and post exchange (PX). The camp market was in Incheon. The U.S. Army Service Command in Korea (ASCOM) was located at that camp and it is where some of the women's Filipino husbands worked until 1965 when their contracts were terminated. Some couples met in Busan and moved to Incheon where their Filipino husbands were later assigned. In sum, three came from Busan in 1956, another three came from Incheon in 1965–1969, and one from Seoul via Vietnam in 1972.

The Korean women who married Filipinos belonged to a group whose radius of activities happened to overlap with these Filipino men. The Korean women interviewees met their Filipino husbands while they worked as clerks or saleswomen in the PX or camp clubs. One woman met her husband at her sister's house, which was a kind of black market for PX goods. The common factor among these women was probably that they were young female laborers entering a new type of service market in Korea, although their educational backgrounds and economic situations varied.

There were two women who were adopted, one to her father's friend in Gwangju and the other to her uncle in Samch'ŏk. In their adoptive families, they served as housemaids and both ran away from home. One went to Busan with her friend and found a job working for the club of Camp Hialeah through a Korean military staff meeting at the cold noodle restaurant where she had been working. The other, however, tried to live temporarily with her grandfather in Hŭnghae and then her mother in Yŏngdŏk, before going to Busan where she was seen by a relative, caught, and sent back to her uncle's house. There she was introduced to her future Filipino husband by her cousin who was a nurse at a hospital.

For other women, male family members went missing during the Korean War period. Their fathers were deceased, missing, or left home after losing their wives and getting remarried. Many of their grown-up brothers were also deceased or missing. The oldest brother of one woman had left Korea to study in the U.S. In her case, her family members could not stay together but split into a couple of groups while moving back and forth between Samch'ŏk, Seoul, Jeju-do, and Taegu, after her family left Haeju in North Korea before the Korean War broke out. After marrying a Filipino man in Taegu, she and her new family continued to move to Ŭijŏngbu and Saigong to follow her husband's company contracts with the U.S. Army before final settlement in Manila. There was also one woman who first married a Korean man, a schoolteacher, in 1950. She also left her birthplace of Kimch'ŏn, moved to Seoul to study, and moved again to Daegu for evacuation and married life. However, her husband abandoned her and their newly born daughter and left home for Jeju-do to join a communist group during the Korean War. Later she then happened to marry a Filipino man.

Thus, besides frequent movement in a time of social turmoil, another common factor in these women's lives was the absence of adult men in the family when they were young. Even though there may have been some living family members, they happened to scatter and unite according to the circumstances. Young women belonging to families without a "male head of family" couldn't help but work and seek husbands who could support them during the war and in the post-war period.

Their marriages with Filipino men who were Asians, not too foreign, and earned good salaries in U.S. money could be considered a satisfying choice in their situation at that time. At least Ha-young, Sun-young, and Suk-hee, among the five Korean women whom I could directly interview, thought their decision on intermarriage with a Filipino was right at that time and even now. They felt that their Filipino husbands were quite handsome, and considered them kind and considerate. Meanwhile Ok-ja, whose Filipino husband was a serious alcoholic, recollected that she just followed what her uncle decided as an adoptee, and Hyun-sil, whose Korean husband went missing during the war, seemed to regret this remarriage with her Filipino husband because she had to leave her daughter from the first marriage in Korea.

Korean men who married Filipino women in the Philippines in the 1950s, such as Pak Y., seemed to marry Filipinos because they happened to be in the Philippines during the liberation period of S. Korea and "were stuck in" the chaos of that time. Meanwhile, Korean women, more or less, who married Filipino men in Korea in the 1950s seemed to marry Filipinos "to escape from" the poverty and catastrophic situation of Korea by establishing their own families. This comparison suggests that these Korean women made their own personal choices in deciding their international marriages, unlike the majority of young Korean women in those days.

However, their personal choice of international marriage had been prompted by two common social factors in their life situations during the Korean War period, as mentioned above. First, their families lost their male members at home, either fathers or elder brothers, whether they passed away, remarried, joined the communist group, went missing, or moved to the U.S., etc. Second, under this kind of situation without "male heads of families," these women were compelled to work in newly introduced service jobs relating to the presence of the U.S. military camps in Korea. By marrying Filipinos these Korean women could fulfill social responsibilities of building families under more desirable conditions from their standpoint. Contrary to their frequent moves within Korea, there was little change in their residence after emigration to the Philippines, which showed that their international marriages stabilized their lives through establishing their own families. However, they had launched a very unfamiliar journey of life in the Philippines with their choice of international marriage.

## LIVING AS KOREAN MARRIAGE MIGRANT WOMEN IN THE PHILIPPINES

Now I introduce their journey of these women to the Philippines, how they made a living in the Philippines, how they built new family relations and social networks in the Philippines under considerably disconnected circumstances from Korea, and how the globalization trend in Korean society affected their ethnic affiliation.

Korean wives who left Korea in the 1950s boarded U.S. army airplanes to go to the Philippines via stopovers such as Okinawa and Tokyo. They recalled the heat of tropical weather and the palm trees of the exotic scenery as their first impressions of the Philippines. Unlike Korea in the 1950s and 1960s, there were lots of cars and goods in Manila. Most husbands of the interviewed participants worked as vessel captains or electricians back home in the Philippines after expiration of their contracts with the U.S. Navy. The Filipino husbands regularly went abroad for extended periods as part of their work, and their Korean wives spent much time alone taking care of the children. Surely, the Korean wives felt lonely and isolated as strangers unable to adjust to local ways or, given the language differences, communicate freely with locals, especially in the early years. Some of them said they went to the pier where vessels with Koreans entered, to see and talk to Koreans in Korean in order to relieve homesickness.

During the long absences of their Filipino husbands, it would have been expected that the Korean wives needed help and support from their husbands' family members. However, half of these women stood apart from their Filipino in-laws in cases where the Filipino-in-laws lived far away in the provinces or if the Filipino in-laws expected financial support from the Filipino husbands who had regular cash income from working abroad. There were also two couples who split due to domestic violence and a husband's new marriage abroad. However, as divorce is not allowed under Philippine law, the women had to remain in their legal marriages and their husbands kept a connection with their children. The children born of these couples in the Philippines were raised almost as complete Filipinos in terms of language, ways of life, and personal and social relations. However, the two eldest sons, Diwa and Yaron, of the two now-deceased women recalled that they had a difficult time among their peer groups in school in Korea and in the Philippines as well. When I interviewed Sun-young at Yaron's house and Yaron told me this, however, Sun-young noted that mothers didn't seriously notice this kind of children's difficulties. Anyhow, Yaron and Diwa graduated from top colleges in the Philippines and are now working as a medical doctor and a business consultant, respectively, by utilizing their networks with Koreans in the Philippines.

In the previous section, I mentioned the Korean news article which introduced 6 male and 25 female internationally married Koreans in the Philippines in 1967 (*Kyŏnghyangsinmun* January 28, 1967). According to my interviews, Ha-young, who came to the Philippines in 1956 from Busan, heard at the Korean Embassy's New Year's Party in the late 1950s that there were around 80 Koreans in the Philippines. The Korean Ambassador in the Philippines, Yu Yang-su, also recollected in his memoir that 150 Koreans welcomed President Pak Chŏng-hŭi in 1966 (Yu 1988, 33). This massive gap in the number of Koreans from Korean newspapers can be explained by the fact that in reality the number of Koreans in the Philippines included significant numbers of Korean women married to U.S. military personnel assigned to U.S. camps in the Philippines. Sun-young, who came to the Philippines in 1969 from Incheon and joined welcoming President Chŏn Duh-hwan in 1981 at the Manila airport, remembered that two big buses were needed to bring people and that almost all of them were Korean intermarried women with the majority from the Clark and Subic U.S. camp sites. However, these Korean women married to U.S. citizens in the Philippines hardly communicated with other Koreans in the Philippines. Taken together, there were about 20–30 Korean women who married Filipinos during the Korean War and moved to the Philippines and at least 10–12 of those women formed an acquaintance group in the 1970s.

Most of these Korean women lived on their husbands' regular salaries. However, Ok-ja couldn't receive enough money from her husband and had to work herself. She recounted impressive stories of how skillful she was at planning, working, and selling home-made children's clothes in the early years. Suk-hee also thoroughly planned for and opened a restaurant, even though the couple had savings and her husband belonged to a moderately rich family, because her husband became jobless after returning from Vietnam. Meanwhile, Ha-young started her study in high school after raising two sons until early school age and she even finished college with a major in optometry. Further study was her ardent dream and what her husband promised to her when he proposed marriage in Korea. She opened her own small eyeglass shop but it didn't stay open for long.

It was these same Korean women who were responsible for opening Korean restaurants and supermarkets in Metro Manila from the early 1960s on. Since the 1961 opening of the first Korean restaurant in Manila, K's house,[10] many other businesses have opened and closed, including well known eateries such as Arirang, Korea house, Korean town, the Merville supermarket and others. Most of these restaurants were opened in Manila but the Merville supermarket was located in the new residential district in

Parañaque city, near the airport. There, some of the Korean women purchased lots for housing and even bought cemetery plots near each other. It seems that in the late 1970s and 1980s, when Japanese tourists surged into the Philippines and the number of Korean residents also started to increase, that the Korean restaurant business thrived. Suk-hee, who had capital and also living experiences abroad in Vietnam before coming to the Philippines, opened her first Asian restaurant in 1974, but soon changed it to a Korean restaurant, which even opened a second branch in the late 1970s. This kind of tourism boom drove some Korean marriage migrant housewives into the labor market. Korean restaurant owners tended to prefer to hire Korean intermarried women as managers since they could understand the Filipino language and local culture. Ha-young, Hyun-sil, and Sun-young worked as hall managers at Suk-hee's restaurant; Ok-ja tried to run a restaurant twice and worked as a tour guide under a Japanese name; and Yaron's mother joined the ownership of a supermarket and ran a restaurant for some time. Diwa's mother also opened a restaurant and then worked as a guide for Japanese tourists during the 1980s. In fact, running restaurants and guiding Japanese tourists or Korean visitors were closely related roles and mutually helpful to each other, because tour guides could bring their clients to restaurants as customers. Some of the Korean marriage migrant women were also involved in "buy and sell" businesses with local products or Korean products later on with increasing visits of Korean businesspersons.

These Korean women interacted with each other when having fun, such as singing along and dancing, playing cards or a slot machine, eating and drinking outside, etc., especially in the heyday of the 1980s. They shared videotapes of Korean soap dramas, cassette tapes of Korean pop songs, and Korean food and goods. For example, Suk-hee, the owner of a restaurant, specially ordered and distributed a Korean styled daily pad calendar to these Korean women every year. For this reason, the women's employment relationships looked bilaterally favorable to each other in the sense that both employers and employees were thought to help counterpart Korean wives of Filipinos who were in the same boat. Suk-hee used the term of *p'illip'in manura* (Filipinos' wives) to name themselves to distinguish their group from Korean couples within the Korean communities in the Philippines.

Before the 1980s, the Korean wives of Filipinos had felt isolated from Korea literally, from local Filipino society culturally. This kind of common experience of being isolated made them allied together for working and having fun. This common sense of being isolated and allying together presumably became the basis for them to keep their own "Korean-ness" as sharing their lives in the Philippines regardless of their titular nationality. As the number of Korean students and Korean company expatriates increased in the 1980s, Korean restaurants operated by Korean marriage migrant women commonly functioned as network hubs for newcomer Koreans where people met each other and exchanged information. Sometimes these Korean women offered boarding rooms especially for Korean students in higher education. However, as the size of the Korean community grew, these intermarried women no longer represented Koreans in the Philippines. Newly established Korean language schools were mainly operated for children of Korean couple families. This was partly because these Korean women became relatively few in number compared to the newcomers and because their children were considered to belong to Philippine society by the Korean community according to the patrilineal norm.

## RE/CONNECTING TO KOREA AND REINFORCING KOREAN IDENTITIES

It took quite some time for most of the Korean marriage migrant women to re-connect with their natal families in Korea once they had moved to the Philippines. Before the late 1980s it was difficult to make international calls, the Korean government regulated trips abroad, and most of these women were engaged in childcare and their family budgets were also insufficient. Only some of the women involved in the retail trade were able to visit Korea. Opportunities for these Korean women to visit Korea more regularly started only in 1989 when the Korean government liberalized Koreans' trips abroad and held the First World Korean Festival. It was also a time when they were released from the duty of caring for their retired husbands and their children, who were now building their own families. Most of them enjoyed visiting Korea during the 1990s and 2000s to meet their family members and relatives, talk in Korean, eat various Korean foods, and visit places of memory.

Hyun-sil's case is rare because she could visit Korea for the first time already in 1968 while accompanying her stepbrother who visited the Philippines on the way back to Korea after studying in England. She wanted to meet her ex-Korean husband and her Korean daughter at that time but her female cousins strongly dissuaded her from contacting them. Later, she found that her Korean ex-husband had reported her as dead to the Korean government. Hyun-sil could finally meet her Korean daughter in 1989 when the Korean daughter visited the Philippines as Korea liberalized its citizens' travel abroad. It was only in 2003 that Hyun-sil could visit Korea again with her Filipino daughter after her Filipino husband had passed away. She would have been eligible for overseas Korean visas (F-4) but she could not apply for one because her resident registration record had been terminated by the death report. She and her Filipino daughter had visited Korea as tourists and stayed as undocumented foreigners in Korea until her daughter was caught by an immigration crackdown in 2009. Hyun-sil's case shows how vulnerable internationally married Korean women in the old days were in keeping or reclaiming their Korean citizenship and legal affiliation with Korea, when male family members denied them these rights.

Sun-young, Diwa's mother and Korean-born Diwa, being different from Hyun-sil, could get overseas Korean visas and visited Korea often to maintain their visas. It was in 1992 when Sun-young visited Korea for the first time after moving to the Philippines. She was so excited at seeing her sisters again and wandering over the country to visit places and people that she stayed for two years straight. She usually spent her time helping her sister or others who ran restaurants when they needed a hand. Diwa received their overseas Korean visas in 2002 and visited Korea every two years to renew their visas. Yaron, who had moved to the Philippines as an elementary school student like Diwa, also wanted to apply for this visa but failed. He had to get documentation to prove that his mother was a Korean citizen because she had already passed away in 1997. However, he was unable to find his mother's family register by himself in Korea and the Philippine embassy also had not kept records of his mother's marriage registration.

The other three women, Ha-young, Suk-hee, and Ok-ja, did not consider applying for an overseas Korean visa. Ha-young visited Korea in 1986 for the first time and reunited with her sisters after many twists and turns. Since then she has repeatedly visited Korea and stayed each time as long as her tourist visa allowed until her eldest sister passed away. Suk-hee and Ok-ja also visited Korea more than twice but less often than the other women, because almost all of Suk-hee's siblings lived in the U.S. and Ok-ja had no siblings and close relatives in Korea.

Even though the Korean citizenship of these Korean internationally married women was nominally lost when they became Filipino citizens through marriage registrations, they have never thought it affected their Korean-ness. It seems that their Korean ethnic identification has held steady and been even been fortified as a generation going through the process of building a modern nation-state with the Japanese occupation, division of Korea and the Korean War. Aside from their revisiting Korea, the rapid growth of the Korean community in the Philippines in the 2000s also provided these Korean marriage migrant women with various "nutriments" to reinforce their Korean ethnic identities. Now they can easily meet Koreans, converse in Korean, access Korean mass media, purchase Korean food and commodities, etc., in the Philippines.

It must be due to the reversed positions of Korea and the Philippines in terms of GDP rank since the 1970s, as shown in the introduction, which increased these women's desires to visit Korea, rather than causing their Korean families to wish to move to the Philippines. After the early 2000s, furthermore, Korean soap operas and K-pop gained popularity and well-off young Korean students were obviously present in the Philippines. The second or third generation of these internationally married couples in the Philippines is also getting more interested in obtaining or strengthening their Korean ethnic identities.

In fact, sharing the same ethnic identities with their children seemed an unattainable goal for foreign mothers who were unable to teach the Filipino language or guide their children's school lives. Localized children hardly spoke Korean, their mothers' mother tongue, and seem to have had difficulty identifying themselves as Korean, even though they love their Korean mothers and feel positively about their mother's country, Korea. However, some of their interethnic children like Diwa and Yaron, who had grown up in Korea, happened to be quite interested in "obtaining" Korean ethnic identities.

Hyun-sil's daughter is another example. She desired to live in Korea and her wish came true as she worked in Korea for several years but without proper documents. According to Hyun-sil, her daughter fell in love with Korean soap operas and songs and she identified herself as Korean more than Filipino. Her daughter may have seen luxury and glamour in Korean soap operas and songs, but she surely also saw reality when she worked in Korea. She may have found meaning, hope, and even pride in modern current Korean style. Some of these women's children and grandchildren also became interested in learning Korean after discovering the "Korean wave" or making their own Korean friends independent of their mothers' families. For example, Sun-young's youngest daughter became interested in learning Korean when she started to watch Korean soap dramas. Sun-young's second daughter's family in the U.S. became close to a Korean family through a friendship with the daughters of both families, who are school friends. As the two families met often, Sun-young's daughter and granddaughter asked Sun-young more about Korea and started to learn the Korean language.

It can be said that these Korean women's ethnic identities as Koreans have been substantial, regardless of the existence of the overseas Korean visa or their frequency of visiting Korea. This is because they grew up in Korea during the colonial and nation-state building period and shared the common sentiment of this period. They emigrated to the Philippines at a time when the nation of S. Korea had experienced the tragedy of a fratricidal war and they have lived through the heyday of nationalism. As Geertz accentuated the primordial sentiment of ethnicity (Geertz 1973), Korean-ness is irreversible and unalterable for these Korean marriage migrant women because being Korean was given by blood line and imprinted by acculturation.

However, as they happened to meet more Koreans both in the Philippines in the 1980s and later in Korea as well, their own Korean ethnic identities abroad as "Filipinos' wives" among Koreans in the Philippines started to be manifested. This sense of belonging to the "Filipinos' wives" group is based on their being wives of Filipinos and naturalized Filipino citizens, being differentiated from most of the Koreans in the Philippines. In fact, their

Korean ethnic identities seem to be assembled from four categories: ethnic origin (Korean), gender (woman), generation (the Korean War generation), and spouse's ethnicity (Filipino husband). Here the categories of gender and the spouse's ethnicity are crucial criteria, due to Korean patrilineal cultural norms, upon which these women have to build up their own Korean ethnic identities.

Meanwhile, Korean ethnic identities of the next generations have become varied, flexible, and changing, from identifying as overseas Koreans, as newly converted interethnic Americans, Filipino Hallyu (Korean wave) fans with a Korean ethnic background to disinterested Filipinos in Korea. It seems, however, that the more the world globalizes, the more the interethnic second generation distinguishes themselves in some way as a group more attached to Korea than as other Filipinos or Asian Americans.

## CONCLUDING REMARKS

Migration is engendered by the events of the time and by reflecting the social legitimacy of both the origin and destination countries (Oishi 2005). The hierarchy among nations and migration policies, including nationality laws, are crucial factors in determining the migrants' gender and to shaping the migrants' ways of life. The life stories in this chapter on Korean women married to Filipinos show how an individual migrant's destiny and their intergenerational destiny are still in large part determined not only by their birth nation's economic position, but also by critical sociocultural-historical factors, such as gender ideology embedded in kinship norms and nationalistic notions.

In some contexts of gender ideology that allots public and private domains by sex, getting married for women is not a matter of choice but an option to survive. When hardship during the war period was combined with absence of male heads of families in the patriarchal society, some Korean girls participated in new type of service labor in and out of the U.S. camps where many Filipinos also served as civilian workers. At that time, the Korean women in my interviews decided upon their marriages with Filipinos on their own accords and recognized their decisions as "natural" and "reasonable" given their circumstances. Based on this fact they can be considered uncommon, modern, independent women, but that is not their image in Korean society. Rather, it seems the ethno-patriarchal lineage of Korea and the national reversal of fortunes with the Philippines has led to their becoming an "unseen" group of overseas Koreans in a less developed country.

However, the Korean ethnic identities of these Korean marriage migrant women of the Korean War period in the Philippines have been maintained and have even been reinforced as time passed. First, they belong to the generation of the liberation period of Korea in which nationalism has been thought to be accepted by blood and heart. Second, their own identities as Filipinos' wives, as Korean ethnic identities emerged through developing a mutual help network and from daily socializing when the Korean community in the Philippines, grew. Thirdly, the globalizing and developed Korean society made them keep their Korean-ness by supplying numerous Korean commodities, services, and human contacts. Those three dimensions occured at different times and were independent of each other, but affected these Korean women abroad by reinforcing their Korean ethnic identities: as belonging to the Korean War generation, as being Korean women married to Filipinos, and as being matrilineal ancestors of an interethnic generation. These women's experiences, which have taken place along with the rapid changes in modern Korean society, illustrate the complexities involved in interpreting a sense of belonging in this globalizing and trans-border era.

## NOTES

1. I deeply thank my interview participants who willingly recollected and shared their life stories with me for this research. I send them all my best wishes.
2. This chapter is a combined and revised version of my previous two journal articles in Korean: Kim, M. (2015a), "se pŏnŭi kkum: han'guk chŏnjaenggie p'illip'in namsŏnggwa kyŏrhonhan han'guk yŏsŏngŭi saengae iyagi" (A Life Story of a Korean Woman who Married to a Filipino Man during Korean War) in *Han'gugyŏsŏnghak* (*Journal of Korean Women's Studies*) 31(3): 103–137; and Kim, M. (2015b), "1900nyŏndae ch'ojungban'gi p'illip'inŭi haninijue taehan sŏngch'aljŏk yŏn'gu" (Reflecting on Korean Emigration to the Philippines in the Early and Middle 1900s) in *Sahoewa yŏksa* (*Society and History*) 107: 251–284.
3. The Philippine air carrier, Philippine Airlines (PAL), started service to Seoul in 1991.
4. The WHO office in Manila was established in January 1973 but was vacant until 1981. Since the first Korean regional director of the Western Pacific Regional Office was appointed in 1989, Koreans' participation has increased. The ADB office opened in 1966 in Roxas Boulevard and moved to Mandaluyoung into a new building which was designed in 1983 and completed in 1991 by SOM (U.S. architectural firm) while subcontracting with Hyundai, a Korean company.
5. From an interview on July 15, 2013, in Makati.
6. President Pak's visit to the Philippines in 1966 was to participate in the seven countries' summit meeting on the Vietnam War.
7. For example, there were 4 Filipinos among 27 non-American foreigners to whom Seoul National University conferred honorary degrees from 1948 to 1962, and Bueno, who is mentioned in the text, is one of them (*Kyŏnghyangsinmun* March 2, 1963).
8. The U.S. Navy started to recruit Filipinos as vessel crews as early as 1898 when the Philippines were transferred to the U.S. from Spain. The number of Filipino workers in the U.S. Navy reached up 5% of the U.S. Navy population during the 1920s and 1930s (Espiritu 1995, 14–15).
9. Many Korean women, who were married to Filipinos during the Korean War, immigrated to the U.S. or have passed away, and there were only six women alive as far as I know when I visited the Philippines in 2013. I interviewed five of them except one who could not talk due to advanced illness at the time. The names of the interview participants in this paper are pseudonyms.

10. On the matter of what was the first Korean restaurant in the Philippines, some people do not accept K's house because of its Japanese co-ownership and the existence of hostesses in the restaurant.

## REFERENCES

Choi, Young-jae. 2000. "YS chŏnggwŏn haeksimsilssega hoegohanŭn munminjŏngbu 5nyŏn (Reflecting five years of Civilian Government by YS Keyman)." *Sindonga (Magazine dongA)*, December 2000: 230–47. http://shindonga.donga.com/Library/3/01/13/100815/1.
Department of Tourism (The Philippines). 2011. *"2011 DOT Year End Report.* http://www.tourism.gov.ph/files/2011%20DOT%20Year%20End%20Report.pdf.
Espiritu, Yen Le. 1995. *Filipino American Lives.* Philadelphia: Temple University Press.
Geertz, C. 1973. "The Integrative Revolution: Primordial Sentiments and Civic Politics in the New States:" In *Interpretation of Cultures*, 255–310. New York: Basic Books.
Giddens, Anthony. 1991. *Modernity and Self-identity: Self and Society in the Late Modern Age.* Cambridge: Polity Press.
Han'guktongnibundongsap'yŏnch'anwiwŏnhoe, ed, 2005. *Han'guktongnibundongŭi Yŏksa (The History of Korea's Independence Movement)*, vol. 55. https://search.i815.or.kr/Degae/DegaeView.jsp?tid=dg.
Kim, Do-hyung. 2015. "Tosan anch'anghoŭi 'yŏhaenggwŏn'ŭl t'onghae pon tongnibundong haengjŏk (A Study on the An Chang-ho's Independence Activities through His Passports)." *Han'guk tongnibundongsa yŏn'gu* (*Journal of Korean Independence Movement Studies*) 52: 35–63. Seoul: Institute of Korean Independence Movement Studies.
Kim, Minjung. 2015a. "Se pŏnŭi kkum: han'guk chŏnjaenggie p'illip'in namsŏnggwa kyŏrhonhan han'guk yŏsŏngŭi saengae iyagi (A life story of a Korean woman who was married to a Filipino man during the Korean War)." *Han'gugyŏsŏnghak* (*Journal of Korean Women's Studies*) 31(3): 103–137. Seoul: Korean Association of Women's Studies.
Kim, Minjung. 2015b. "1900nyŏndae ch'ojungban'gi p'illip'inŭi haninijue taehan sŏngch'aljŏk yŏn'gu" (Reflecting on Korean emigration to the Philippines in the early and middle 1900s). *Sahoewa Yŏksa* (*Society and History*) 107: 251–284. Seoul: Korean Social History Association.
Kim, Myongsob, and Yang, Joonseok. 2014. "Sŏurollimp'ik yuch'iŭi chŏngch'ioegyosa— 981nyŏn sŏurŭn ŏttŏk'e ollimp'ik kaech'oegwŏn hoektŭge sŏnggonghaenna? (The political and diplomatic history of the Seoul Olympic bid—How did Seoul win the bid in 1981?). *Kukchejŏngch'inonch'ong* (*The Korean Journal of International Studies*) 54(4): 271–302.
Kutsumi, Kanako. 2007. "Koreans in the Philippines: A Study of the Formation of Their Social Organization." In *Exploring Transnational Communities in the Philippines*, edited by V.A. Miralao and L.P. Makil, 58–73. Quezon City: PMRN (Philippine Migration Research Network) and PSSC (Philippine Social Science Council).
*Kyŏnghyangsinmun.* May 8, 1962. "Kŭnyang patkinŭn natpukkŭrŏun igug (異國) ŭi tongjŏng (同情)—pigija (比記者) dŭl mogŭmundong (募金運動)" (Foreigner's sympathy should not be taken for granted: Fund-raising campaign by Filipino journalists).
*Kyŏnghyangsinmun.* December 21, 1962. "Nunmure paksugalch'ae (拍手喝采)" (Cheering and Clapping with Tears).
*Kyŏnghyangsinmun* March 2, 1963. "Hakhae (學海) ŭi pyŏl chisŏngŭi sanmaek (山脈) paksa (博士)" (Ph.D., Stars on the Sea of Scholars and Mountains of Intelligence).
*Kyŏnghyangsinmun.* October 25, 1966. "Manilla chŏngsanghoeŭi (頂上會意) wa paktaet'ongnyŏng (朴大統領) ŭi kijoyŏnsŏl (基調演說)" (President Pak's Keynote address at Manila Summit Conference).
*Kyŏnghyangsinmun.* January 28, 1967. "Asea (亞細亞) ŭi han'gugin (韓國人) (3): p'illip'in" (Koreans in Asia [3]: The Philippines).
*Kyŏnghyangsinmun.* February 3–28, 1977. "Heoe (海外) e sanŭn han'gugin (韓國人) (120): sarainnŭn p'illip'in iminsa (移民史) pagyunhwa (朴允華) ssi(1)-(5)" (Koreans living abroad [120]: Pak Yun-hwa, Living History of Migration to the Philippines [1]-[5]).

Ministry of Foreign Affairs (Korea). 1989, 1995, 2007, 2017. "Chaeoedongp'o Hyŏnhwang (Current Status of Overseas Compatriots)." www.mofa.go.kr.

Moon, Seungsook. 2005. *Militarized Modernity and Gendered Citizenship in South Korea.* Durham, NC: Duke University Press.

Oishi, Nana. 2005. *Women in Motion: Globalization, State Policies, and Labor Migration in Asia.* Stanford, CA: Stanford University Press.

Romulo, Beth Day. 1974. *The Philippines: Shattered Showcase of Democracy in Asia.* Lanham, MD: M Evans & Co.

*Tongailbo.* April 9, 1924. "Taedonggongsandangdaehoe (極東共産黨大會)" (The Far East Communist Party Convention).

*Tongailbo.* January 5, 1959. "Kukchegyŏrhon (4): pirubin (比律賓) namsŏng" (International Marriage[4]: Filipino men).

*Tongailbo.* March 27, 1962. "Sinimbidaesa (新任比大使) 'pueno'ssi ch'ŏga (妻家) ŭi nara han 'gug(韓國에)" (New ambassador, Mr. "Bueno" coming to his wife's nation).

*Tongailbo.* December 28, 1962. "'Maksaisai' chŏngsin (精神) ŭl pugak (浮刻)" (Highlighting the spirit of President Masaysay).

*Tongailbo.* June 27, 1963. "Syŏlli, sangch (傷處) 'ŏe ch'iyu (治癒) ŭi" (Healing Touch for Wounds by Typhoon Shirley).

The World Bank. n.d.. *GDP Per Capita (Current U.S.$).* https://data.worldbank.org/indicator/NY.GDP.PCAP.CD?end=2017&locations=KR-PH&start=1960.

Yeo, Jiyeon. 2002. *Beyond the Shadow of Camptown: Korean Military Brides in America.* New York: New York University Press.

Yu, Yang-su. 1988. *Taesaŭi ilgijang (The Ambassador's Diary).* Seoul: Sumunsŏgwan.

Yuval-Davis, Nira. 1997. *Gender and Nation.* London: Sage Publications.

# Afterword

## Transnationalism Studies and Its Challenges — The View from Asia

## Brenda S.A. Yeoh

The processes behind globalization, migration, and development have fueled a new spatial order of interconnectivities among nations, communities, families, and individuals across the globe. The mobility of ideas, knowledge, images, commodities, and people, as well as the uneven transgression of national borders in today's globalizing world, may well be liberating or emancipatory at times, but may also reinforce existing social ideologies, including those of the nation-state. While there has been phenomenal expansion of the scope and depth of literature interrogating the links between mobility, migration and the formation of transnational identities in recent years, much still remains to be done in reconceptualizing fluid lives and interconnected societies in a rapidly globalizing world. Focusing primarily on migrations and mobilities within, as well as in and out of, Asia, this afterword discusses three challenges at the forefront of debates in transnationalism studies, using the case of Singapore as illustration where appropriate.

First, we need more innovative vocabulary and ways of understanding which are more reflective of grounded realities in a world of quickened motion. While traditional migration research has privileged more permanent forms of migration and issues of settlement, adaptation, and assimilation in host societies, the time-space compression brought about by rapid advancements in transport and communication technologies, as well as the flexibilisation of contemporary life and work cultures under neoliberal capitalist conditions, are beginning to move the focus to more temporary modes of

migration. Migration as a household livelihood strategy or a pathway expressing personal aspiration is now within reach of an increasingly broad
spectrum of socio-economic classes, as the tagline of budget airline Air Asia
would have it, "Now Everyone Can Fly." Today, migrations in and out of
Asia, for example, by and large do not take the form of permanent ruptures,
uprooting, and settlement, but are more likely to be transient and complex,
ridden with disruptions, detours, and multi-destinations and are founded on
interconnections and multiple chains of movement. The growing scholarship
on temporary migrations in the Asian context covers a variegated range of
peoples—professional and managerial elites, contract workers, undocumented migrants, student migrants, marriage migrants, retirement or lifestyle
migrants, frequent flyers—and draws attention to implications for identity,
citizenship, and notions of "home." Indeed, this broad range of people on the
move, with different aims and aspirations and under widely differing conditions, is also reflected in this volume focused just on transnational mobility in
and out of Korea. The chapters cover Korean immigrants in the United
States, female Korean migrants doing business in Japan, Korean healthcare
workers in Germany, Korean activists in Japan, young Korean women living
or studying in the West, Korean transnational adoptees, Korean-Chinese students in Korea, Soviet-Korean returnees or *koryŏ saram*, Korean-American
returnees, Korean women who have married Filipino men, and Asian marriage migration in Korea. In this context, the conceptualisation of *emigration*
as a form of permanent departure from a home-nation and conversely the
notion of *immigration* as a form of full incorporation and permanent settlement in a host-nation needs to be rethought to accord more provisionality and
flexibility to people movements, as well as the relationship between people
and nation-states. As Toro-Morn and Alicea (2004, xxi) note, "the demarca-
tion line between 'sending' and 'receiving' countries is no longer a clear-cut
line between core and periphery."

    In defining emigration as "don't look back exit for a new existence else-
where" and the "converse and historical complement of diaspora," Sanjek
(2003, 327–328) is able to point to several "unambiguous instances of historical emigrations," but only with the benefit of hindsight as human intentions
at the point of exiting may be unclear or change. With the proliferation of
transnational connectivities, multidirectional mobilities and hybridized identifications in a globalized new order, emigration as a unidirectional people
movement of non-return is likely to become even more provisional and ambivalent. Indeed, at the turn of the new millennium, discourses on emigration
among home countries in the developing world have generally taken on more
positive connotations. While individuals who leave the People's Republic of
China were once regarded as "traitors" within state narratives, such mobility
is now encouraged for certain groups as a strategy to tap business potential
inherent in the development of diasporic networks (Nyiri 2004). In the case

of overseas students, the key policy is encapsulated in the "twelve-word approach" of *zhichi liuxue, guli huiguo, laiqu ziyou* (meaning "support study overseas, encourage returns, guarantee freedom of [international] movement") (Xiang 2003, 29). In the case of the Philippine state, turning citizens into labor commodities in the global marketplace by institutionalizing employment abroad through the Philippine Overseas Employment Program has become a major strategy to address poverty and unemployment, and to siphon in remittances vital to the Philippine economy (Tyner 2004). With over a million Filipinos annually deployed to take up work in foreign countries and roughly ten percent of its population abroad, the Philippines has positioned itself within the new international division of labor as a major source country of workers, supplying workers of varying skill levels to over 100 countries (Asis 2005, 27). This is accompanied by a consistent state discourse where "all the presidents from Marcos to Macapagal-Arroyo" have lauded overseas contract workers as the nation's "new heroes" (Asis 2005, 27). At the same time, imaginaries of the "nation," i.e., the "trans-territorial nation state," as Guarnizo and Smith (1998, 8) put it—based on a shared ethnicity—continue to be drawn upon to protect the integrity of the nation and sustain its longevity. There is also the assumption here, as Aguilar (2004, 100) puts it, that "at their destinations, emigrants will be transnationalists" who would engage in transnational circuits—both emotional and material—to contribute to the development of their "homelands."

Among host-countries, however, the phenomenon of "emigration becoming immigration" is viewed in far more ambivalent terms. In the early 1990s, the Emigration Dynamics in Developing Countries Project, funded by the International Organization for Migration and the United Nations Population Fund, was initiated to address "widespread concern" about "the increasing numbers of refugees, irregular migrants and asylum seekers" from the South "grasping the emigration option as a last chance for survival and moving, uninvited, to . . . developed countries" (Appleyard 1998, 1). This view has gathered pace and in recent years taken on more complex inflections. A key observable trend in many host-countries around the globe, for example, concerns the heightened visibility of the immigration debate in the public arena. On the one hand, Turner (2007) argues against a post-national version of "flexible citizenship" in an age of increased mobilities and instead follows Shamir (2005, 199) in proposing a reconceptualization of globalization "not as a system of liquid mobility" but one that also produces "closure, entrapment and containment." He notes that anxieties over terrorism and urban violence have created a "fear of diversity," triggering processes of "enslavement" and "new forms of enclosure" involving complex and sophisticated systems ranging from bureaucratic barriers, legal exclusions and registrations to the use of forensic medicine and bio-profiling. On the other hand, more optimistic accounts of the impact of rapid immigration on the urban landscape show that "immigrant-led spaces also function as important economic generators in the urban economy and contribute to the sense of cultural diversity and cosmopolitanism" (Price and Benton-Short 2008, 36–37). Li (1998), for example, describes "ethnoburbs" as suburban ethnic spaces characterized by both vibrant ethnic economies and strong ties to the globalizing economy, while Chacko (2008) uses the term "sociocommerscape" to denote ethnic commercial centers instrumental in the revitalization of declining urban areas in postindustrial cities.

Amidst such complexities, approaches to understanding the place of immigrants in host countries, however, have not kept pace and are, to a large extent, still based on notions of assimilation, acculturation, and integration, measured primarily by spatial segregation/concentration, linguistic change and intermarriage, where the immigrant-host, minority-majority relationship is understood in terms of race/ethnicity/religion (Vasta 2007; Koopsmans 2016). The inadequacy of such approaches has been discussed by scholars who point to the tendency in research on integration and multiculturalism to rely on a view of society as made up of discrete ethnic groups living side by side and developing fairly autonomous trajectories (Vertovec and Wessendorf 2006). Instead, Vertovec (2007) argues that framing interactions between different social groups in terms of interethnic relations alone fails to come to grips with the "super-diversity" of immigrant societies today, where inter-group difference runs the gamut of cross-cutting axes including not only race/ethnicity but also place of origin, age, gender, human capital, language, religion, legal status, etc.

In short, immigration has become a compelling force not only in increasing diversity in cities and other places of reception, but also introducing more complex diversifications—new patterns of inequality and segregation/concentration, new encounters of intimacy and prejudice, new modes of hybridity and fusion, and new practices of coexistence, cosmopolitanism, and bridge-building—for which we have yet to formulate a vocabulary and discourse beyond the unimaginative language of assimilation, acculturation, and integration which will help us make sense of the emerging phenomena. As Hall (2017) argues in the context of European nation-states, going forward the challenge is to understand the processes of migrant-led diversity-making as moored to the "conditions of power produc[ing] violent social stratifications" that are "increasingly endemic" to a "brutal migration milieu." Here I pause to take a closer look at the migration dynamics in Singapore.

Training the analytical lens on Singapore as an example of a globalizing city shaped (if not produced) by migration, conditions of "super-diversity," or what has been called the "new pluralism" reflecting the complex intersectionality of class, race, nationality, and residency status, are part of the structure of everyday transactions, encounters, and landscapes. Goh (2008), for example, observes that the new pluralism is reinforcing the old conjunction of race and class in the new globalized economy. Thus, in Singapore, while the largely Chinese professional class competes with hastily naturalized immigrant Chinese and Indian professionals to hobnob with white expatriates possessing privileged residency status, these groups are serviced by working-class Chinese, Indian, and Malay Singaporeans in different economic sectors, and everyone live in spaces built and maintain by Indian, Indonesian, and Filipino immigrant workers with minimal legal protection.

In Singapore, identity markers based on race continue to be significant in official discourses and informal spheres, even as the racial arithmetic of the four ancestral races—Chinese, Malays, Indians, and "others"—have recently given way to a more complex discussion of racial hyphenations, permutations, and combinations. Despite the salience of racial categories in influencing the tenor of human relationships, it is human capital differentiation or the "skills divide" which most significantly shapes the conditions under which transnational migrants are admitted into the city-state and impinges on their everyday experience of the city. On the one hand, among the unskilled or low-skilled migrant worker population admitted into the city-state on short-term work permits as disposable labor without any residency rights (Yeoh 2006), their presence in the everyday landscape is most keenly felt in the form of "weekend enclaves," social and commercial landscapes containing migrant concentrations which are transient in nature. Mainly confined to workplaces (such as construction sites, or Singaporean homes in the case of foreign domestic workers) during the work-week, large numbers of migrant contract workers congregate temporarily in strongly ethicized enclaves over the weekend. Some examples include Little India/Serangoon Road which attract Indian and Bangladeshi workers; Little Manila in Lucky Plaza, right in the heart of the Orchard Road shopping belt, for the Filipina domestic workers; and Little Thailand for Thai workers at Golden Mile Complex in Beach Road. Foreign worker gatherings have also sprung up in open spaces near shopping malls and train stations in public housing estates, the residential heartlands where the majority of Singaporeans live. These weekend enclaves and foreign worker gatherings are often viewed negatively or with unease by Singaporeans who consider them a form of "intrusion" into "their own backyards": some have openly expressed their displeasure and asked the authorities to step up security measures in these places while others wondered whether these workers could be relocated to out-of-sight locations such as offshore islands (Yeoh 2018, 243–244). In a similar vein, debates about whether foreign domestic workers should be allowed into private clubs or use the swimming pools in condominiums are indicative of the spatial politics of exclusion at work in the global city, dangerously reminiscent of discriminatory "dogs and Asians not allowed" policies prevalent in the colonial era. These voices reflect a "use and discard" sentiment among the general population who want foreign workers to do the work that citizens shun, but at the same time wish that these workers can be erased from the landscape.

On the other hand, at the other end of the skills spectrum, migrants of the professional and managerial class are also making their mark on the landscape. Nationality- or ethnicity-based enclaves have sprouted in private residential areas such as Woodlands (Americans), Serangoon Gardens (French and Australians), Tanjong Rhu and Meyer Road (Indians), West Coast (Japanese), and East Coast (Koreans), often in the vicinity of their respective country's international schools. Their presence has significantly altered the retail landscape in the residential estates, transforming "old-school shops selling joss sticks and simple grocery items" into alfresco eateries, upmarket specialist shops, modern convenience stores or supermarkets, wine shops, and new beauty and wellness services that attract a "more diverse 'globe-trotting' crowd" or serve a "cosmopolitan clientele." While there is a certain degree of resentment that these so-called foreign talent take away jobs, are paid too much, and enjoy all the privileges of living in Singapore with none of the responsibilities that citizens bear, there is also acknowledgment that the Singapore economy currently needs foreign talent to enhance its global competitiveness and keep pace with global changes. The influx of well-heeled expatriates also boost property prices and rental yields reaped by homeowners, as well as increase exposure to other cultures including the welcomed addition of a wide range of international cuisines into Singapore's restaurant scene (Yeoh and Lam 2017). Not only does the social heterogeneity resulting from multiple streams of migration have a transformative effect on the tapestry of everyday spaces such as shopping malls, hospitals, offices, campuses, places of worship, and street-life in general, it also opens up opportunities for the new and spectacular. As Prime Minister Lee Hsien Loong elaborates:

> Today we get people from all over the world too. We have people from Turkey, there are Portuguese, somebody from Venezuela, somebody from Morocco, even a Korean or two, some Russians. And they add colour and diversity to this society. So our cuisine is something special. Singaporeans love food. You want Korean ginseng chicken, you can get the real thing cooked by a Korean. You want Arab food, you go to Arab Street, you can eat shawarma, which is shish kebabs. You can smoke the hubble-bubble, the waterpipe. Now harder because new rules on no smoking. But it's something different for Singapore. . . . And we have other customs too. Recently there was a splendid wedding in Singapore. The groom came riding on a white horse. He was a Marwari, it's an Indian group, Indian businessman, very successful caste. So the zoo is now thinking of going into the service of providing horses and elephants for weddings. (quoted in *The Straits Times* 19 July 2006)

In short, as Singapore's bifurcated labor-immigration regime demonstrates, understanding the immigrant experience in a postcolonial city deeply "inscribed with a race-culture" (Chua 2009, 242) still requires attention to a number of issues: the diversification of how difference and similarity are conceived across multiple registers; the inequalities produced by inclusionist/ exclusionist projects that attempt to domesticate certain transnational subjects (foreign talent), while distinguishing other foreign bodies (foreign workers) as transgressors of the nation; and, more importantly, how "contact zones of fear" between strangers may be transformed into "comfort zones among neighbors" and freed from the power and prejudice of "arbitrary definition and identification" (Sennett 2001).

Second, as transnationalism studies give weight to the effects of "multiplying forms of mobility," there is a need not to "lose sight of the importance of localities in people's lives" (Oakes and Schein 2006): both *situatedness in* and *connectedness across* different spaces and places are simultaneous moments in the same account. "Place" is not just "the backdrop for motion" (McKay 2006, 197), but mobility and migration produce "porous places" which are linked to a larger network of relationships. Instead of starting off with a binary where the "global" is presumed to be that which moves, while the "local" is that which is fixed, we need to focus instead on the complex space between the global and the local where relations of (im)mobility are forged and reworked, and over time, productive of particular cultures of (im)mobility. As Cresswell (2006, 2) observes, "mobility" and "immobility" are not just ontological opposites but bound through "relational politics" and "given meanings within contexts of social and cultural power." Not only are "mobility" and "immobility" entangled terms, but it is important to give attention to "different forms of mobility" and to take into account that "the same mobility trajectories can have radically different spatio-temporal outcomes for different subjects, creating striated routes and velocities, blocked futures, liminal presents and renegotiated life scripts" (Robertson, Cheng and Yeoh 2018, 622).

In order to understand the dynamic between *situatedness in* and *connectedness across* different spaces and places, scholars have argued for a stronger focus on the embedded, embodied, and material quality of the migrant-local interactions in the spaces and places of everyday life. Similar to Amin's (2002) call for ethnographies which highlight the "local micropolitics of everyday interaction," my work (mainly with Shirlena Huang) on transnational domestic workers in the context of Singapore have focused on the politics of the contact zone. In Yeoh and Huang (1999), we began work on the complex negotiations of gendered identity between employer and employee within homespace drawing on Mary Louise Pratt's (1992, 7) definition of a "contact zone" (situated in the context of colonial encounters in her work) as "an attempt to invoke the spatial and temporal copresence of subjects previously separated by geographic and historical disjunctures, and whose trajectories now intersect." A "contact" perspective "emphasizes how subjects are constituted in and by their relations to each other . . . not in terms of separateness or apartheid, but in terms of copresence, interaction, inter-locking understandings and practices, often within radically asymmetrical relations of power." Paid domestic labor has often been interpreted as com-plicity on the part of women employers in "simply perpetuat[ing] the sexist division of labor by passing on the most devalued work in their lives to another woman" and "escap[ing] the stigma of 'women's work' by laying the burden on working women of color" (Romero 1992, 131). What has been given less attention is that far from the unilateral transfer of one woman's immutable burden to another, the nature of that "burden" undergoes transla-tion in the context of copresence as each woman repositions and redefines herself within the web of domestic practices vis-à-vis their own worlds and each other's. While employers and transnational domestic workers are "worlds apart" in many ways, they also participate in negotiations around similar issues around mothering: both sets of women often justify resorting to "substitute mothering" to seek material betterment for their families, both have removed themselves physically from the reproductive burden of their own households but do not entirely escape the multiple ties that bind women to the domestic world, and both struggle with "distance mothering" (although this occurs on different scales). Contrary to the idea of "home" as a place of "stability, oneness and security," treating the home as a contact zone where gendered norms and domestic practices are constantly negotiated between women, between "self" and "other," shifts the perspective to one of seeing "home" as a place "where one discovers new ways of seeing reality, frontiers of difference" (bell hooks, quoted in Massey 1994, 171).

Our continued work (Yeoh and Huang 2010; Yeoh et al. 2017) turns attention to the relational politics of mobility and immobility within home-space in the globalizing city of constant motion. Against the conventional notion of home as "a private, secure location, a sanctuary" and a place "where inhabitants can escape from the disciplinary practices that regulate our bodies in everyday life" (Johnston and Valentine 1995, 99), we argue that the home should be conceived as a locale where (im)mobility has to be constantly negotiated vis-à-vis written and unwritten rules governing the "place" of different individuals. It is by examining the contested nature of space and mobility (Cresswell 2006; Hannam, Sheller and Urry 2006) among those involved in the production of the "domesticity" of the home that we attempted to unpack its materiality, specifically in terms of a politics of space and mobility, focusing simultaneously on the forms of dominance employers wield and, the strategies of *resistance*, as well as compliance, domestic work-ers demonstrate. The complexities of spatialized politics played out between employer and worker through little tactics—negotiations over ground rules,

timespace mappings, no-go sites, and the shifts between front and back regions—as well as larger, more dramatic strategies, from struggles over the
telephone and other social networking tools to escaping spatial confinement,
sometimes with tragic ends, produces the "home" as a highly variegated
space where power relations are continually and endlessly reproduced and
inflected amidst the mobilities and non-mobilities of a global city. Ironically,
migrant domestic workers who themselves are the active subjects, even pio-
neers, of transnational mobilities may experience, at a different scale, far
more disciplined forms of fixity when they are relocated in the "home"
within global cities.

Third, as transnationalism scholars challenge the myopia of methodological nationalism and contemplate comparative and connective multi-site research, this needs to go hand in hand with forwarding a socially progressive
agenda for a more inclusive approach, requiring more conscious commitment
to extend the dialogue beyond the Anglo-American world to connect with
scholars and researchers elsewhere in sustained engagement with cosmopolitan (collaborative, bridge-building) practices of knowledge production. It
follows that our research practices have to evolve to embrace the quickened
pace of mobilities and the heightened sense of transience, simultaneity, and
otherness experienced by the mobile (and non-mobile) subject within inter-
locking lifeworlds. This requires us to go beyond the single case in our
research and to seriously contemplate multi-site research, to develop comparative transnational frameworks, to be aware of the connectivities across
scales, and to be wary of methodological nationalism (Wimmer and Glick
Schiller 2002).

We need to equip ourselves for the task of boundary-crossing, a task
which I believe goes hand in hand with forwarding a socially progressive
agenda for a more inclusive approach. To more fully take on methodologies
which valorize connectivities, comparative frames and multiple sites, we
need also a more conscious commitment to extending dialogue beyond the
Anglo-American world to connect with scholars and researchers elsewhere, a
more sustained engagement with cosmopolitan (collaborative, bridge-building) practices in the production of post-colonial knowledge (Yeoh and Ramdas 2014), as well as a willingness to invest time and resources in learning
languages and to spend extended time in the field to get under the skin of a
place beyond the Anglo-American world. In this way, research practices
which valorize connectivities and question boundary lines that divide would
ultimately contribute towards dismantling institutionalized practices which
reproduce racisms, nationalisms, and social privilege, and pave the way for a
more inclusive approach in our work as migration researchers.

# REFERENCES

Aguilar, Filomeno V. 2004. "Is There a Transnation? Migrancy and the National Homeland among Overseas Filipinos." In *State/Nation/Transnation*, edited by Brenda S.A. Yeoh and Katie Willis, 93–119. London: Routledge.

Amin, Ash. 2002. "Ethnicity and the Multicultural City: Living with Diversity." *Environment and Planning A* 34: 959–980.

Appleyard, Reginald Thomas. 1998. *Emigration Dynamics in Developing Countries* (4 vols). Aldershot: Ashgate.

Asis, Maruja M.B. 2005. "Caring for the World: Filipino Domestic Workers Gone Global." In *Asian Women as Transnational Domestic Workers*, edited by Shirlena Huang, Brenda S.A. Yeoh and Noor Abdul Rahman, 21–53. Singapore: Marshall Cavendish.

Chacko, Elizabeth. 2008. "Washington, D.C.: From Biracial City to Multiethnic Gateway." In *Migrants to the Metropolis*, edited by Marie D. Price and Lisa Benton-Short, 203–225. Syracuse, NY: Syracuse University Press.

Chua, Beng Huat. 2009. "Being Chinese under Official Multiculturalism in Singapore." *Asian Ethnicity* 10(3): 239–250.

Cresswell, Tim. 2006. *On the Move: Mobility in the Modern Western World*. London: Routledge.

Goh, Daniel P.S. 2008. "From Colonial Pluralism to Postcolonial Multiculturalism: Race, State Formation and the Question of Cultural Diversity in Malaysia and Singapore." *Sociology Compass* 2(1): 232–252.

Guarnizo, Luis Eduardo and Michael Peter Smith. 1998. "The Locations of Transnationalism." In *Transnationalism from Below*, edited by Michael Peter Smith and Luis Eduardo Guarnizo, 3–34. New Brunswick: Transaction Publishers.

Hall, Suzanne M. 2017. "Mooring 'Super-Diversity' to a Brutal Migration Milieu." *Ethnic and Racial Studies* 40(9): 1562–1573.

Hannam, Kevin, Mimi Sheller and John Urry. 2006. "Editorial: Mobilities, Immobilities and Moorings." *Mobilities* 1(1): 1–22.

Johnston, Lynday and Gill Valentine. 1995. "Wherever I Lay My Girlfriend, That's My Home: The Performance and Surveillance of Lesbian Identities in Domestic Environments." In *Mapping Desire: Geographies of Sexuality*, edited by David Bell and Gill Valentine, 88–103. London and New York: Routledge.

Koopmans, Ruud. 2016. "Does Assimilation Work? Sociocultural Determinants of Labour Market Participation of European Muslims." *Journal of Ethnic and Migration Studies* 42(2): 197–216.

Li, Wei. 1998. "Anatomy of a New Ethnic Settlement: The Chinese Ethnoburb in Los Angeles." *Urban Studies* 35(3): 479–501.

Massey, Doreen. 1994. "A Place Called Home?" In *Space, Place and Gender*, edited by Doreen Massey, 157–174. Minneapolis: University of Minnesota Press.

McKay, Deirdre. 2006. "Introduction: Finding 'The Field': The Problem of Locality in a Mobile World." *The Asia Pacific Journal of Anthropology* 7(3): 197–202.

Nyiri, Pal. 2004. "Expatriating Is Patriotic? The Discourse on 'New Migrants' in the People's Republic of China and the Identity Construction among Recent Migrants from the PRC." In *State/Nation/Transnation*, edited by Brenda S.A. Yeoh and Katie Willis, 120–143. London: Routledge.

Oakes, Tim and Louisa Schein. (eds.) 2006. *Translocal China: Linkages, Identities and the Reimagining of Space*. London: Routledge.

Pratt, Marie Louise. 1992. *Imperial Eyes: Travel Writing and Transculturation*. London: Routledge.

Price, Marie D., and Lisa Benton-Short. 2008. "Urban Immigrant Gateways in a Globalizing World." In *Migrants to the Metropolis*, edited by Marie D. Price and Lisa Benton-Short, 23–47. Syracuse: Syracuse University Press.

Robertson, Shanthi, Yi'En Cheng & Brenda S. A. Yeoh. 2018. "Introduction: Mobile Aspirations? Youth Im/Mobilities in the Asia-Pacific." *Journal of Intercultural Studies* 39(6): 613–625.

Romero, Mary. 1992. *Maid in the USA* . London: Routledge.

Sanjek, Roger. 2003. "Rethinking Migration, Ancient to Future." *Global Networks* 3(3): 315–336.

Sennett, Richard. 2001. "New Capitalism, New Isolation: A Flexible City of Strangers." Accessed 2019, February 16. https://mondediplo.com/2001/02/16cities.

Shamir, Ronen. 2005. "Without Borders? Notes on Globalization as a Mobility Regime." *Sociological Theory* 23(2): 197–217.

Toro-Morn, Maura Isabel, and Marixsa Alicea (eds.). 2004. *Migration and Immigration: A Global View*. Westport: Greenwood Press.

Turner, Bryan. 2007. "The Enclave Society: Towards a Sociology of Immobility." *European Journal of Social Theory* 10(2): 287–303.

Tyner, James A. 2004. *Made in the Philippines: Gendered Discourses and the Making of Migrants.* London: Routledge.

Vasta, Ellie. 2007. "From Ethnic Minorities to Ethnic Majority Policy: Multiculturalism and the Shift to Assimilationism in the Netherlands." *Ethnic and Racial Studies* 30(5): 713–740.

Vertovec, Steven. 2007. "Super-diversity and Its Implications." *Ethnic and Racial Studies* 30(6): 1024–1054.

Vertovec, Steven, and Susanne Wessendorf. 2006. "Cultural, Religious and Linguistic Diversity in Europe: An Overview of Issues and Trends." In *The Dynamics of International Migration and Settlement in Europe*, edited by Karen Kraal, Marinus J.A. Penninx and Maria Berger, 171–199. Amsterdam: University of Amsterdam Press.

Wimmer, Andreas, and Nina Glick-Schiller. 2002. "Methodological Nationalism and Beyond: Nation-State Building, Migration and the Social Science." *Global Networks* 2(4): 301–334.

Xiang, Biao. 2003. "Emigration from China: A Sending Country Perspective." *International Migration* 41(3): 21–48.

Yeoh, Brenda S.A. 2006. "Bifurcated Labour: The Unequal Incorporation of Transmigrants in Singapore." *Tijdschrift voor Economische en Sociale Geografie* [Journal of Economic and Social Geography] 97(1): 26–37.

———. 2018. "Transnational Migrations and Plural Diversities: Encounters in Global Cities." In *Routledge Handbook of Asian Migrations*, edited by Gracia Liu-Farrer and Brenda S.A. Yeoh, 238–249. Abingdon: Routledge.

Yeoh, Brenda S.A., and Shirlena Huang. 1999. "Singapore Women and Foreign Domestic Workers: Negotiating Domestic Work and Motherhood." In *Gender, Migration and Domestic Service*, edited by Janet Momsen, 277–300. London: Routledge.

———. 2010. "Transnational Domestic Workers and the Negotiation of Mobility and Work Practices in Singapore's Home-Spaces." *Mobilities* 5(2): 219–236.

Yeoh, Brenda S.A., and Kamalini Ramdas. 2014. "Gender, Migration, Mobility and Transnationalism." *Gender, Place and Culture* 21(10): 1197–1213.

Yeoh, Brenda S.A., Marie Louise Platt, Choo Yuen Khoo, Theodora Lam, and Grace Baey. 2017. "Indonesian Domestic Workers and the (Un)Making of Transnational Livelihoods and Provisional Futures." *Social and Cultural Geography* 18(3): 415–434.

Yeoh, Brenda S.A., and Theodora Lam. 2017. "Postcolonial Migration and Social Diversity in Singapore." In *Migrant Cross-Cultural Encounters in Asia and the Pacific,* edited by Jacqueline Leckie, Angela McCarthy, and Angela Wanhalla, 151–166. Abingdon: Ashgate.

# Index

acculturation, 31, 190, 198
agency, 11–12, 19, 33, 47, 53, 79, 119,
    123, 126, 158
Ahmed, Sara, 34
Allen, Horace, 150, 151
Amerasian, 107
An Chungkŭn, 159, 160, 168, 170
Army Service Command in Korea, 183
artivism, 24, 32–34
ASCOM. *See* Army Service Command in
    Korea
*The Asia Kunglun*, 157–158; aims of,
    161–165, 166; Japanese authors of,
    165; and the "Korea problem,"
    167–168; and the new world order, 168;
    publication of, 162; reception of, 166
Asian Solidarity Society, 161
Asiatic Exclusion League, 150
aspiration, xi, 4, 79, 86, 89–90, 92, 120,
    125, 161, 196
assimilation, 26, 49, 72, 195, 198; policy,
    158, 159, 165
*Aussiedler*, 131

banal racism, 13
Bauman, Zygmunt, 4, 6
Beck, Ulrich, 4, 6
belonging, 6, 15, 18, 20, 23–24, 26, 34,
    160; in-betweenness of, 28, 54; loss of,
    16; non-belonging, 14, 17, 19, 30; sense
    of, xii–xiii, 6–7, 17, 20, 23, 29, 31, 34,

42, 119, 121, 123, 190, 192; space and,
    18, 26, 34, 45, 121; un-belonging, 27
biopower, 29–31, 30
birth search and reunion, 23–34
body, 29–30, 50
brotherhood, 28
business: ethnic, 83, 88, 186–187;
    gendered, 90–92

Cai Peihuo, 168–169
care, 40–42, 52, 89, 188; deficit, 39, 69;
    recipients, 41, 46–47, 50, 53. *See also*
    healthcare work
career development, 82
*Chaoxianren*, 115
*Chaoxianzu*, 115. *See also Chosŏnjok*
China: activists from, 157, 164–165; New
    Culture Movement in, 164; pan-
    Asianism in, 158, 160–161
*ch'inilp'a*, 160
Ch'oe Ungpong, 167–168, 170
Chosŏn dynasty, 24, 26, 30, 31, 150
*Chosŏnjok*, 116–117, 134–135;
    globalization of, 125–126; identity,
    117–119, 123; relationship with *Koryŏ
    saram*, 136–138, 139; relationship with
    South Koreans, 138–140, 142
citizenship, xiv, 23–24, 27, 57, 58, 62–64,
    72
Commonwealth of Independent States, 99,
    102

# About the Editor and Contributors

**Yonson Ahn** is professor, chair of Korean Studies, and deputy executive director of the Interdisciplinary Centre of East Asian Studies (IZO) at the Goethe University of Frankfurt, Germany. She received her PhD degree in women's and gender studies at the University of Warwick in 2000. Gender and migration, with a focus on transnational nurse migration and transnational marriage migrants, is her major research interest, along with the Korean diaspora and sexual violence associated with armed conflict. Her work has been published in a range of journals including the *European Journal of Women's Studies* and *Comparative Korean Studies*. Her recent book is entitled *Whose Comfort? Body, Sexuality and Identities of Korean "Comfort Women" and Japanese Soldiers during WWII* (2019).

**Minjung Kim** is professor of cultural anthropology at Kangwon National University. Her research focus is migration and gender, and family. She has done field research on Filipinas' lives in a rural village in the Philippines and in Korean society. Recently she has been researching overseas Korean women's mobile lives and diaspora identities. Her recent articles, among others (in Korean), are "Contribution to the Fatherland and Recognition as Koreans Overseas" and "Korean Women Married to Filipino Migrant Workers in the 1990s and Another Type of 'Multicultural' Family." She is now working on a book about gendered migration of Filipinas in Korean society and also an edited book about overseas Koreans' mobility, gendered experiences, and belonging between nation and family.

**Youna Kim** is professor of global communications at the American University of Paris, France, and joined from the London School of Economics and Political Science, where she had taught since 2004, after completing her PhD at the University of London, Goldsmiths College. Her books are *Women, Television and Everyday Life in Korea: Journeys of Hope* (2005), *Media Consumption and Everyday Life in Asia* (2008), *Transnational Migration, Media and Identity of Asian Women: Diasporic Daughters* (2011), *Women and the Media in Asia: The Precarious Self* (2012), *The Korean Wave: Korean Media Go Global* (2013), *Routledge Handbook of Korean Culture and Society* (2016), *Childcare Workers, Global Migration and Digital Media* (2017), and *South Korean Popular Culture and North Korea* (2019).

**Jieun Lee** is assistant professor of women's, gender, and sexuality studies at Wake Forest University. Her research examines the intersections of diaspora with race, class, gender, sexuality, ethnicity, and nationality embodied in theater and performance through feminist theories. Jieun has published articles and reviews in *Theatre Annual, Theatre Journal, Ecumenica, New England Theatre Journal, Journal of Japanese and Korean Cinema, Puppetry International*, and *International Journal of Korean Studies*. She is currently working on her book about Korean transnational adoption represented in contemporary theater and performance art in South Korea, the United States, Europe, and Scandinavia. Jieun holds a PhD in theater and performance studies as well as a graduate certificate in women's studies from the University of Georgia, where she taught at the Institute for Women's Studies. She is also a volunteer translator for the South Korean feminist journal *ILDA* and a member of the Feminist Research Working Group of the International Federation for Theatre Research.

**Seonok Lee** is visiting researcher at The Center for East Asian Studies Groningen and instructor at the Media Studies at the University of Groningen, the Netherlands. She recently received her PhD in sociology from the University of British Columbia, Canada. Her doctoral dissertation examines how the production of race and racial hierarchies is deeply intertwined with economic migration and global capitalism in contemporary East Asia.

**Dukin Lim** is a PhD student in social and international studies at the University of Tokyo. She is currently working at Peace Research Institute, International Christian University, as a research assistant. Her research is about ethnicity, gender, and social integration of highly skilled Korean female migrants in Japan. She published the chapter "Korean Women's Life Course after Divorce" in *International Migration in Progress: The Sociology of Modes of Incorporation* in 2017 and "Divorced Newcomer Korean Women in Japan: The Decision to Remain in Japan, Work and Lifestyle Adjustments" in *Rethinking Representations of Asian Women: Changes, Continuity, and Everyday Life* in 2016.

**Dolf-Alexander Neuhaus** holds an MA in Japanese studies and history and is finishing a PhD in history/Japanese studies/Korean studies that deals with regional networks among Korean and Japanese Protestants during the late nineteenth and early twentieth century at Freie Universität Berlin, where he also teaches courses as an adjunct lecturer. He is a freelance writer and journalist on Japan- and Korea-related topics. Neuhaus has worked as a research fellow at the Institute of Korean Studies, Goethe University Frankfurt am Main, Germany. From 2011 to 2015, he was a research fellow at Freie Universität Berlin, Institute for Japanese Studies. He has been a visiting research scholar at the Institute for Advanced Studies on Asia and the Institute of Social Science, University of Tokyo, and at the Institute of Korean Studies, Yonsei University in Seoul, South Korea.

**Wayne Patterson** is professor of history at St. Norbert College in Wisconsin. He received an undergraduate degree in history from Swarthmore College and graduate degrees (two MAs and a PhD) in history and international relations from the University of Pennsylvania. He has been a visiting professor of Korean history in the United States (Harvard University, the University of Chicago, the University of Pennsylvania, the University of California-Berkeley, the University of Kansas, and the University of South Carolina), in Hong Kong at Hang Seng University, in the Philippines at the University of the Philippines-Diliman, and in Korea (Korea University, Ewha University, Yonsei University, Sogang University, and Chonnam National University). He is the author of fifteen books on modern Korea and modern East Asia.

**Changzoo Song** is senior lecturer in Korean and Asian studies at the University of Auckland in New Zealand. He completed his PhD in political science and Korean studies at the University of Hawai'i at Manoa in 1999. His academic interests include the politico-cultural dimensions of nationalism, changes in nationalist ideology in Korea, and Korean diasporic communities in the global context. His current research is on the relationship between homeland and Korean diasporic communities, particularly Korean Chinese and Soviet Koreans; the dynamics of nationalism and multiculturalism in Korea; and comparing ethnic return migrations of Korean Chinese and Soviet Koreans. His most recent published articles and book chapters include a chapter in the volume *Diasporic Returns to the Ethnic Homeland: The Korean Diaspora in Comparative Perspective* (2019).

**Stephen Cho Suh** is assistant professor of sociology and women's & ethnic studies at the University of Colorado–Colorado Springs. Suh completed his PhD in sociology at the University of Minnesota–Twin Cities in 2016. His scholarly interests lie at the intersection of race, ethnicity, gender, migration, and culture, especially in relation to Asian Americans and the Korean diaspora. He has researched the phenomenon of ethnic return migration through the experiences of U.S.-raised Korean American "returnees." His current research examines the culinary entrepreneurship of 1.5 and 2nd-generation Korean Americans in the U.S. and South Korea. He has works published in outlets such as the *Ethnic & Racial Studies, Journal of Asian American Studies, Men & Masculinities*, the *International Review for the Sociology of Sport*, and *The Society Pages*. He is a co-editor of the forthcoming *Koreatowns: Exploring the Economics, Politics, and Identities of Korean Spatial Formations*.

**Ruixin Wei** is a doctoral candidate in the department of Korean Studies at Goethe University Frankfurt, Germany. Her research interests surround ethnic identity, transnational migration, and youth mobility in the contexts of China and Korea, focusing especially on Korean Chinese.

**Brenda S.A. Yeoh** is Raffles Professor of Social Sciences at the National University of Singapore (NUS) and research leader of the Asian Migration Cluster at the Asia Research Institute, NUS. Her research interests include the politics of space in colonial and postcolonial cities, and she also has considerable experience working on a wide range of migration research in Asia, including key themes such as cosmopolitanism and highly skilled talent migration; gender, social reproduction, and care migration; migration, national identity, and citizenship issues; globalizing universities and international student mobilities; and cultural politics, family dynamics, and international marriage migrants. She has published widely on these topics, and her recent books include *Transnational Labour Migration, Remittances and the Changing Family in Asia* (2015, with Lan Anh Hoang), *Contested Memoryscapes: The Politics of Second World War Commemoration in Singapore* (2016, with Hamzah Muzaini), *Asian Migrants and Religious Experience: From Missionary Journeys to Labor Mobility* (2018, with Bernardo Brown), and *Handbook of Asian Migrations* (2018, with Gracia Liu-Farrer).

www.ingramcontent.com/pod-product-compliance
Lightning Source LLC
Chambersburg PA
CBHW022310280326
41932CB00010B/1049